Peter Rees has had a long career as a journalist covering federal politics and as an author specialising in Australian military history. His books include *Anzac Girls*; *Desert Boys*; *Lancaster Men*; *Bearing Witness: The Remarkable Life of Charles Bean*; and *The Missing Man: From the Outback to Tarakan, the Powerful Story of Len Waters, Australia's First Aboriginal Fighter Pilot*, and he is a co-author with Sue Langford on *A Week in September: A Story of Enduring Love from the Burma Railway*.

GUTS AND GLORY

PETER REES

ABC
BOOKS

Aboriginal and Torres Strait Islander readers are advised that this book contains names and images of Indigenous people who have died.

 The ABC 'Wave' device is a trademark of the Australian Broadcasting Corporation and is used under licence by HarperCollins*Publishers* Australia.

HarperCollins*Publishers*
Australia • Brazil • Canada • France • Germany • Holland • India
Italy • Japan • Mexico • New Zealand • Poland • Spain • Sweden
Switzerland • United Kingdom • United States of America

HarperCollins acknowledges the Traditional Custodians of the lands upon which we live and work, and pays respect to Elders past and present.

First published on Gadigal country in Australia in 2025
by HarperCollins*Publishers* Australia Pty Limited
ABN 36 009 913 517
harpercollins.com.au

Copyright © Peter Rees 2025

The right of Peter Rees to be identified as the author of this work has been asserted by him in accordance with the *Copyright Act 1968*.

All rights reserved. Apart from any use as permitted under the *Copyright Act 1968*, no part may be reproduced, copied, scanned, stored in a retrieval system, recorded, or transmitted, in any form or by any means, without the prior written permission of the publisher. Without limiting the exclusive rights of any author, contributor, or the publisher of this publication, any unauthorised use of this publication to train generative artificial intelligence (AI) technologies is expressly prohibited. HarperCollins also exercises its rights under Article 4(3) of the Digital Single Market Directive 2019/790 and expressly reserves this publication from the text and data-mining exception.

HarperCollinsPublishers
Macken House, 39/40 Mayor Street Upper
Dublin 1, D01 C9W8, Ireland

A catalogue record for this book is available from the National Library of Australia

ISBN 978 0 7333 4422 0 (paperback)
ISBN 978 1 4607 1817 9 (ebook)

Cover design by Hazel Lam, HarperCollins Design Studio
Front cover image courtesy Australian War Memorial (E03355). France, 20 September 1918. Teams of the 59th Battalion playing rugby football during a brief rest from the fighting at Barleux. Back cover image courtesy Australian War Memorial (P00001.022). Solomon Islands, 1 December 1945. Desperate finish to a sprint race at a combined Anzac sports meeting at Bougainville Island.
Author photograph by Peter Rees
Typeset in Bembo Std by Kirby Jones
Printed and bound in Australia by McPherson's Printing Group

For
Oliver and Hamish
Elliot, Phoebe
and Georgia

Dare to dream – and dare to commit.

Contents

World War I

1	Players by Nature	3
2	And the Pyramids Watched	8
3	The Red Rag	14
4	Cricketing Bombs	26
5	Slingshot Thunderbolts	37
6	The Game Changes	45
7	Somewhere in France	50
8	Bowling Against the Wind	58
9	Surely the Moment for a Test Match	70
10	Put Our Scores on the Board!	83
11	All Dressed Up and Nowhere to Go	91
12	A Golden Decade Begins	101
13	The Noble Art	107
14	The Awesome Oarsmen	117
15	A Fighting Force	123

World War II

16	The Old and the New	139
17	Tout Juste	145
18	An End to the Good Times	158
19	The Changi Tests	165
20	Not Just a Diversion – a Lifeline	173
21	Mates	181
22	The Demon	191

23	Kriegies	199
24	Playing for Australia!	212
25	Black Magic	215
26	Conjuring Victory	225
27	The Victory Tests	232
28	When Success Turns Sour	241
29	Mate Against Mate	249

Post–World War II

30	Running Hard	257
31	Vung Tau	265
32	The Paradox	276
33	They Don't Unteach You	283
34	Even a Warped Bat Will Do	295
35	Fighting Back	303
36	Just a Game of Football	309

Epilogue	317
Acknowledgements	321
Notes	325
Bibliography	353

World War I

I

PLAYERS BY NATURE

You couldn't miss Big Jack Massie. At 193 centimetres tall and weighing 95 kilos, Jack was a formidable presence. Success came easily. He had represented New South Wales in cricket, rugby union, athletics and rowing, and was a crack shooter. In 1914 he won the State Amateur Heavyweight Boxing title, one of his close mates describing how his sheer physical presence struck terror into an opponent in an elimination bout. Halfway down the aisle to the boxing ring Massie's opponent 'looked up, saw this man-mountain standing in the ring, with his grey blanket-coat, hesitated, turned round and went back to his dressing room'. Years later, another of his friends described him as having 'the body of a God'. Somehow, he also found time with his studies at Sydney University to win the gold medal in the School of Engineering.

At twenty-four, an already brilliant career was about to be capped by his selection as a Test cricketer, to open the bowling for Australia. His left-arm pace and swing bowling terrorised batsmen and had snared him ninety-nine first-class wickets. Many regarded him as the best bowler in Australia and a certainty for the next Australian Test team. Among astute judges, celebrated Test spinner Arthur Mailey rated him the best left-arm bowler of all time.

Here was a sportsman who captured the imagination of Australians in the early Federation years; someone for whom sporting glory was so natural it fitted like a glove; someone so gifted that despite the privilege and family wealth he had been born into, the new nation could identify with him as someone who would carry their country forward. Indeed, his father, Hugh Massie, had top-scored in Australia's 1882 victory against England, from which the Ashes legend was born. His son now seemed poised to add to the family's cricketing achievements.

On 4 August 1914, Jack's life changed forever when Great Britain declared war on Germany. The declaration meant Australia too was at war. Thirteen days later Jack walked into a Sydney recruitment depot to enlist in the new Australian Imperial Force, as a second lieutenant and assistant adjutant to the 4th Battalion AIF. He prepared to sail to war.

The Australian government had pledged 20,000 Australian troops to join the fight. Six days after recruiting offices opened at army barracks around Australia, men flooded in to sign up. The number was so high that recruitment officers were forced to turn men away. The first four months of the war saw more than 52,000 men join the AIF, with another 4000 joining the navy.

Pro-war articles in newspapers and posters built an expectation of battlefield success. Sportsmen in uniform were the exemplars of the new army of heroes, and Jack Massie was among the earliest to volunteer. Although qualified to join the Royal Engineers, he chose to become a footsoldier in the infantry. Here was a sportsman turned warrior, one who typified the initial recruits portrayed by the official war correspondent, Charles Bean:

> The first fine rush to enlistment brought to the 1st
> Australian Division a class of men not quite the same as

that which answered to any later call. All the adventurous roving natures that could not stay away, whatever their duties and their ties; all those who plunged heads down into war, reckless of anything else, because it was a game to be played and they were players by nature.

There was a widely held view that sportsmen were easily the best equipped for war; their prowess on the football field, cricket pitch, track, swimming pool or boxing ring gave them a natural advantage through honed fitness and sharpness of reflexes. This belief was millennia old. In ancient states in Asia more than 2000 years ago, martial arts emerged as a training tool for war when physical strength was critical to battle the enemy in close contact. As the twentieth century dawned, nation states understood that personal fitness, team sports and patriotism were critical in an army. In Australia in 1900, Victorian politician John Thompson told a function in Hamilton that one of the local men volunteering for the Boer War in South Africa was 'prominent in all manly sports … there was no schooling that brought up a man for the battlefield equal to that'.

The belief was a formative influence at the new Royal Military College Duntroon in Canberra, where the first commandant, Major General William Throsby Bridges, acknowledged the value of sporting activity as 'a means of maintaining health, and as an assistance to discipline'. More broadly, there was the notion of its contribution to leadership: 'an officer who has led his men to victory in a football match will be more devotedly followed by them in a sterner field.'

In the *Winner* newspaper, a senior football official spoke of a peculiar esprit de corps among sportsmen: 'Their religion, so to speak, is to be thorough, and never to know when they are beaten.' From the early days of the colony, the military had embraced the adoption of sport. As far back as 1806 soldiers helped to establish cricket in Australia when a match between two British regiments in Sydney attracted 2000 spectators. In 1851, a tract of land near Victoria Barracks in Sydney was granted to the army for use as a cricket ground. Known as Moore Park, for many years it was the main location for cricket matches in Sydney. In 1870, the tract of land morphed into the Sydney Cricket Ground (SCG).

The link between sport and war was thus laid down. In Melbourne's *The Australasian* a few months after war broke out, a columnist pondered how the different classes of sport had responded to the crisis: '... there may be no particular reason why athletes should volunteer in greater proportional numbers than other members of society, except that their aptitude, youth, strength, physical fitness and dash, stamp them as the makings of ideal soldiers.'

There was early talk of forming a Commonwealth Sportsmen's Battalion to follow Britain's example. However, such units would not appear until later in the war, when the initial enthusiasm for enlistment had waned. Nonetheless, from the start there was pressure on the nation's sportsmen to enlist, to 'train together, embark together, fight together'. The sport didn't matter. Footballers, cricketers, rowers, sailors, jockeys, boxers, golfers and even lawn bowlers were all exhorted to live up to Henry Newbolt's 1892 poem, 'Vitaï Lampada', and to '"Play up! play up! and play the Game!"'

Playing 'the greater game', as one newspaper described war, would eventually cost Australia's sportsmen dearly. Bullets and scything shrapnel may not discriminate, but in 1914 patriotism held sway.

In September, the first Australian shots in World War I were fired when an expeditionary force headed to the German territories in New Guinea to shut down radio transmitters. During the advance towards the German wireless station on New Britain, Able Seaman William Williams was shot. Fighting to save him, a former schoolboy athletics and rugby champion and now doctor in the Australian Army Medical Corps, Captain Brian Pockley, gave up his Red Cross armband and carried Williams to the rear himself. Without this protection, Pockley too was shot. Both men died, becoming the first Australian casualties of the war.

With the German radio stations destroyed and their outposts in New Guinea captured, the expeditionary force effectively became an occupation force. With only a little guard work to do there was growing disenchantment. A game of rugby helped fill in the time. Private Ralph Robertson, who had formerly captained the New South Wales Australian Rules side, represented his company in a football kicking competition. '6 kicks, drop and place, from the half-way and 25 flags. We were well beaten, much to our disgust, and also to that of our friends, who had us in a double at 20 to 1. You should try dropkicking in military boots.' And so began an Australian wartime tradition of gambling on the sporting abilities of mates in uniform – and playing football in army boots.

The Australians were now on the move. On 1 November 1914 a convoy of thirty-eight ships carrying 30,000 men left Albany for an undisclosed location. Men on board watched the coast of Western Australia fade into the darkness and sailed off to war. 'Some of the country's very best men and most valuable assets,' thought Tom Richards, another early volunteer. He was thirty-two years old, big, fast and versatile: a rugby union star who had, uniquely, represented both the Wallabies and the British Lions. He signed on with the 1st Field Ambulance and, after just eight weeks' training, boarded HMAT A14 *Euripides*. Once on board, he noted in his diary: 'When one looks over the troops as they stand around, their height and physique are admirable, their age is thoroughly mature and their faces, though hard and weather-beaten, are very determined and strong looking.' He added that 'the present cricket season and the coming football season must suffer in consequence'.

2

AND THE PYRAMIDS WATCHED

For a month as they crossed the Indian Ocean and sailed through the Suez Canal, the men of the First AIF played deck cricket, boxing and tug-of-war before arriving at Port Said on 3 December 1914. They immediately moved to Cairo, where a base at Mena was established, a camp housing more than 20,000 men. It was a vast training facility in the shadow of the Giza pyramids about 16 kilometres from the Egyptian capital. The Light Horse also established a camp at Maadi, on the edge of the desert south of Cairo. Around mid-January, another 10,000 Australians arrived, and nearby, 10,000 New Zealanders were also newly encamped.

They had been cooped up on ships for several weeks, so it was no surprise that the urge for football was irrepressible. The Australians took to the field for the first time just sixteen days later at the Gezira Sporting Club for an Australian Rules match. The crowd, largely British expats, were bemused by the sight before them: they had never seen anything like it – a mad scramble resembling neither rugby nor soccer, because it was neither. Football certainly, but played under Australian rules, and rarely seen outside Australia.

The ground was a dirt bowl and there were injuries aplenty, but to the Australians it did not matter. In this joyful expression of youthful Australian exceptionalism, war seemed far away. On the field were two teams chosen from the 2nd Field Company Engineers, Victoria. The captain of one, Sapper Harry Matheson, had been a half-forward for the Collingwood Magpies in the Victorian Football League (VFL). He was among those who had rushed to enlist. He wrote home that playing football in Egypt was 'not all beer and skittles' as the ground was hard and grassless. 'Without any training and under such conditions, you can imagine the tired limbs that eventually sought repose at the Pyramids nine miles away.' Matheson felt proud that he was captain of the winning team, 'and that it was a ball carried from Australia which was the first booted through the goals by one of the "Fighting Magpies" in Egypt'.

It was natural that further Australian football games would follow the first match at the Cairo stadium. Teams from A Squadron, 4th Australian Light Horse, and the 2nd Field Ambulance fought it out before a large crowd at the ground a month later, on 22 January 1915, with the Light Horse winning with a goal on the final siren. *The Australasian* published an account of the match some weeks later, noting spectators had mistakenly believed that the game was a cross between soccer and rugby, but 'nothing is further from the fact, as the game's principal features are not embodied in either of the other codes'. The paper soberly noted that Field Ambulance forward Clyde Donaldson, an Essendon rover, was now 'playing at higher stakes, and may his dash remain undiminished'.

Regardless of sporting background, the training was necessarily intense, the men carrying 35-kilo packs on their backs, enduring mock fights through sand and under a broiling sun, followed by night marches before being pronounced 'Fit for War'. With venereal disease on the rise, military and civilian authorities looked to give the men 'a healthy, decent alternative', as the

Young Men's Christian Association (YMCA) put it in early 1915. Sport provided the answer. Besides football, brigade military sports were organised at Mena, where a stadium was erected, and boxing contests staged. With 100,000 horses for the Light Horse regiments transported from Australia to Egypt, horse racing inevitably emerged. While polo ponies were in short supply, there were plenty of donkeys that could be drafted for polo.

Despite the excitement generated in sport that accompanied the arrival in Egypt – even extending to state-based teams competing in lacrosse – there were pangs of homesickness. Letters and local papers were eagerly received, bringing news of home and providing an ongoing link to sporting news. The 8th Battalion's Corporal Hector Hallam, a farmer and athlete in Victoria's Wimmera, wrote from Mena to his local paper saying that 'the boys are still wearing the old blue and white, for our regimental colours happen to be blue and white. Would you kindly give my best wishes to the Lowan Footballers and tell them I hope to be back for the final.' Hallam added that he had had four fights in the soldiers' stadium. 'I won three and lost one, being beaten by the champion of the force.'

Under the shadow of the Great Pyramid of Cheops, Tom Richards played several hard-fought rugby union matches. He explained that these games meant as much to players and followers as any international game at the Sydney Cricket Ground. 'Whether the ground was crusted with sun-baked mud, that rashed and cut all unwary players, or several inches deep in heavy, black mud, depended entirely on the rise and fall of the wondrous "Father" Nile.'

To have the chance to play on Nile Delta country stirred Richards with awe, and playing under the Great Pyramid, towering 146 metres above them, conjured images of gladiatorial contests of old. 'To us, it was the finest test of physical fitness that we knew of.' Richards thought the men played with the same vigour and dash as that of a rival inter-town match or, with a dramatic flourish, as if they were in an amphitheatre, where any lack of determination meant 'thumbs down, which, in turn, meant death to the losers'.

Richards was a football traditionalist whose sentiments lay strongly with rugby union rather than rugby league, the new game formed after the 1908 split with union. He mused in his diary that there was a time when he did give some thought to playing league for the money, 'but I am now very thankful that I did not do so'. One of league's key figures, Sergeant Ted Larkin, was also in Cairo with the AIF 1st Battalion. Larkin was a former Wallaby who had faced a touring New Zealand All Blacks team in 1903 before joining the professional code. When the league plunged into financial crisis, Larkin quit the police force to become the new code's secretary, turning around its fortunes to ensure its future. In 1913, Larkin was elected to the New South Wales Parliament as a Labor MLA, with a bright future in politics ahead of him. With the outbreak of war he enlisted, believing that his role should be to say 'come on', rather than encouraging others to 'go on'. In August, he told the New South Wales Parliament: 'I consider this a critical time for our Empire, and I deem it the duty of those holding public positions to point the way.'

It was natural that Larkin and Richards should meet, as they did on 5 February 1915 when Richards called on Larkin in camp. Later that night Richards wrote in his diary of the meeting, describing Larkin as 'a peculiar type of person' to be an MP, and then went further: 'He played football the other day and boomed the miserable game in the Cairo press. I can't see how the Australian Government is going to be strengthened or even run on honest lines when this type of man can secure recognition and a seat in the House.' Richards' acerbic assessment of Larkin was likely sparked by their contrasting positions on amateur and professional football. Richards had long embraced the amateur values of rugby union, dismissing professional sport as 'not having the same honour or enthusiastic achievement' as amateur sport, while Larkin could see nothing wrong with earning money from the game.

In this waiting period, interstate rivalry was soon sparked in Australian Rules football. On 23 January 1915, a quasi State of Origin match saw 'gunners' of the West Australian 8th Artillery Battery and the Tasmanian 9th Artillery Battery take the field, with the Tasmanians winning by 2 points in a close match. The Sydney-raised 3rd Artillery Battery, 1st Field Artillery Brigade, took on the Adelaide-raised 10th Australian Infantry Battalion at the Cairo stadium. Some weeks later, a detailed account of the match was published in *The Observer*, Adelaide, complimenting the infantrymen for the way they kept plugging away at goal. 'The [first] quarter was very fast, and at the finish the heat was telling a little on the players.' But they found renewed energy and by the third quarter the 'Infantrymen were at it hammer and tongs right from the jump'. A 'skyscraping mark' saw the infantry put the result beyond doubt, winning 16.10 (106) to 6.8 (44). South Australian honour was appeased.

These matches played in an exotic location quickly ensured they took root in the national legend, inevitably crossing years later into filmic history. In Peter Weir's 1981 movie *Gallipoli*, a key theme is the connection between sport and war. In an early scene, at the Kimberley Gift footrace, an army recruiter for the Light Horse calls war 'the greatest game of all'. The film's central character, Archy, claims that athletes have a special responsibility to join up because of their physical prowess. At the footrace, a whistle blows to start the contest; at Gallipoli, that moment is echoed by an officer blowing a whistle to send men over the top. The footrace is portrayed as a test, rivalry playing out on the sporting field rather than the battlefield. It was a contest that formed bonds of mateship that continued onto the battlefield. The role of the runner was critical in the fighting that followed at Gallipoli – and central to the film's tragic ending.

A highlight was playwright David Williamson writing himself into his own script and onto the screen in an Aussie Rules match between Victoria and Western Australia. With the pyramids in the background, football fanatic Williamson became an Australian soldier in a cameo performance playing a ruckman, with Mel Gibson's character watching on and caustically dismissing him as 'That long thin streak of Pelican shit'.

At least one critic at the time made his displeasure clear by calling the scene astonishing and self-indulgent and saying that it was 'appalling that it was kept in the film'. Such criticism missed the point: the scene captured the post-Federation spirit of optimism that marked the first wave of young Australian troops readying to fight in the early days of World War I. Importantly, it portrayed a moment when military folklore graduated to the screen. Football played against the backdrop of the pyramids *did* happen, and as these wonders of the ancient world watched on silently, the filmed scene ensured that that reality would be recognised for generations to come. But there was a graver reality: Gallipoli was not far away.

3

THE RED RAG

There was a joyous rumour in the Light Horse camp at Maadi that made Trooper Cliff Halloran of the 6th Regiment take note. 'We will be on our way to the front shortly,' the former journalist wrote, adding that the rumour had been circulating for three days and had been the cause of much happiness. 'There is hardly a man in the camp who would not rejoice if we were to start packing at once.'

But first there was an important matter to attend to: the commander of the 2nd Light Horse Brigade, Brigadier General Granville Ryrie, had prizes to hand out after a recent brigade sports meeting. The awards coincided with a concert at the stadium attended by 3000 people to honour the presence of the 1st Australian Light Horse Brigade, who had left their Heliopolis camp for a four-day bivouac at Maadi with their comrades in the 2nd Light Horse Brigade. According to Halloran, Ryrie gave a 'sturdy fighting speech … for the benefit of you residents of Egypt' that Australia had 'come to fight, and to fight as soon as ever they let us'. The prizes awarded were for:

- Officers' 100 yards championship
- Other ranks' 100 yards championship
- Tug-of-war
- Wrestling on horseback
- Balaclava Melee
- Machine-gun competition
- Stretcher-bearers' race

'Bull' Ryrie, forty-nine, was a Boer War veteran, pastoralist and conservative federal MHR for North Sydney. On the day war was declared, 4 August 1914, he wrote to his wife, saying that 'after thinking for 11 hours ... I feel I must offer my services' to the war effort, otherwise 'I couldn't look men in the face again, especially some of my political opponents whom I have accused of disloyalty. I simply cannot hold back.' His 2nd Light Horse Brigade, comprising the 5th, 6th and 7th Regiments, was part of three brigades of Light Horse initially formed for the war.

Ryrie was a big man physically, with a personality to match. He remained a member of Federal Parliament throughout the war. On board ship after the convoy of troops left Australia and as senior officer in charge, his goal was to ensure the men were physically ready with endless drilling for the fighting ahead. Of greater interest to the men were the inter-regimental boxing contests. Besides being a noted horseman and marksman, Ryrie was also a formidable boxer, who twice had been runner-up in the New South Wales amateur heavyweight championship. In Parliament on one occasion, he had objected to the remarks of a Labor senator and challenged him to a fight, but common sense on the part of the senator prevailed and a reconciliation ensued. On board the transport *Suevic*, Ryrie had issued a challenge to take on all-comers. There were no takers. He had to settle for the role of referee.

Once at Maadi, as at Mena, a stadium was erected and boxing contests held thrice weekly. One of Ryrie's men,

Trooper Charlie Rowe, 5th Light Horse Regiment, wrote to his local paper in Charters Towers, the *Northern Miner*, about life at Maadi. Among his friends in camp was Tom Richards, 'and some more of our good old Towers sports'. Charlie wanted the townsfolk to know that Trooper Ted Reynolds, twenty-five years old, a noted Charters Towers amateur boxer, had fought for the 2nd Brigade championship, winning on points after fifteen rounds.

What irritated the men was the often-discourteous attitude displayed by the local British civilian community when they met at various sporting contests, ranging from football and lacrosse to hockey and cricket. This caused a Light Horse sergeant to complain of the behaviour of cricketers at the Gezira Sporting Club. 'They do not invite us to have a cup of tea, nor do they condescend to talk to us except about the match in progress.' The rigid Anglo-Egyptian class structure was alive and well.

After several weeks in camp at Maadi learning more of army life, the men were becoming restless and eager for action. With never-ending drill and rumour after empty rumour about impending action at the front, Ryrie knew he had to keep the men focused. Cliff Halloran wrote from Maadi complaining about the lack of physical exercise and how unfit some of the men of his regiment were.

> When we come to do a bayonet charge over the sand in the course of our drill, we are done after going 50 yards, and in some cases less ... In the case of the 6th Australian Light Horse, there was no attention paid to physical exercise on the boat trip from Australia to Egypt, and that was why so many of the troopers of that regiment left the ship very much on the soft and fat side. Goodness only knows how they would have managed had they been required at once for hard work.

Ryrie's answer to both restiveness and the flabbiness turned to more sports days, race meetings, football and ever-popular boxing contests. As the official historian of the Light Horse campaign, Henry Gullett, wrote after the war, Ryrie's 'excellence in all physical exercise despite his weight and age' quickly won the respect of his troops.

Finally, the move was on. Richards noted, 'The fellows were cheering and singing last night at the thought of soon getting onto some proper service instead of hanging about this expensive and robbing town of Cairo on so small an allowance.' In the countdown to departure, football matches were finally organised on successive days at Mena, a windstorm notwithstanding.

Ryrie's insistence on the physical condition of the men paid dividends. After their weeks of training in the desert, Charles Bean concluded, the 1st Australian Division was already emerging into one of the finest fighting units any soldier could wish to see. 'Hard work,' Bean wrote, 'cheerfully undertaken day after day in toilsome sand and heat in the true spirit of "playing the game", has gradually manufactured a fighting force of which Australia may be intensely proud.' Bean's idealism, so redolent of simpler times, was about to be tested in the unimaginable ferocity of the first modern industrial war.

In early March 1915, Australian troops began landing at Lemnos, around 100 kilometres from the Gallipoli Peninsula, with the aim of becoming part of the occupation force if British and French battleships managed to capture the Turkish forts along the Dardanelles Strait. The mid-March naval attack failed disastrously, with more than 700 sailors lost, three battleships sunk and another three disabled. A new plan to invade the Gallipoli Peninsula with a ground force was approved and the date of 25 April 1915 was set.

The night before the landing, Tom Richards wrote in his diary of a grim briefing to the medics in the 1st Field Ambulance about the anticipated heavy casualties. Sobering though it was, he professed, 'I don't feel the coming danger any more than I have felt anxious the night before an international football match.'

The 10th Battalion's Tom Whyte, a champion sculler from Adelaide, was also writing that night to his fiancée and was there the next morning as the Australians made their way to the Gallipoli shore. Having represented South Australia at several interstate rowing championships, Whyte was a natural choice to row the men ashore. His mate Arthur Blackburn, a battalion scout, recalled that the battalion was divided into two parts, one of which landed before daybreak, and the other later in the morning, when dawn had broken. Whyte was in the second contingent, when the men in the landing craft approached the shoreline in the morning light. According to Blackburn, no one was more cheerful than Whyte. 'He was joking and laughing all the way to the shore.' Such was the easy confidence and determination of the champion rower who had a crucial role to perform. As Blackburn described it:

> The dangers of such a task were so apparent that officers hesitated to order men to expose themselves to the work of rowing. Tom immediately grasped the situation, and, as everyone knew he would, volunteered his services as a rower, as the boat crept in towards the shore the fire became hotter and hotter. The men towing had a terrible time, but they stuck to it in a way which was absolutely magnificent. Just as the boat touched the shore Tom slipped over on to the bottom of the boat, and it was then discovered that he was badly hit.

Whyte was immediately taken to the hospital ship, *Gascon*, but died from his wounds before the ship reached a military hospital in Egypt. He was buried at sea. Blackburn had no doubt that it was 'largely due to the courage and endurance of Tom and his fellow rowers in all the boats that everyone was landed with the minimum of loss'. It was only decades later that Whyte's letter to his fiancée was given to the Australian War Memorial. In it, he wrote:

> I thought of writing this in case I went under suddenly. Not that at present I have any thought of not seeing you again but in case of accidents. As this is only intended to reach you in the event of my death you will know that my thoughts will have been of you right until the end. May this letter never be necessary. But the thought that hurts worst of all is of you and your sorrow.

When the first account of the landing at Gallipoli on the morning of 25 April 1915, the focus was less on the sorrow of those lost and more on the 'fine athletic type' of the Australian soldier. The public's imagination was immediately captured by the heroism and disregard for personal safety. The sheer determination of the Australians sent the English war correspondent Ellis Ashmead-Bartlett into overdrive. His florid account was the first to reach Australia, and was published in the morning press on 8 May 1915: 'They waited neither for orders nor for the boats to reach the beach, but, springing out into the sea, they waded ashore, and, forming some sort of rough line, rushed straight on the flashes of the enemy's rifles.' The Australians were, Ashmead-Bartlett said, a 'race of athletes'.

The nation thrilled at this extraordinary account of military achievement by heroic Australian troops, sparking an immediate increase in volunteer enlistments. The sporting analogy was irresistible, with one journalist writing:

> The way the troops landed at night in boats, stormed an almost vertical sea cliff and then held their ground for fifteen hours, called for possession of swimming power

maybe, running ability, general hardihood, and tenacity of purpose begotten of trained oarsmanship, playing in ruck, cross-country running and Warrnambool to Melbourne, Goulburn to Sydney pedalling.

On its front page in Sydney, *The Referee* sports newspaper splashed with the sporting analogy, lauding the 'deeds that thrill by our athletes and sportsmen', whose 'rushes of the football field' were replicated 'with the bayonet against the Turks'.

Charles Bean's report was published nine days later, on 17 May, and while more sober in tone than Ashmead-Bartlett's, it nonetheless struck a similar chord.

> Bullets struck fireworks out of the stones along the beach. The men did not wait to be hit, but wherever they landed they simply rushed straight up the steep slopes. Other small boats which had cast off from the warships and steam launches which towed them, were digging for the beach with oars. These occupied the attention of the Turks in the trenches, and almost before the Turks had time to collect their senses, the first boatloads were well up towards the trenches. Few Turks awaited the bayonet ... The Third Brigade went over the hills with such dash that within three quarters of an hour of landing some had charged over three successive ridges. Each ridge was higher than the last, and each party that reached the top went over it with wild cheers ... the feat which will go down to history is that first Sunday's fighting, when three Australian brigades stormed, in the face of fire, tier after tier of cliffs and mountains.

The Gallipoli landing saw the loss of many sportsmen among the 752 Australians who died on or about 25 April. 'Bull' Ryrie tried to put the deaths into context, writing to a friend: 'Despite the tragic side of the landing here the element of what may be called war-sport was not wanting.' The metaphor linking war and sport mirrored Bean's belief that Australian country life had hammered out of the old stock a new man who was 'a tall, spare man, clean and wiry rather than muscular ... a certain refined ascetic strength'. Even the British had to agree with Bean's assessment, with one officer writing:

> The Australians are a wonderful race, and the physique of the men is splendid. Everything they do is done thoroughly. They lack discipline as we know it yet have a discipline that is not so common with us, namely, a rotter and waster is not allowed to comfortably exist. They are an exceptionally formidable weapon, for when they fight, they go on like wild men, never showing fear or attempting to go back. They perform the most extraordinary and hair-raising deeds that history can record, all the time to a flow of very sanguinary and strong language. What a superb Army.

Bean had a penchant for sporting imagery, which emerged in his account of the role of the 1st Battalion's Major Blair Swannell at the landing. A Boer War veteran, Swannell, thirty-nine, had played for the British Lions and, after settling in Australia in 1905, for the Wallabies. Swannell was a rough and at times a dirty forward on the field and, having enlisted again, approached Gallipoli with the same determination. According to Bean, as Swannell waited on the troopship *Minnewaska* to land, he said he felt sure he would be killed, 'for he realised that he would play this game as he had played Rugby football – with his whole heart'. Once ashore, one of Swannell's troops, Sergeant Harry Mitchell, wrote, 'He wanted to be in it. We will never forget the rush he made leading us up to the first rest after landing. There certainly was no fear in that man's make-up.' As enemy bullets whipped among his men, Swannell knew they had to mount return fire. Spying a sniper, he ordered a man alongside him to shoot him and gave him the range. As Bean described it, 'while kneeling in order to show his men how to take better aim at a Turk, he was shot dead'.

In an early dispatch from Gallipoli, Bean wrote of Swannell: 'He fought that day as a footballer fights in a good Rugger scrum — as he had fought in many an interstate and international match — and you cannot say more than that.' Tom Richards wrote in his diary a few days later: 'I am really grieved, as "Swanny" with all his faults etc was quite all right, though he was a character seldom met.'

Bean wrote glowingly of another footballer at the landing, the prominent Sydney rugby league identity Sergeant Ted Larkin. He knew Swannell from their playing days but were polar opposites in personality, lifestyle and views on the future of the professional game. While Swannell was flamboyant and gaudy, Larkin was a staid family man. At the landing Larkin led his men to the heights above the beach, and around 3 pm led them in an advance against a Turkish position. Corporal Charles Lawler, who was with Larkin at the time, later wrote, 'It must have been shrapnel that got him for we were charging under bursts of shrapnel, and there was very little rifle fire. Teddy was well up in front, but I can't tell you any details, for we had all gone mad.' Larkin's brother Martin was killed nearby. In contrast to Tom Richards' assessment of Larkin, Bean wrote that Larkin was 'a man with a fine influence in his battalion' and concluded that he had been cut down by machine-gun bullets.

Jack Massie was among those who scrambled ashore on 25 April. A few days later, he wrote to his mother. 'We have had a pretty rough time since we landed. We have been in the trenches for 10 days now without a spell and are not likely to get one for a considerable time, I think. The men had to dig day and night at first for a week and were very done at the end of it.' He reassured

Major Blair Swannell (back left) with fellow rugby-playing 1st Battalion AIF officers. AWM C02130.

her, 'We are being fed well, and if it was not for the damned noise would get a good sleep.' A few days later, he wrote that 'the best bit of luck we have had is that the Navy landed us a mile or so north of where we were to have landed by mistake. We could never have lived in the place where we were to have gone.'

With a promising cricket career ahead of him, Jack was especially conscious of the need to protect his bowling arm, his left. Thus, he decided to give the enemy an incentive to shift their aim away from his left to his right arm by tying a red rag to it. The ruse appeared to work, with just two minor wounds in June and July. But then came Lone Pine. Over four days in August, beginning on the 6th, Anzac units fought a ferocious battle in an attempt to force a breakout from their perimeter on the heights of Chunuk Bair and Hill 971. While the main Turkish trench was taken within 20 minutes of the first charge, the Turks regrouped, and four days of intense hand-to-hand fighting followed. Seven Australian VCs were awarded amid more than 2000 AIF casualties.

As the 4th Battalion Adjutant, Massie led a counterattack on 7 August, the red rag still tied around his right arm to attract attention. But the ruse could do nothing to stop machine-gun bullets from smashing into his left shoulder, puncturing a lung and breaking ribs. His left shoulder blade was splintered, his only consolation being the immediate award of the Distinguished Service Order for outstanding gallantry in action.

Hospitalised in Alexandria, Massie wrote home after doctors operated on his shoulder. 'They found that the bullet knocked my ribs about a good bit after which it got foul of my left shoulder blade and fooled it about a bit before coming out.' The injury was serious enough for him to be repatriated to Australia. During the voyage home he was promoted to captain, mentioned in despatches and awarded the French Croix de Guerre. Over the next few months his wounds healed. He was determined that his war was far from over and waited to return.

Not least at Lone Pine, as historian Bill Gammage noted, men used the language of sport to describe the game they were playing, comparing the tension before battle with that before a football match, or describing their time in the line as an innings. 'At Lone Pine a soldier looked at the calico patches on his mate's back and commented, "Fancy going on the field without our numbers".' Sporting imagery was prevalent at Gallipoli from the earliest days. On 19 May, Lieutenant Wally Hale commented, 'I think it is wonderful how our boys love fighting. It is just the same as sport. Australia can hold its own against the world … in sport … in fighting.' Hale would die in the Third Battle of Ypres, Belgium, in October 1917.

Meanwhile, in Australia the debate over professional and amateur sport was passionate and led to sometimes unseemly bouts of one-upmanship between the rugby codes in Sydney as to whose players – professional or amateur – were more patriotic. There was also a split in Melbourne between the Victorian Football League and the Victorian Football Association. The reason was simple: a power struggle fuelled by money between VFL's stronger and wealthier clubs which did not want to share their higher gate takings with the VFA's weaker clubs. The outbreak of war saw the VFA suspend competition while the VFL continued to operate, heightening their already antagonistic relationship. The patriotism of sportsmen who continued to play came into question.

4

CRICKETING BOMBS

The news of the heroics at the Gallipoli landing gripped the nation's imagination. A recruiting upsurge followed. Rival film companies recreated scenes of men wading ashore and scaling cliffs, using soldiers from the army camp at Liverpool; one filmed at Obelisk Bay in Sydney Harbour, the other not far away at Tamarama beach. Both premiered within weeks, and although re-enactments, the films were greeted enthusiastically by audiences, giving enlistments a bump, at least for a while.

However, before long, a disparity in recruitment emerged, essentially between amateur and professional sportsmen. In Sydney, *The Referee* reported in August 1915 that 90 per cent of first-grade rugby union players had enlisted; in Melbourne, 774 VFL-level players enlisted; while across the country, soccer players enlisted in droves. Among them was James 'Judy' Masters, twenty-three, a precociously talented player from Balgownie, on the New South Wales South Coast, where soccer flourished among British coalminers drawn to the Illawarra mines. Just how he earned the moniker of 'Judy' is unclear, but as the seventh of thirteen children, the Masters family believes that his boisterous older brothers gave him a girl's name because of his gentle demeanour.

Judy may have been gentle but working in the mines from the age of thirteen also made him tough. While slimly built and just 175 centimetres tall, he was all muscle and bone. By fifteen, he was playing first-grade soccer with Balgownie. At the same time, he played rugby union, and in his spare time played the cornet in the town's band. A centre forward, he was already a star when he enlisted as a private on 1 June 1915 in the wake of the sensation of the Gallipoli landing.

Judy sailed for Gallipoli just a few weeks later with the 19th Battalion. As a bandsman, he was automatically designated a stretcher-bearer. Writing home to his brother, he soon saw the reality of life on the peninsula: the flies, heat, dysentery and the bloated bodies of the dead – and the constant menace of being 'popped over' by sniper fire. Amid this, Judy swam in the waters of Anzac Cove. Like Tom Richards, he was impressed by the willingness of the men to ignore the battery of Turkish guns known as 'Beachy Bill' that rained shrapnel on swimmers. Judy told his brother: 'If the Turks saw a mob swimming, they put a shell right amongst them, although our boys took no heed of them, being so dirty and lousey they took the risk for a swim. My mate and I never missed a date, sneaking away when there was nothing doing.' Such was the shock of reality for footballers – amateur and professional alike – who patriotically answered the call. But prejudices persisted.

Football, of course, was as hot a topic at Gallipoli as it was in Australia. In *The Australasian* the columnist J.W. was pleased that amateur sportsman 'have nobly answered the call of the blood', while that same call had fallen on the deaf ears of the professional athletes, for which they stand 'openly condemned'. With Shakespearean flourish, he put the question to this class of sportsmen: 'Why has not the blood of all quickened at the thought and knowledge of the heroic deeds that are daily done by men of our own race in the blood-soaked trenches?'

J.W. believed that all codes of football produced the best raw material to ready the soldier for war. The qualities of self-reliance, discipline, dash and the capacity to give and take punishment were necessary qualities in the soldier. 'The sport itself is mimic warfare. But the selfish part of human nature, backed up by inept management, is robbing the Empire of some of its best fighting material.'

These values, cultivated in the English public school system, had found a natural home in Australian private schools catering for the middle to upper class. 'Muscular Christianity', as it was known, was based on the philosophy 'that man could enhance his moral character through physical endeavour', which encouraged 'a fusion of ideas with notions of imperial duty, national identity and military imperatives'.

Rugby union – the code of choice among private schools – was the embodiment of this ideology; enlistment in the army was seen as the natural next step for the code's amateur players. Posters proclaimed: 'This is what you've been doing for the majority of life, you've been playing football, now go and play the greater game.' The enlistment of rugby union players was so effective that early in the war, competition in Sydney was suspended.

An exemplar was Syd Middleton, from Glebe in Sydney, who enjoyed a stellar sporting career in rowing and rugby union. His gold medal at the 1908 Olympic Games in London was the highlight of his four-Test rugby union career, which saw him captain the Wallabies on three occasions. Having retired from rugby in 1911 to concentrate on rowing, Middleton went on to win a silver medal at the Stockholm Olympics in 1912 and in the same year was part of the eight that won the Grand Challenge Cup at the Henley Royal Regatta in England. On landing at Gallipoli as a second lieutenant in August 1915, he wrote: 'There are dozens of footballers of lesser fame and lower grades knocking about. I meet them every day.'

In Sydney, however, rugby league continued unabated, with enlistment from the code's ranks standing in stark contrast to the numbers from union. Unlike union, league players were from predominately working-class areas, often with young families to support, and were more pragmatic in their views about sport in a time of war. As historian Michael McKernan put it, 'sport meant entertainment and pleasure, an exciting break from the monotony of urban work'. As such, sport needed no further or more serious justification. The influential *Bulletin* magazine took umbrage, asserting that 'war and football are rivals, and there is no room for both … Every footballer is a possible soldier, so the winter game will have no excuse this year for showing itself in public.'

At Gallipoli, photographer Ernest Brooks managed a rare but blurry photograph of British soldiers playing football late one evening as the Turks shelled background territory under the Achi Baba height that dominates the Gallipoli Peninsula. In an interview held by the Imperial War Museum in London, British private Thomas Baker talked of playing soccer on a rudimentary pitch.

> There was a piece of land where the teams used to play football and there was not one shell hole on that piece of ground, not one. It was hard and sandy somewhat and you could play good football on there. They'd got goalposts made up – they made them out of bits of trees, you know. They looked a bit raw, but they was standard sized – no nets, just the posts. They marked out along the side, you know, by marking in the sand for the lines, no whitewash or anything like that. We stripped right down, because we hadn't got much in the way of clothes so we didn't have to wear very much. One side wore shirts and the other side didn't wear any, so that it was no trouble for the referee to sort them out.

The Australians were located around 20 kilometres away from the British in much more rugged country, and Tom Richards commented that 'football matches were out of the question at ANZAC'. But one afternoon he was astounded to see a football floating through the air as he came over from Brown's Dip towards White's Gully. 'I set off down into the blind valley and joined in with a number of Victorians who had brought the ball from Egypt with them.'

Despite the rough terrain, the Australians couldn't resist having a kick around. Padre Tom Bennett, attached to the 22nd Battalion AIF, noted in his diary on 19 November 1915 that during a bombardment from the Turks, 'our men cheer a miss and go on kicking the football'. Sometimes the contact between the Turks and Diggers was more personal, such as an incident witnessed at Lone Pine by Colonel Jim McKinley.

> There was an awful lot of sniping going on from both sides and I was standing alongside one of the riflemen and he was having a shot at a Turk who was evidently digging a trench fifty or sixty yards away. Every time the shovel came to the top, our soldier had a shot at it and the Turk of course decided to show our rifleman exactly how he was scoring. If he missed, he waved his shovel from side to side, and on one occasion he put a bullet through the middle of the shovel. The Turk held the thing up, 'Good on you, Aussie, you got a bullseye that time.'

The strongly held belief that sport prepared the soldier for battle was best exemplified by the photograph Brooks captured of the Australians as they practised throwing the aptly named 'cricket ball grenade', which weighed 1 pound 11½ ounces (780 grams or about five times the weight of a cricket ball). With bomb throwing a crucial skill in a campaign where opposing trenches

Diggers practising bomb-throwing. AWM G00406.

were sometimes only a few metres apart, Bean commented, the 'good cricketer is the man for the bomb'.

Indeed, according to Tom, a good arm could throw them 30 yards.

When news of the diggers' skills filtered back home, it caught the attention of Test cricketer Arthur Mailey. A friend invalided from Gallipoli after suffering a shrapnel wound told Mailey about the feats of Jack Massie, who had thrown bombs without rest for ten hours. The men in the trenches 'saw no one his equal at throwing bombs'. 'Needless to say, [Massie] could not have made such an impression on all around, if he had not had the splendid training in cricket he received at school and University,' Mailey, who had played with him for New South Wales, enthused. Not only had Massie been able to bowl at high pace, even at school he could throw a cricket ball more than 100 yards (110 metres). At Gallipoli, according to his friend Alex Wilkinson, he 'toyed with the idea of being the first to throw a grenade into … Constantinople'.

Victorian Sheffield Shield cricketer Frank Lugton, twenty-one, was another of those who put his cricket talent to good use as a bomb thrower, by being put in charge of a grenade party. In a letter home, he drew on the language of cricket to describe 'a couple of close shaves' he had had. 'Just had the bails rattled once or twice, but not enough to knock them off. As long as they don't get closer I am satisfied.' The 'bails' were all but removed by a shell explosion which buried him for six hours, and then in a narrow miss when a Turkish sniper's bullet shot the bolt from his .303 rifle.

Cricket was never far away from Bean's reporting on Gallipoli. After one afternoon in July, Bean mused,

> One could not get it out of one's head that it was a holiday afternoon at home, and that the occasional smack that rang out of the hills above our heads was the good, healthy sound of a cricket bat with plenty of wood behind it, and that some local club must have been having its evening practice. Then down it came – shells of every sort, feeling, I think, along the hilltops for our batteries rather than for the bats.

Again, after witnessing the slaughter of the 10th Light Horse during the August offensive at the Nek, Bean wrote, 'The best loved leaders in sport ... then rushed straight to their death. Wilfred [Harper] ... was last seen running forward like a schoolboy in a footrace.'

Undaunted by war and terrain, a little-known 'Test' match was played on a makeshift pitch at a rest camp between Outpost No. 3 and the sea on 15 October 1915. The two teams comprised men from each of the three regiments from the 1st and 3rd Australian Light Horse Brigades, who had been withdrawn from the line for a period of rest. Among them was Corporal Leslie Sutherland, 1st Light Horse. A keen cricketer, he played when he could in Cairo before arriving at Gallipoli in May. Sutherland noted that a 60-pounder battery was alongside the rest camp and was in action most of the time. He would later recall:

> The Aussies were supposed to rest so their thoughts naturally turned to sport – football and cricket. Officers and men were sent to Lemnos to beg borrow steal some kit. They, with Australian zeal, produced it. Various football matches were arranged and unusually ran for about 20–30 minutes. Bully and biscuits doesn't build long winded forwards.

Only one 'Test' was played as the brigades had to return to the line. The match was recorded on two traditional, if rudimentary, scoresheets. Sutherland was a member of the team chosen to represent the 1st Light Horse Brigade, and top-scored with 18 runs in the total of 75. In reply, the 3rd Light Horse Brigade managed 56 runs, with Trooper Frank Bach (10th Regiment) top-scoring with 17.

While the details of this game remained buried in the archives of the Australian War Memorial, there was another notable cricket match at Gallipoli that has echoed down the years. With the campaign all but over, the troops were being evacuated from Anzac Cove under a plan drawn up by Brigadier General Cyril Brudenell White. In what would be the most successful operation of the campaign, the Turks were lulled into thinking that the lack of activity was part of preparations for winter.

Taking some final photographs of Gallipoli before the evacuation was completed on the afternoon of Friday, 17 December, Charles Bean called on the 2nd Battalion's Lieutenant Colonel Walter Cass, who, he noted in his diary, had arranged a 'smoking fatigue'. As part of Brudenell White's deception tactics, a party of men were detailed to smoke and lounge about Artillery Road corner where the Turks could see them from

Gaba Tepe, the headland they held about 2 kilometres to the south of Anzac Cove. Their role was to carry water 'like stage soldiers' round the road and then back again. Bean thought it the 'most extraordinary fatigue we have had at Anzac'. The Turks saw the loiterers and began firing, putting three shells onto the road where they were. Bean noted that the smoking fatigue 'retired but presently came out again and manfully smoked like heroes' as the Turks began shelling again.

Bean continued walking to Bolton's Ridge and onto Shell Green, which he noted had originally been 'a fair-sized cotton field on which at the time of the Landing was a thin crop of bushes flecked with the white cotton tufts'. These were soon trampled down to leave 'the only piece of flat ground' at Anzac Cove. Light Horse troopers were now putting it to good use. To the cricket tragic Bean, what he saw could only have gladdened his heart: 'I found the Light Horse playing cricket on Shell Green while shells were flying overhead.'

Major George Macleay Macarthur-Onslow, commander of the 7th Light Horse Regiment, whose dismounted troops had been on Gallipoli since May, had arranged the game as a

Captain Ray Stanley's photo of the Shell Green cricket game. AWM P12584.006.

distraction during the evacuation. Bean wrote in his diary that Macarthur-Onslow was batting, and his photo captured him, with bat inelegantly outstretched, seemingly driving the ball through mid-on, and possibly being caught. Major Harold Suttor, 7th Light Horse, noted that the Turkish gun battery Beachy Bill sent 'shells whizzing overhead during Major Onslow's innings, but the Turks didn't manage to actually bowl anyone out'. As the shells continued to rain down, play finally had to be abandoned for the afternoon.

While Bean's photo has been cited as the sole evidence of the game, at least two other photos were taken: one by Padre Bennett, and the other by Captain Ray Stanley, officer commanding a 2nd Light Horse Brigade signal troop. The Stanley photo was captioned, 'The day before we left. Passing the time away. Col. Onslow batting'. Remarkably, the Bennett image on a glass lantern slide was hand coloured in an effort to capture the moment in an age before colour photography became common.

Granville Ryrie was among those who watched as the cricket ruse played out on Shell Green. 'We had a game of cricket on Shell Green ... and when shells whistled by we pretended to field them. The men were wonderfully cheerful and seemed to take the whole thing as a huge joke,' he wrote to his wife.

This was a period of intense activity. Between 8 and 20 December 1915, 90,000 men were secretly embarked from Suvla and Anzac Cove. On the final night of 19–20 December, the last 10,000 men were evacuated, the withdrawal accomplished without incident or casualties. This was the one great success of an otherwise disastrous campaign that needlessly cost the lives of some 8700 Australian men, 3400 New Zealanders, 22,000 British, 27,000 French and 57,000 Turks. And was marked at the end by a game of cricket.

The scoresheets from the 'Test' at Outpost No 3.

5

SLINGSHOT THUNDERBOLTS

Weary and still in shock after the Gallipoli debacle, the Australian troops were shipped to Lemnos, a low and largely treeless Mediterranean island that offered, however brief, a place to heal and reflect. Tom Richards caught the mood: a mere few weeks in the Gallipoli trenches – the land of 'shiver, shell and hell' – was long enough to 'make an old soldier of any young man ... The loss of life I would not at all mind if we only had a fair, sporting chance.'

Richards had seen enough at Gallipoli to reject the modern concepts of war. The men who died there he saw as victims of 'murder' and 'terrible crimes', the responsibility for which he laid at the feet of the British government. At heart he was a sportsman, and this was reflected in his bitter assessment. He hankered for a war defined by 'honest open hand-to-hand or man-to-man conflicts where the bravest man gets the upper hand, where the strongest arm and the noble heart wins the honour and gratification of the country'. He bemoaned that this view of war was old fashioned and out of date and reluctantly accepted the stark reality that there was no sporting chance in modern war.

A short interlude on Lemnos provided breathing space for bodies to heal and spirits to revive – and to play football. This was despite the medical assessment that the men were too exhausted for sport. A rugby match between two teams from Richards' Field Ambulance unit was arranged. 'The surface was hard and flat, and the game drew a crowd. I padded myself up a lot as usual, and though we won I kept well out of the way and finished up unmarked while many of the fellows were badly rashed and bleeding.' On Christmas Day 1915, three different codes of football were played – a diversion for players and spectators alike.

A football game four days later exemplified, for Richards, 'the true sporting instinct, the fairness of the Australian character'. An old Greek farmer with a small pony laden with two huge baskets of oranges had passed by the field, causing several of the Australians to comment that he 'was a cruel beggar to burden the animal' in such a way.

> I saw the pony had fallen underneath the heavy load and the Greek was shouting, kicking and beating the poor brute which could not rise, try honestly though it did. The attention and dissension of the men was turned and hurled on to the old Greek who persisted in beating the pony. The soldiers, taking compassion on the pony, approached ... but in doing so a basket of oranges lost its balance and fell all over the ground. The soldiers naturally scrambled round and got every orange before the Greek could recover any.

Much football was played on Lemnos that included all codes. Private James McKenzie noted in his diary an Australian Rules match between the officers and NCOs against the men, commenting, not without some glee, 'The men win.' Judy Masters was glad to have a chance to play soccer again over the

Christmas–New Year period. 'There was a camp of Tommies and we had a couple of games of football against them.'

Private Jimmy Clarken, the Australian and Glebe and Randwick rugby union forward, was attached to the 3rd Australian General Hospital, and was pleased to note that there was a ground for football and cricket, which were 'on the bill of fare every day, Saturdays especially'. And he was full of praise for the Anzac nurses. 'The nurses make all the difference; we have over 100.' But life on the windswept island, he noted, was difficult. 'It blows like the devil here, and we often get out of a morning to find some of tents clean bowled, and it is no joke being roused out about 3 a.m. to rescue some of the sisters.'

The interlude on Lemnos ended with the AIF regrouping in Egypt. Despite the overflowing wards in the Australian hospitals in Cairo, where doctors and nurses struggled to deal with the thousands of wounded soldiers from Gallipoli, football was still important – at least for the male staff. They needed a break from the long hours they had worked in the makeshift wards since the landing eight months earlier. As the troops arrived from Lemnos, orderlies and doctors played rugby at the Gezira Sporting Club, with No. 1 General Hospital defeating No. 2 General Hospital 9–3.

On his arrival in Cairo, Tom Richards was soon back on the field, describing how he almost enjoyed playing rugby on a ground which was either rock hard or soft sand. Being tackled was infinitely preferable on the sandy patches. Richards felt the bruises next day. That didn't stop him from lacing up the boots again with the 1st Field Ambulance team six days later, this time for a 14–0 win over the 5th Field Ambulance. Richards would play just one more match in Cairo, his team losing to an Engineers side by 9–6.

While the question of sportsmen joining the AIF may have been a live debate back home, the troops in Egypt were nonetheless very aware of it. In January 1916, Private W. Murphy wrote from Heliopolis to *The Referee*, exemplifying this:

They say that the sports are not enlisting as they ought, but there is no doubt of the statement being false. One has only to go round the different camps here, and he comes across fellows who are connected with some branch of sport or other. You see some either kicking the football about or having a smack with the cricket bat ... Last night I went up to the 1st Light Horse camp to see Tibby Cotter. He is looking in the pink, and has had some great experiences on the Peninsular, and his regiment was the last to leave the historic place.

Albert 'Tibby' Cotter, thirty-one, was a nuggetty, 172-centimetre-tall former Australian Test fast bowler, capable of terrifying pace, estimated by observers at the time as reaching 100 miles per hour (160 kilometres per hour) – enough to regularly break stumps. In a nine-year international career that changed the way fast bowlers approached their task, he played in twenty-one Tests, taking eighty-nine wickets at an average of 28.64 runs. After Victor Trumper, he was considered the most popular cricketer in Australia, and his use of a fearsome bouncer three or four times an over intimidated batsmen and saw him labelled as 'distinctly dangerous to life and limb'. The English journalist Charles Alcock sniffed: 'One hardly expects to see this sort of bowling in a Test match. His bowling is not so much to be described by the word deadly as by that other word dangerous.'

A bookkeeper, Cotter enlisted in the 12th Light Horse Regiment on 15 April 1915. Photos of him in uniform adorned newspapers and recruitment posters, affording great publicity to the AIF in its urgent bid to build an overseas army.

Although his recruitment medical revealed his vision was rated at the minimum standard and, as a city boy, having no great riding ability, he was accepted into the Light Horse and embarked with the 3rd Reinforcements, 12th Light Horse Regiment, from Sydney on 9 August 1915. After briefly taking part in the final months of the Gallipoli campaign, Tibby waited in Cairo for the forthcoming Palestine campaign.

Yet another cricketer in camp was all-rounder Herbie Collins, twenty-seven, already a New South Wales Sheffield Shield player, and attached to the 6th Company Army Service Corps. As a lance corporal, he would serve as a driver in France; once the war ended, he would captain the Australian Test team. Nearby, wrote Private Murphy, was Lieutenant Charlie Kelleway, 1st Battalion AIF, who played twenty-six Tests for Australia between 1910 and 1928, and was Tibby Cotter's schoolmate at Forest Lodge Public School in Sydney. Cricket writer Ray Robinson would later comment that Collins 'had an implacable trench warfare style that in difficult times earned admiration from his own side, put bowlers on the road to exasperation and sent onlookers through the doors of bars'.

The match between Murphy's ASC unit, the 20th, and the 5th Reinforcements of the 25th Battalion, took place on 8 January 1916. Murphy thought the credentials of his unit's eleven looked on paper good enough to play any team. Describing the playing conditions, he complimented the effort that Sydney first-grade player Billy Unsworth had put into forming and rolling to create the all-important wicket. He wrote: 'You can imagine the work entailed in making a playable wicket on a sandy and desolate place as the Sahara Desert, on which our camp is pitched.' The ASC team scored 168 runs and dismissed the 5th Reinforcements for a paltry 76.

At the Gezira Sports Club in Cairo, in March 1916, an AIF team took on an English Yeomanry side captained by Colonel J.W.H.T. Douglas, who had captained the England team that won the 1911–12 Ashes. (Australian fans, bored by his slow scoring, dubbed his initials 'Johnny Won't Hit Today'.) This was an unofficial 'Ashes' match. Some of the Australian team were from the small headquarters staff left in Egypt after the Gallipoli evacuation, and the rest were Light Horsemen training for the campaign. In particular, the Australians had an ace up their sleeve – the redoubtable Tibby Cotter.

The match against the English was the perfect time for him to uncoil his slingshot thunderbolts. Recounting the match in a Melbourne newspaper after the war, the columnist 'Sergeant' wrote that the desert sand, 'watered and stamped with tibbin by the Kamleelah wallahs', made a pretty fair concrete pitch. The English Yeoman, all officers, took the field in spotless flannels.

> The officers were always punctilious about appearance and cleanliness even in the desert. How they carried their boudoirs about in the desert was a marvel. Our team looked like a mob of Murrumbidgee whalers who had lost their swags. A few of the officers were in khaki slacks and shirts, and the other ranks wore their old blue-grey flannel shirts, riding strides with the knees out for the most part, no leggings, and their knitted socks hanging down over their ankle boots.

The Australians won the toss and had a bat. They managed only 57, with Douglas getting most of the wickets.

> Then the Yeomanry took block. That's about all they did take. Tibby Cotter ... bowled with the wind behind him, and the Tommy officers never saw which way he went. They just walked in and out in a dazed manner. We had four men behind the stumps to stop any risk of byes getting into double figures.

Colonel Clive Single, a first-grade cricketer in Sydney, bowled a mix of slow and medium spin from the other end. Together, Cotter and Single bowled the Yeomanry all out for 4, including one bye. 'Who is this Cotter man?' the English kept asking, according to the newspaper account. 'Douglas had spotted

Cotter the first time he made his characteristic long run before bowling but thought it wise not to break the news to the batsmen beforehand. They took it like sportsmen when they knew. It hardly seemed fair.' A Test cricketer cleaning up the English while on active service made Tibby Cotter the type of recruit that the army could only dream of – especially as the casualty count worsened.

This was not the only victory the Australians scored over the British during this post-Gallipoli period. Besides cricket, intense rivalry developed between the Australian and British cavalry about who had the best horses. To settle the score, a 'Cavalry Desert Olympics' was arranged between the two armies. The Australians were confident, having complete faith in their strong and hardy stockhorses, called Walers, a cross between thoroughbred and semi-draught horses. They had speed, strength and stamina.

Three events were to be held to test the horses' ability, the riders' ability and their combined ability. Lieutenant Guy Haydon, 12th Light Horse Regiment, and his horse, Midnight, were chosen to represent Australia. Unusually, the army had reluctantly agreed for Guy and his younger brother, Barney, who was also a lieutenant in the 12th, to take their own horses from the Haydon family's Hunter Valley property to the war. Guy had a special bond with Midnight, a jet-black Waler with a white, three-pointed star like a tiara on her head. Guy, who had been a schoolfriend and teammate of Jack Massie's at Shore in Sydney, was an excellent horseman and trained Midnight well in his duties around the family station back home. When the two brothers were sent from Cairo to Gallipoli in August 1915, they had to leave their horses behind. Guy and Midnight were finally reunited, enabling them to join forces as the Australian representatives.

The first event was a short-distance sprint race over 440 yards (400 metres). Unbeknown to the British, Midnight was by the champion sire Tester, whose progeny were rarely beaten in the short-distance Bridle Spurts back in Australia. Guy and Midnight won the event at a canter, easing down at the finish after establishing a commanding lead to give Australia a 1–nil lead. The second contest was a utility Flags event involving obstacles, with the riders using their swords to complete tasks against the clock. Again, Guy and Midnight prevailed, winning the event with a clear round in the quickest time to stretch Australia's lead to 2–nil. The third event was an equitation test involving the dressage movements.

The British were confident they would win this event as at home there was a focus on this type of more formal equine movements. Again, they underestimated Guy and Midnight. Being a fine all-round horseman, Guy had trained Midnight in her early years back on the farm. She would move off his legs while performing the bush tasks such as opening gates, to stop, back, extend and to do flying changes. To the astonishment of the British, Guy won narrowly to give Australia a 3–nil victory. Guy and Midnight were the heroes of the Australian Light Horse. Their success created a cultural shift in the respect the British cavalry had for the Australians. As the desert campaigns evolved, the British acknowledged the tougher, bush-reared Australian horses had come into their own. In fact, they rated the Walers to be some of the finest cavalry horses ever seen. Of this the Australians had little doubt – whether it be a charge under arms or a complex dressage event.

6

THE GAME CHANGES

Large concentrations of Australian reinforcements began arriving in the Étaples region of northern France as the Anzac focus moved to the Western Front in the first half of 1916. There were sixteen hospitals and a convalescent centre that could cater for 22,000 sick or wounded soldiers. Once in France, training began immediately and was necessarily physically demanding. Private Gerald Evans, 9th Battalion, a saddler from Rosewood in Queensland, recalled the training at his camp at Étaples, under the direction of an English sergeant major who shouted: 'They say you cannot drill the Australians, but I like training them.' It is clear from Evans' account just how important an adjunct sport was in the training regimen:

> We would do an hour's physical training, and it was willing, a one-hour lecture which was on the rifle, Mills bomb, mortar or Lewis machine gun, then back on the hard training ... Then there was the obstacle course. You were lined up and told it was a course and off you went. You had to jump a trench, run to a wall and scramble over

it without any toehold, then on to an 8 ft. drop, and if you jibbed you got pushed over by the ones behind.

Physical demands such as these developed endurance, strength and aggression, qualities that played out recreationally, and could be enjoyed in an atmosphere of team spirit.

By Easter Sunday, 23 April 1916, the Australian Field Ambulance units were stationed at Sailly-sur-la-Lys, a support base in north-central France where units were stationed in the lead-up to the Fromelles battle three months later. It gave Richards the chance to catch up with old rugby mates from Wales who were in the British army and camped nearby. The Welsh convinced him to stay for a drink, bringing out wine, whisky and cigarettes. 'They were not long in finding out my name and my footer performances and a cheery welcome followed.' While there, Richards played his first game of rugby in France, against the 3rd Field Ambulance. It was played on a cow field, where the 'grass was lovely and soft, but so slippery that one could not venture to move sharply.' With his team winning 15–0 before an enthusiastic crowd, Richards rated the game as one of the most pleasant he had played.

The disillusionment with how the British were running the war, however, continued unabated. The Australians had already been given a taste of what lay ahead in the early fighting across the old towns and villages in the northern French countryside. The idea of sport at such moments was far from their minds; survival was the order of the day. Yet when the immediate crisis waned, sport took the focus away from the fighting, however briefly.

Another match for Richards followed, this time between the 1st and 3rd Field Ambulance units on a ground where there were neither goals nor sidelines, and with grass more than half a metre high in places. The conditions were not conducive to good football but nevertheless led to a curious game. The 1st Field

Ambulance team was one try to nil ahead at half-time, and by the end of the match they had scored another three tries to none.

> But the strange part was that the ball could not be seen in the long grass and the men kicked yards away from the ball and fell down where they thought it was when rush stopping. I played fullback and enjoyed it very much indeed, but when it came to dribbling rushes and I could not see the ball, there were anxious moments you might depend. A fellow was laid out and none of our players noticed it, he was practically lost in the long grass.

Along with Richards, James Gibb, nineteen, was one of 20,000 Australians in the Armentières sector. A stretcher-bearer with the 7th Field Ambulance, he loved his football – any code would do. He kept a diary in which he noted the games he played and watched. 'We return from Bois Grenier to Ft Rompu – A new "soccer" ball gives us plenty of sport,' he wrote on 24 June 1916. And plenty of sport there was. Over the next three weeks he recorded various football games, both rugby and soccer. On 10 July his team won a rugby game 9–6, and soccer 3–2. 'Myself a scorer in soccer. Great Day.' These days of sport in late June and early July 1916 would soon be treasured.

In the early morning of 1 July 1916, the war on the Western Front erupted in carnage when more than 100,000 British infantrymen leaped from their trenches in the country north of the River Somme to attack German troops. Within twenty-four hours, the British army would suffer the worst day in its history, with more than 57,000 casualties, including nearly 20,000 soldiers killed. All to gain just 8 square kilometres of territory. A war of attrition set in along the Western Front.

A few days later, across the Belgian border at Neuve-Église, ambulance units prepared to move to the Somme. Given a break on 6 July to play cricket and football, they were suddenly bombarded by German shells. Richards noted that around 8.40 pm three of his mates had been killed while walking along the main road. 'These are the first casualties in France amongst our unit.' Despite such attacks, sport did not stop. Two days later the ambulancemen played football between the unit's 'A' and 'B' sections. Richards noted: 'The rivalry was intense throughout and the barracking terrific as the game has long been talked about and there was wholesale betting going on with "A" favourites. The game was very fast indeed and the play very clever all round.' A day later Richards took to his diary with a cricket match in progress while the German guns were 'thundering all around'.

That same day 'A' and 'B' sections resumed hostilities, this time at cricket, with a big win for the 'B' team, scoring 238 runs to 118. 'They now feel happy and compensated for the defeat at football,' Richards observed. For the next two months there would be no time for sport. 'They came to fight. They know that many will never come out of France again ... Our men do look fine, too. Their physique will take them where no other soldiers on earth could get.'

On the Somme from late July into early September 1916, troops of the 1st, 2nd and 4th Australian Divisions attacked at Pozières and Mouquet Farm, and although they captured some ground, this came at the cost of severe casualties. News of how the Australians had fared at Pozières after the 1st Division attacked German positions on 23 July began to filter through. Among the wounded a day later was Judy Masters, shot through the shoulder. He was taken to No. 5 Australian General Hospital in Rouen. He would not rejoin his unit for another four months.

All three AIF Divisions, 1st, 2nd and 4th, fought at Pozières, suffering heavily during nineteen attacks launched over forty-two days. Australian casualties totalled a staggering 23,000 men, of whom 6800 were killed. The nation reeled from news of this slaughter, which followed the earlier disaster on the night of 19–20 July at the Battle of Fromelles, in which more than 5500 Australians were casualties, including nearly 2000 dead. In his account of Fromelles, and with a heavy heart, Charles Bean drew on a cricket analogy to describe the fighting, in which 'the Australians, up on the parapet, flung their missiles like cricketers throwing at a wicket'. However, this was no longer a game.

7

SOMEWHERE IN FRANCE

As a youth, Albert Jacka was shy. Nonetheless, he was intensely competitive and gifted in sports such as boxing, cycling and football. Having enlisted in September 1914 in the 14th Battalion AIF, the twenty-two-year-old landed at Gallipoli on 26 April. Less than a month later, on the night of 18–19 May, he single-handedly captured a Turkish trench during a Turkish counterattack on the Allies' position at Courtney's Post, thus becoming the first Australian to be awarded a Victoria Cross in the war.

In June 1916, the 14th Battalion was shipped from Egypt to the Western Front in France. Newly promoted to lieutenant, on the night of 6 August 1916, Jacka moved into the line at Pozières with his unit. As dawn broke, German troops overran part of the line. Jacka rallied his men and charged, recapturing a section of trench, freeing a group of captured Australians and forcing the surrender of some fifty Germans. Jacka was wounded in the neck and shoulder and subsequently taken to a London hospital. Awarded the Military Cross, his bravery moved Charles Bean to describe Jacka's action as 'the most dramatic and effective act of individual audacity in the history of the AIF'. Captain Edgar

Rule, a friend, who also was the 14th Battalion's historian, was moved to write that Jacka possessed 'courage, high personal honour, and outstanding manhood – equal to that of the greatest heroes of antiquity'. Jacka's feats would 'stir the blood of Australians for all time'.

Jacka's heroics saw him immediately elevated into exalted territory; he had become a Homeric hero. Here was a soldier who represented everything that the Australian army needed at a time when the terrible casualties on the Western Front saw recruitment slump. With the need for reinforcements increasingly desperate, enlistment figures could not keep pace. Efforts redoubled to boost recruitment, with Jacka promoted as the 'spirit of the Anzac', and his 14th Battalion now known as 'Jacka's Mob'. His image appeared on recruiting posters, in magazines and newspapers. One powerful poster featured Jacka standing tall with his rifle and bayonet, while in the background sportsmen in various codes were enjoying themselves. The message was blunt: 'Enlist in the Sportsmen's Thousand' to 'show the enemy what Australian sporting men can do'.

A similar campaign advocating the formation of 'Sportsmen's Battalions' had been part of the British scene since the war's early days. In Australia, high-profile sportsmen who did enlist to acclaim in the sporting fraternity included, as described earlier, Jack Massie, Tom Richards, Tibby Cotter, Herbie Collins, Judy Masters and Jacka. Test batsman Charlie Macartney, and future Test cricketers Bert Oldfield, a stretcher-bearer in the 15th Field Ambulance, Jack Gregory, a Field Artillery lieutenant, Nip Pellew, a captain in the 27th Battalion, and 101st Battery gunner Johnny Taylor were among others. Yet another was Hughie Mehegan, ex-champion lightweight boxer of Australia, who enlisted as a driver with the 22nd Company, Australian Army Service Corps.

As the fighting on the Western Front in 1916 dragged on, the need for reinforcements was ever more urgent. However, the government, by legislation, could not compel Australian citizens to serve overseas. Labor Prime Minister Billy Hughes concluded that conscription was the only answer, despite it being strongly opposed by his own party in the Senate. Hughes decided, therefore, to take the issue directly to the people with a plebiscite. After a bitter and furious debate which split the nation, Australians went to the polls on 28 October 1916, to decide if they were in favour of the government having the power to conscript for overseas service. The referendum was narrowly defeated, with 1,160,033 votes against and 1,087,557 votes in favour. In the ensuing political fallout, the Labor Party split, and Hughes formed a breakaway party – the Nationalists.

On the same day the nation voted, a unique Australian Rules exhibition match between the 3rd Division AIF and the AIF's Combined Training Units was played in London. The match was suggested by Major General John Monash, in command of the AIF 3rd Division, and supported by Brigadier General Sir Newton Moore, general officer commanding AIF depots, United Kingdom. It was organised by the former Olympic swimmer Lieutenant Frank Beaurepaire.

Monash granted a holiday to his troops who were training on the Salisbury Plain. While no sportsman himself, he understood the hold that sport had on Australians, not least the passion of Victorians for Australian Rules football. After the war, Monash would tell a Melbourne dinner that all responsible AIF commanders early in the war were impressed with the importance of sport. The YMCA and the Australian Comforts Fund sent liberal amounts of sporting equipment. Every unit had its teams, and what never failed was the appeal to their sportsmanship – the same inspiration they took into battle. Whether war or sport, 'It's up to you to play for your side' was a message that all understood.

Londoners were intrigued by the prospect of the exhibition match. *The Winner* newspaper in Melbourne commented that the game, played at the Queen's Club in London, was the first occasion on which two 'really expert teams had been pitted against one another on English soil'. The match drew more than 3000 spectators, the majority of whom were Australian soldiers taking advantage of the holiday that Monash had granted.

A report on the contest in *The Winner* observed that the teams comprised 'fine exponents of Australian football – men who have shown exceptional skill on the fields here'. The report added that the game seemed have been a fast and even exhibition, despite such handicaps as a lack of training and the time to develop combinations. When the game was over, the Third Australian Division team won 6.16 (52) to the Combined Training Units' 4.12 (36).

The London correspondent of *The Winner* wrote that since the arrival of the Anzacs there had been an odd match here and there of the Australian game but nothing at all comparable in importance with Saturday's game.

> Every man seemed imbued with the desire to show the possibilities of the Australian national game. Undoubtedly, they realised that the crowd was a critical one – that portion of it which consisted of lovers of Rugger and Soccer. There was another portion made up of staunch Anzac adherents of both teams, and their enthusiasm was a thing to remember.

The game drew favourable coverage from the London papers, including *The Times*, which observed that the Australians had combined soccer and rugby, with the rules designed to make the game a fast one, and 'it has certainly the look of being that'. Also notable were the two hand-stitched footballs used in the game, which were made by Corporal Claude McMullen, a leatherworker in Melbourne before the war. In a letter to *The Winner*, McMullen revealed that he had also made the first

LESSONS OF THE GREAT WAR.
Australian Rules Amended.

Football when the boy come home.

WOOLOOMOOLOO KIWIS LOSE THE PREMIERSHIP.

"On the third day we exploded a mine under our opponents' goal."

DISCRETION THE BETTER PART OF VALOUR.

FORCE OF HABIT
Private Bidjim takes cover instead of defending goal

SPORT AND WAR.
The advantage of the High Mark.

Pte. Ballup, of Wangaratta Dingbats F.C., collects a souvenir

Cartoons by Australian artists Fred Leist, Will Dyson and Laurie Tayler for the London match program.

football for the Australian Divisions in Egypt. Altogether, since enlisting he had made 216 footballs – known affectionately as 'The AIF Ball'.

McMullen's footballs were prized at the front line, enabling matches to be organised as the brutal European winter of 1916–17 set in. Besides footballs, there was also the problem of proper playing fields, especially the larger ovals required for Australian football. Not to be denied a game of footy, the Western Australia–raised 44th Battalion resolved the problem by devising their own game. Called 'mobbing', it was played with a hessian bag filled with straw and had no rules other than that the bag could not be kicked, the object being to force or throw the bag through the opposition's goal. The game's appeal was that it could be played on any ground.

A week before the London match, another game was held 'somewhere in France', as a letter to *The Winner* revealed. Private Lou Baker wrote that his unit had received and accepted a challenge for a game 'of the old toeball', and 'yesterday the team and barrackers, about 27 all told, set off in a three-ton motor lorry for the ground, some nine miles south from here, and four miles from the front line. Our chaps scraped home on time by three points, 7-13 to 7-10, amidst tremendous noise from the on lookers.'

A few weeks later, Lieutenant Lionel Short, a former journalist on *The Argus* in Melbourne who was attached to the 23rd Battalion, wrote of a football match on a Western Front battlefield between officers and NCOs:

> The playing field is within shell range. Every inch of it has been won from the enemy by the hardest fighting, of which evidence lay all around. The centre was marked by two enormous shell holes, with two 5.9 shells (unexploded) lying beside a hand bomb at the bottom of one. Other shell holes lay towards the goal posts. Indeed,

the ground might have been prepared for a billiard match so amply was it provided with pockets. Some damaged wire entanglement, a small mound, and a few half-filled sandbags assisted to complete the picture of warfare.

There was a light fall of snow on the ground that was melting fast in the warm sun of February 1917. At 2.30 p.m., with the band playing 'I Want to Go Home' and with guns booming in the distance, the game began under the control of an umpire with a 'look of worry on his face'. Short observed that the look of the players on the field would not have pleased the eye of an Essendon barracker.

> But they were just out of the trenches, where it is not possible to buy the shorts, shirts, and stockings that make up the uniform of the footballer. Instead, the officers wore sheepskin jerkins with socks over their puttee-less legs, the NCOs had their issue cardigans, and all wore cap comforters.

Although there were some skilled players on the field who had played at senior levels in Melbourne, they had had little chance to practise. This contributed to a lack of fine marking and long kicks, together with poor passing, which too frequently was to the other side. Adding to the challenges the players faced was the melted snow, which 'made the ground as slippery as a banana skin'. As the players began the second quarter, with the NCOs leading, Short observed:

> It was a sadly altered group of men that faced each other for the second bout. With mud on faces hands and clothes, they stood breathing heavily. Trench life does not make for soundness in wind and muscle. But the gameness that had carried them so far into the world's turmoil sustained

> them in this trial of skill. The heavy members in the commissioned ranks – and some were hefty – charged down on the little members of the opposing side, who only escaped a roll in the slimy mud by nimbleness and dexterity.

Short thought the umpire provided the 'star turn' of the afternoon.

> With fine speed he had followed up the ball which was fast rolling towards a deep and snow-filled shell hole. As he neared the crater his foot slipped on its edge. To the astonishment and delight of spectators and players he disappeared nearly from view, rolling over and over to the bottom of the hole, where he lay in the soft snow.

Short rated the match a 'most stupendous game'. Each player had contributed to that 'most astonishing match on that most astonishing ground', with the NCOs winning six goals to two. The afternoon was but a brief, unforgettable interlude.

That night the officers and sergeants did an inspection before the next tour of duty in the trenches. Short was certain that 'the game had carried their thoughts vividly back to those happy days when football was played in certain Melbourne suburbs they called "home". And it is in such happy thoughts and memories that we soldiers live.'

On the field that day there was a grim reminder of the war: behind the goalposts at the southern end was a small heap of earth – the grave of a dead soldier with the simple inscription, 'To Unknown British Heroes'. Short was moved to record this poignant scene as the 'saddest and most realistic touch of all'. Such scenes were now beginning to appear all too quickly across the Western Front: white wooden crosses seemingly sprouting at will. Before long, seven of the men who played in the London exhibition game would be among them, somewhere in France.

8

BOWLING AGAINST THE WIND

The sight before Major General Harry Chauvel, commander of the Australian and New Zealand Mounted Division, brought gales of laughter. In the unforgiving environment of Sinai and Palestine this was a rarity, and it was the camels that did it. The scene was a desert sports carnival at El Arish, a northern town in the Sinai Peninsula, on the Mediterranean coast, in early 1917. The carnival involved Light Horse regiments and companies of the Imperial Camel Corps (ICC), among whom were Australians originally intended as reinforcements for Light Horse regiments in the Sinai and Palestine campaign.

The camels were the stars at ICC sports carnivals. Egg-and-spoon races, wrestling and tug-of-war were all contested on camelback and, after watching the camels compete at the El Arish carnival, Chauvel wrote to his wife:

> I have never seen anything so funny as musical chairs on camels, the men had to ride bareback round a big ring, while the music was playing. When it stopped, they dismounted and led their camels up to the sandbags. As a camel dislikes being hurried beyond all things, and objects

to going out for a walk when he is being led, it was not always the smartest men who got the chairs. You never saw anything so ridiculous as the camels keeping time to the music, and one of them started waltzing in the middle of the ring.

Beyond the hijinks, of course, there was a critical reason for the presence of the camel and Light Horse units. Their goal was the defeat of Turkish forces intent on capturing the Suez Canal, Britain's vital trade link to south and east Asia, and Australia and New Zealand. The first Turkish attack on the canal had been easily repulsed in February 1915, but now, after the end of the Gallipoli campaign, Turkey had the troops to launch a new drive to capture the waterway. British and dominion forces stood in their path.

The second Turkish advance on the canal began in mid-July 1916 and culminated in the Battle of Romani on 4–5 August. Although outnumbered, the Allied forces defeated the Turks, who, despite several dogged rearguard stands, were forced all the way back to their outposts on the Palestine frontier. Turkish defences at Magdhaba fell on 23 December, and those at Rafa on 9 January 1917. Both were captured at bayonet point. Allied occupation of the Sinai Peninsula was completed with the capture of the last small garrisons of Turkish forces in February 1917. This ensured the security of the Suez Canal and opened up the Palestine front. As the Allied forces regrouped in preparation for what would be a history-making campaign in Palestine, sports meetings were a focus of much-needed relaxation.

At one point, this involved a regatta and water sports meeting at Ismailia, which included sailing, rowing, swimming and diving. There was also a tub race, walking the greasy pole, a mop fight, a tug-of-war in boats and a duck race, the rules for which read: 'A duck will be thrown into the water and given a start. Competitors will then dive into the water and try to catch the duck. Competitor who catches the duck wins and also keeps the duck.'

Harry Chauvel arranged a race day, the Desert Column First Spring Meeting, at Rafa on 21 March 1917. It was held on the battlefield at Rafa, an amphitheatre of green grass where they had fought only weeks earlier. The course-setters avoided the filled-in trenches in erecting the big sandbag and scrub jumps, while the Walers were groomed amid gaiety and excitement from the riders. As a pipe band played, the mood for the Rafa Races was like a picnic race meeting back home, with one important difference – nearly every horse competing had carried his owner in the battle fought where they were now racing.

Chauvel, a successful amateur rider in his younger days who was known throughout the force for his horsemanship, was one of the race stewards. He provided a prize of five guineas for the Anzac Steeplechase, entering his own horse, Ballie, in his groom's name. Other races on the card were the Sinai Grand National, the Syrian Derby, the Promised Land Stakes, the Border Plate and the Jerusalem Scurry for mules. The troops were enthusiastic in their preparations for the big day, recreating as much as was possible in the desert the various elements that were part and parcel of a racecourse at home, including an enclosure, totalisator, jumps and a marked course. Trophies were ordered from Cairo and a program printed. The meet was a great success, raising more than £200 for charities. The horse that won the Sinai Grand National had been wounded three times in battle. In a letter to his wife after the event, Chauvel wrote:

> We have had a great day today the races at Rafa and I don't know when I have enjoyed a day's racing so much. The course was lovely, beautiful green grass in a large natural amphitheatre right bang in the middle of the battlefield of Rafa! – the Turks' trenches and rifle-pits needed a little dodging when laying out the course but that was all, and

the jumps were sand-bag walls with brushwood on top. My Division won five out of the eight horse races and, out of the other three, one (the Anzac Steeplechase) was won by a 3rd L.H. Brigade horse. My own horse "Ballie" ran third in the Anzac Steeplechase ... I think it was very creditable of our horses considering there were so many English hunters and well-bred horses about.

With the love of horses shared by Australians, New Zealanders and Englishmen, and the strong competitive spirit between brigades and divisions, more carnivals and gymkhanas would follow the Rafa meeting. Chauvel did all he could to encourage them when the troops were resting. Anzac Day 1917 provided one such opportunity with, according to Trooper E.A. Lewis, 'a big program of sports' in the desert. That day it was 46°C 'in the shade, with a hot, sandy wind blowing' and, observed Lewis with some understatement, 'it was not too pleasant'. But that didn't stop the men playing football and cricket. He added that Tibby Cotter was with them, and they had a strong cricket team led by Captain Eric Hyman, who at one time played for the gentlemen of England and who was a good bat and an excellent wicketkeeper.

By the time Lewis's letter to *The Referee* had been published, the mounted troops of the Desert Column had been involved in two abortive attempts – on 26 March and 17 April – to capture Gaza, the heart of the main Turkish defensive position in southern Palestine. The attack may have been a failure, but Tibby was commended in the *Official History* for his 'fine work under heavy fire' during the second battle.

Meanwhile, in France, the First Battle of Bullecourt was about to unfold, with Australian troops going into battle under the headstrong British general Sir Hubert Gough in April 1917. Among the Australians was Lance Corporal Richard Overy, who joined the 4th Machine Gun Company after leaving Gallipoli in mid-1916. Overy was a dedicated rugby league fan and had played league from its inception. He was among the first to join a newly formed Company team, calling themselves the Mudlarks, after an Australian bird with a propensity to make nests with sticks and mud – a fitting reference to life in the trenches. They were soon competing against teams raised throughout the AIF and British troops. Never beaten during the winter of 1916–17, they regarded the defeat of the Welsh Guards 3–0 as their greatest victory. A solidly built forward, Overy proved a valuable player, and was duly presented with a gold medallion for his contribution to the team.

However, the Mudlarks' time together was short-lived. On 11 April 1917, the 4th Machine Gun Company took part in the first disastrous attack at Bullecourt. More than 3300 Australian troops were killed, wounded or taken prisoner in this ill-fated attempt to break through the Hindenburg Line. Among the casualties were some of the Mudlarks. With so few players remaining, the team was forced to disband.

Five months later, Overy was wounded near Messines in Belgium and hospitalised with severe gunshot wounds to his buttocks and abdomen. In January 1918, he was repatriated to Australia, taking with him his blue cotton Mudlarks jersey, with the silhouette of the Australian mudlark sewn onto it, and still encrusted with the mud of the team's final game.

Despite the failure of the first attack at Bullecourt, another attack across the same ground was ordered for 3 May 1917. The Australians broke into and took part of the Hindenburg Line, but no important strategic advantage was ever gained; in the two battles the AIF lost 10,000 men. Among the dead in the Second Battle of Bullecourt was a Geelong footballer, Captain Joe Slater. In France, he had played football for the 22nd Battalion. His death played out in an unexpected manner sixteen days later during a VFL match at Corio Oval, Geelong.

At half-time, two recruiting sergeants addressed the crowd, calling for volunteers. The *Geelong Advertiser* reported that the reception they received was hostile, and their appeals produced no volunteers. One spectator cried out that footballers had done their share of supplying recruits, and that the army should turn its attention to the golf links or tennis courts. The *Advertiser* reported that 'a feeling of profound sorrow passed over Geelong last evening' when news of Slater's death became known. Geelong players paid their respects by wearing black armbands in their next game. Poignantly, Slater's fiancée, Nellie, who had joined the Australian Army Nursing Service, only heard the news of his death after the ship carrying her to the battlefields of France docked in Britain.

Among the dead that same day at Bullecourt was the 19th Battalion's Private Norman Callaway, twenty-one. He had made his first-class cricketing debut for New South Wales at the age of eighteen when he joined renowned Test cricketer Charlie Macartney at the crease in February 1915 in a match against Queensland at the Sydney Cricket Ground, with New South Wales in trouble at 3 for 17. Callaway was a cricketing prodigy from the outback New South Wales town of Hay. He soon unleashed a dazzling array of fine strokes, driving and square-cutting on his way to an extraordinary 207. At the other end, Macartney watched the emergence of this young talent, content to let him play the dominant role in scoring, before going on to score 103. Callaway was the first person to score a double century in his initial first-class match and was immediately hailed as a future Test cricketer. However, with the cancellation of the 1915/16 Sheffield Shield and international cricket season, Callaway felt the pressure to join the war effort.

Cricketers who enlisted were lauded, their names adorning 'Sportsmen's Unit AIF' posters. On 17 May 1916, Callaway enlisted and was posted to the 5th Brigade's 19th Battalion and five months later sailed for Britain and the Western Front. Just on a year after he joined up, on 3 May 1917, Norman Callaway advanced with his unit in the Second Battle of Bullecourt. He was last seen sheltering in a shell hole before being hit by shrapnel. Later, it was confirmed that he died that same day, although his body was never found.

Two months later, on the Western Front, battalions of the 3rd Division's 10th Brigade emerged from the Battle of Messines in need of a well-earned rest. Among these was the 40th Battalion. Raised in Tasmania, it had undergone a costly introduction to war at Messines, losing more than 350 men killed or wounded. On 24 June, the battalion bivouacked on the banks of the River Douve, not far from Ypres. There, over the next two weeks, the battalion, along with the 10th Field Ambulance, 10th Machine Gun Company, and 10th Field Company of Engineers, made the most of the warm summer days, with cricket and various sports dominating a daily program that other troops on the Western Front could only have dreamed of.

In his unit history of the 40th Battalion, Frank Green captured the interlude, describing how the military training culminated in a skill-at-arms competition among representative platoons, embracing Lewis gun work, bombing, musketry, bayonet fighting, gas and tactical exercise. With that done, the troops turned to sports events, the chief event of which was an obstacle race. One of the obstacles was swimming across the River Douve. As Green described it, 'About 50 competitors plunged into the stream and stirred up the mud and smell of centuries, which raised a mild protest from the rest of the Brigade.'

Earlier in June at Messines, the heat of battle fell on the 37th Battalion in their first major action. Leading one company up a modest slope under sustained gunfire and a massive gas attack was Captain Robert Grieve, a Melbourne baysider. As the only officer in his company who was not dead or wounded, Grieve made his way through a gap in the wire to attack a machine-gun post. Taking a bag of bombs with him, and throwing as he advanced, he stormed the pillbox, killing two gun crews.

He had been a good left-arm bowler at Melbourne's Wesley College and the Brighton Cricket Club where his accurate medium pacers saw him rated among the leading bowlers of the city's sub-district competition. Grieve was wounded but survived and later wrote to his parents about the action:

> We had run into a pretty tight corner, as you will have read by all accounts, so I had to put all the company under cover in shell holes. Those with me wanted to come on our little stunt and I had to threaten to shoot two of them if they did not obey orders and remain where I told them. Off I went, bowling against the wind and got the usual number of wickets. I was surprisingly lucky when you come to think of it because the first two guns as well as two in rear of them were kicking the dust up all round me. It was not long after this that I got a smack on the shoulder ... it sounded just like the smack of a bullet through a target ... this spun me round two or three times and I fell flop. Crawled into a shell hole and pulled my equipment off.

Grieve was evacuated to England, where he received the VC from King George V later that year. He returned to his unit, but due to illness, had to return home at war's end in 1918.

Elsewhere on the Western Front, Private Reg Telfer, an orderly with the Australian Medical Corps in the South Australia–raised 27th Battalion, embraced the chance to be out of the line and throw himself into a 7th Brigade Sports Day. The pastoral beauty of the small valley between low, steep hills covered with clumps of oak and elm trees held him transfixed. A big program of military sports lay ahead of the several thousand men spread around the grassy field for the various events, which included footraces over distances between 100 yards and 880 yards, long jump and high jump, as well as football kicking and, of course, stretcher-bearing. Telfer, who was thankful for the £100 sent by 27th Battalion Comforts Fund in South Australia for sports equipment, was a keen observer of the day:

> The events came off successfully. The running tracks on the grass got very muddy and could have done with several loads of creekbed sand as could the kicking off place of the football kicking and long jump respectively, but otherwise there was nothing that could be growled at. Machine gunners, signallers, trench mortars infantry, engineers, ASC [Army Service Corps] and Army Medical all jostled together, and rubbed shoulders and by their proximity to one another extracted whatever fun and noisy joy possible from the day. These events all help to keep up the morale of the army and I think the length of the strife needs counter-acting somewhat and in some such way if we cannot have an immediate peace.

But not all the troops there that day found it easy to put the trauma of war to one side and lose themselves in sport. Many chose to lose themselves in grog.

> I'm afraid a pretty large amount of beverage was consumed during the day and the scene around the Sergeants' Mess after the lunch interval resembled more the picture of No-Man's Land after a battle. Thousands of empty bottles lay around the grass and floated down the stream which flowed through the grounds and all along its banks lay the casualties of the day, in all attitudes. But it would be a mistake to think everyone was so, for, for all the screwed ones that one couldn't help noticing, there were the

thousands of quiet, orderly, sober lads enjoying themselves in watching their favourite runners and jumpers endeavouring to capture the premier events of the day.

Charlie Macartney too enlisted, joining the 3rd Division Artillery HQ on 4 January 1916, and sailed for France in May that year with the rank of temporary Warrant Officer. Two months after Callaway died, Macartney was chosen in an Australian army team to play England in an international military match at Lord's. A crowd of 8000 people watched and an Australian band played, with one stand filled with loudly barracking khaki-clad Australians. The AIF team was led by an army doctor from Sydney, Captain Eric Barbour. Having made his first-class debut for New South Wales against Queensland as an eighteen-year-old, Barbour had played twenty-one Sheffield Shield matches for his state and scored 1540 runs at a fine average of 51.33.

Barbour was respected both for his cricketing ability and for his war service as a doctor. He had come close to Test selection when he was named as an opening batsman in the Australian team to tour South Africa in 1914–15 – but this was cancelled, however, due to the looming war in Europe. Enlisting in October 1915, he served first in Egypt, then in England, and would ultimately become RMO (regimental medical officer) of the 1st Field Artillery Brigade in early 1918.

One of the factors that made the mid-July 1917 match notable was that it was the first involving a team representative of the AIF. For Barbour, it was the first of eight second-class games he would play during the war years at the famous ground to raise funds for wounded soldiers and sailors. Besides Charlie Macartney, Barbour's team included another Australian Test star, the quarrelsome Lieutenant Charlie Kelleway. Against them was an England team that boasted several first-class county cricketers and a few current and future internationals, including

Captain Pelham 'Plum' Warner, Patsy Hendren, Percy Fender, Ernest Tyldesley and J.W.H.T. Douglas, who had witnessed the decimation that Tibby Cotter caused his England players in Egypt.

On a London day that *The Referee* in Sydney reported as 'gloriously fine' with the 'famous ground bathed in sunshine', the Australians had first use of the wicket. Macartney and Kelleway opened, and with the score at 7 Macartney was LBW for a duck. As the innings progressed, Barbour and Kelleway steadied the side before Kelleway was bowled for 53. Barbour went on to make 30 in a total of 130. In his account of the match, Barbour described how he was dismissed: 'I tried to jam a yorker hard past point and was beautifully snapped up at fine slip by [Patsy] Hendren.' New South Wales cricketer Cyril Docker came to the crease. A veteran of the Battle of Pozières, he had distinguished himself by leading a charge on German trenches which left sixty enemy dead. Barbour went on:

> Cyril Docker started to make some fine shots after lunch but was stumped off one well out on the off from [Harry] Lee for a dozen. Norman Dean shaped well, but no one else looked like making any, and we totalled 130 – a poor effort on the wicket. Lee took five wickets for 23, a performance which gives an inflated impression of his merit as a bowler. Douglas swung a great deal either way but was never dangerous – he could not get the same nip from the wicket as he could in Sydney …

Barbour's comments about English bowler Private Harry Lee were ungenerous. That Lee was playing at all was extraordinary. He had fought in the disastrous Battle of Aubers Ridge on 9 May 1915, where the British 13th Battalion took a major hit with the loss of 499 of their 550 men. Lee was presumed dead. In fact, he was lying semiconscious for three days in no-man's land, a bullet having fractured his left femur. When the Germans eventually found him and sent him to Valenciennes in a crowded cattle train, the first stages of gangrene had set in. The German Red Cross put his leg in an iron cast. Sent home, he was discharged as medically unfit, with one of his legs now permanently shorter than the other. He resumed playing, determined this would not end his cricket career. In time, he was selected in 'Plum' Warner's team and, despite the difficulty of bowling with a shortened leg, still managed to rip through the Australians.

Not content with his bowling honours, Lee then opened the England innings but was bowled by Macartney for 7 runs. Despite the match loss to England, Barbour noted that Macartney bowled

> as usual, a fine length doing a little either way, and always had the batsman on the defensive ... [but] that the best point of the whole game was our fielding, which was almost flawless. Docker caught Tyldesley off a clipping drive at cover, and I dug one up out of the grass toward the finish.

Barbour had one parting comment about English cricket grounds: 'My impression of Lord's and the Oval? No, they don't come up to Sydney and Melbourne, or nearly so; but both are fine grounds. Lord's, I think, the prettier, and the Oval more of a run-getter's paradise.' These interludes were something to hang on to, a very different reality from events on the other side of the English Channel.

9

SURELY THE MOMENT FOR A TEST MATCH

As towns burned and turned to rubble, and the stark white crosses of the dead sprouted at an alarming pace, the Western Front was no place to be throughout 1917–18. During an eight-week period beginning in September, Australia suffered 38,000 casualties in the Third Battle of Ypres, its heaviest losses in the war. At Polygon Wood Australians played a key role in a crucial Allied victory that opened the way to the tactically important Broodseinde Ridge. But that involvement came at the cost of 5770 Australians killed or wounded.

Among the injured was Charlie Macartney's fellow Sydney first-grade cricketer and future Test teammate Bert Oldfield. Hours after a bombardment, he was found semiconscious and partly buried. Evacuated to England, he would later recall: 'For six months I suffered from shellshock.' Oldfield was among the lucky.

Also on the Western Front was Private Alfred 'Tiny' Ryan, twenty-five years old, from Peak Hill, New South Wales, attached to the 1st Australian Machine Gun Company. Tiny was a shearer and boxer. He was Indigenous, yet when he enlisted, he slipped through the race provisions of the 1903 *Defence Act*, which exempted people who were not 'substantially of European origin or descent' from joining the army. A tall man standing 1.8 metres tall and weighing 109 kilos, he had won a twenty-round fight at Dubbo Stadium marked by 'glorious fighting', according to a local newspaper.

On enlistment, Tiny was the heavyweight boxing champion of western New South Wales. The Sydney *Sun* reported in March 1915: 'Tiny Ryan, the heavyweight pride of the Dubbo and surrounding district, has shouldered a gun, and is just now preparing, at the Liverpool Camp, to go to the front.' At Gallipoli on 1 June 1915, Tiny was wounded when a shell burst along a main trench. 'I was hit by a piece of it, which knocked me flat,' he wrote in a letter to the Sydney *Sun*. He recovered and was back boxing in Cairo by the end of the year, before moving with the AIF to the Western Front. While there he reflected on the death of champion Australian boxer Les Darcy, who was vilified for not enlisting. Denied a passport to go to the US for the official world title, he stowed away on a ship bound for the US on the eve of the 1916 conscription plebiscite. By this time, US had been caught up in war fever. Darcy volunteered for the US Army to avoid further criticism. In the meantime, he trained for the world title. However, Darcy died from a blood infection on 24 May 1917, aged just twenty-one. Tiny was moved to write of Darcy in September that year that he 'did not deserve half the tabooing he got, for, when it is all said and done, there are others who, even in the Australian Forces, are only masquerading in the uniform of a soldier, and are not worth their salt ... when there are gaps to fill in the trenches'.

In the same letter, Tiny expressed confidence that despite 'a close shave or two' he would survive the war and return to Australia to resume his boxing career. 'I don't think they will ever get me now.' But they did, at Polygon Wood on 25 September 1917. In the sporting bible of the time, *The Referee*, boxing correspondent W.F. Corbett wrote a tribute: 'Tiny gone – Tiny, the merry-faced, laughter-loving, light-hearted big boy – for he was only a boy – gone. It seemed incredible.' Corbett added a note from a friend of Tiny's: 'One of the gamest lads that ever donned khaki, and a shining example to the coldfoots who are for ever shrieking about a white Australia.'

There, in the most dangerous place on earth, the diggers played sport – in the quiet times and under the most unconventional of conditions. In early spring 1917, with the ground drying and the sun growing stronger by the day, the troops were feeling the benefit of rest and the change from the everlasting mud. On Anzac Day that year, the 12th Infantry Brigade held a sports meeting near Hennencourt Wood, with £100 prize money. There were thirty events on the program, which, besides the usual sprint races, football kicking and grenade throwing, also included a 'signallers race with despatches on bicycles' along a road.

The next month, a 3rd Brigade sports carnival was also held at Hennencourt Wood, with the 10th Battalion emerging victorious. Captain Walter Belford, 11th Battalion, commented in his battalion history that while his unit 'made a poor showing as far as points were concerned', the battalion was 'now enjoying quiet, peaceful days after the stress of war'. Even divisional sports carnivals were not without their danger, as Belford witnessed a fortnight later during another meeting at Hennencourt Wood. 'During one of the bombing competitions, Lieut. Ray Clarke, the divisional bombing officer ... was dangerously wounded by the premature burst of a bomb.'

Lance Corporal Arthur Moore, 8th Field Ambulance, captured a period of sporting intensity in mid-1917, writing in his diary:

Today we had 44 men out playing in 4 different matches.
2 teams played the 1st Fld Amb. and won, easily. Another team played the 15th F Amb. and lost. Then our soccer

team played the 8 M.G. Coy. and lost by 6–0. Col. Shepherd and most of the officers played cricket.

In May 1917, Charles Bean travelled to old sites south of Bapaume, where he found Australian troops filling in shell holes and levelling part of the previous battlefield to form a field for Australian Rules football. Later in 1917, Bean went to a camp near Neuve-Église, spending the day with the 28th Battalion and noting in his diary: 'Our battalions are full of their football, [and] are just like a lot of Oxford colleges in the October term – more keen on their football for the moment than anything else in the world.'

But just which code of football was a matter of fierce debate among the Australians. Old allegiances to the various codes, and which was better, did not disappear – even as ultimately fruitless attempts were being made in Australia to combine the rival codes into the one game, 'Universal football'. Sometimes, this resulted in a grudging stand-off, as happened in London in September 1917 in two unique matches between the Australian army and HMAS *Australia*. In the first game, played under rugby rules, the army won 9–6. Returning to the field under Australian football rules, the army team led at one stage by 46 to 14, but the naval men finished strongly, only to lose 46–36.

It seemed the desire to play cricket could not be quelled – the more so when the need for a break from the fighting was pressing. And if they didn't have equipment, handcrafting a bat from a branch of silver birch did the job. As with the Australians, the craving for the diversion cricket provided was alive and well with the British troops. Plans were hatched for a match on the Western Front between the two nations. Englishman Cyril Dennys, of the Royal Garrison Artillery, recalled the outcome as the old foes prepared to do battle at the suggestion of the Australians on a rare corner of an unscathed field. With a break in the fighting, the Australians thought it called for a 'test match'.

They found a bit of unshelled ground within reach of their positions and ours. And we, or they, or both, got some equipment – bats and balls and bales and stumps – and we played cricket with them. What the Germans could have thought was going on, I can't imagine. But it must've been reported by some German. Unfortunately, next morning when the Australians were assembling on the cricket pitch and we were on the way to it, they were heavily shelled. Some were killed and some were wounded.

If he had been in London, Tibby Cotter no doubt would have been selected for the Australian teams that played the English that summer of 1917, but he was biding his time in Palestine as a stretcher-bearer with the 12th Light Horse, waiting for the third attempt to capture Gaza. But first there was Beersheba. With two failures behind them, the Desert Mounted Corps adopted a new strategy, based around a feint. The aim was to fool the Turks into believing that another frontal attack was imminent. Instead, the real focus was directed at capturing Beersheba, the eastern end of the Turkish line.

Shortly before the regiment left for Beersheba, Tibby took part in a bowling competition at Tel el Fara. With just a single stump to aim at, he bowled the equivalent of four six-ball overs, hitting the stump with eighteen of those twenty-four deliveries, at speed. Early in the morning of 31 October, Tibby was watering his horse in a wadi at Khalasa when he picked some mud and shaped it into a ball and rolled his arm over before announcing to a mate: 'That's my last bowl, Blue, something is going to happen.'

Later that day Tibby rode into action as a mounted stretcher-bearer in the famous charge of the 4th and 12th Light Horse Regiments, working coolly amid the dismounted fight around the earthworks. The *Official History* remarked that 'he behaved in action as a man without fear'. Trooper Scotty Bolton, 4th Light Horse, saw what happened to Tibby.

> [Tibby] rode up to a field gun that was trotting off in front of us, and they surrendered to him, but just as he went past them one of them pulled out a revolver and shot him dead. He fell off his horse and never moved. Several of our fellows who saw it rushed over with revolvers, and the 4 Turkish drivers came down with no less than 5 bullets in each.

Tibby would be the only Australian Test cricketer killed in action in World War I. He was buried in the Beersheba War Cemetery, one of thirty-one Australians to die in the famous charge. Tibby was not the only Australian sporting hero to pay a price that day at Beersheba. The casualties also included Guy Haydon and his Waler, Midnight, the horse that had stunned the British in the Cavalry Desert Olympics earlier in the war. As she jumped a Turkish trench, a bullet ripped upwards through the black mare's flank, before tearing into Guy's back and lodging near his spine. Guy eventually recovered, but Midnight died on the battlefield.

Guy's brother Barney survived the charge and rode on into town on his horse, Polo, to secure the wells. And then, with the Australians in high spirits, it was time to whoop it up. In a letter to *The Referee*, published four months later, the 8th Regiment's Ern Mitchell, a Port Melbourne featherweight, described the night:

> In the Beersheba stunt the Victorians galloped three miles into action with fixed bayonets. There was a lively time while it lasted, and we were dead beat at the finish; but not so tired, however, that we could not produce the gloves for a bit of sport the same night. Personally, I outpointed Ditchburn, of the Provost Corps, but later lost to Trooper Arnold of Tassy. He was better-conditioned, for he had just lobbed, while six months of bully beef and sand had played up with yours truly.

The occupation of Beersheba was the beginning of the end for the Turkish defensive line. The Allied forces were soon able to outflank the enemy forces in Gaza, and the Turkish resistance in the long-contested city collapsed within the week.

As the war's death toll rose, Australia struggled yet again with the question of conscription to boost recruitment to cope with the continuing heavy losses. Among the men lost on the Western Front was Tibby's older brother, John, forty-one, a private in the 4th Battalion. He was killed at Anzac Ridge, during fighting at Broodseinde on 4 October – just twenty-seven days before Tibby died. John Cotter, who had played cricket with his younger brother in the back streets of Glebe Point, was one of 6500 casualties the Australian divisions suffered that day. A shell had burst in front of him, blowing his leg off at the hip. The stretcher-bearers who went to him could do nothing. While their near neighbour from Glebe, Bert Oldfield, had survived the carnage, the Cotter brothers had not.

The more the need for replacement troops for the Western Front failed to keep pace, the more the moral pressure to enlist intensified. If a sportsman did not enlist, well, they were seen as not fair dinkum. Posters told the story: 'Which picture would your father like to show his friends?' demanded one, showing two images: a soldier with a rifle and backpack, and a languid sportsman in whites, reclining in a deck chair, surrounded by tennis racket, cricket bat, football and, to rub it in, a bottle of wine on a side table. Rowers were urged to 'pull together to victory', sailors to 'weather the storm', and golfers to 'take their caddy and enlist'.

Albert Jacka was not alone in having his image plastered across recruitment posters; Jack Massie and Charlie Macartney appeared together on one AIF recruiting lantern slide for the Sportsmen's Unit. In their cricket flannels, Massie towered over Macartney. 'Some sports now fighting. What about helping

The Jack Massie and Charlie Macartney Sportsmen's Unit lantern slide.
AWM P04366.004.

them,' read the poster, which described Massie as 'N.S.W. Champion Bowler now Bowling in France', and Macartney as 'Australia's Champion Batsman still NOT OUT'.

As the campaign momentum increased, Melbourne's *Arrow* reported a compliment from the skipper of the South Australian Sheffield Shield team, Captain Gordon Campbell, that Massie – 'the Sydney giant' – had 'done magnificent work' after being posted back to France. Campbell, attached to the 3rd Brigade's 10th Battalion, himself featured in the Sportsmen's Unit campaign, as 'a sportsman now fighting' who had 'scored a Military Cross' after his courage at the Battle of Pozières on 24 July 1916. During the fighting, Campbell 'stood on the parapet and threw bombs into the German trench and although wounded in two places, he continued his work until the enemy were driven out'.

The campaign, featuring such figures as Macartney, Massie and Campbell, was authorised by the Defence Department and the Victorian and New South Wales Sportsmen Recruiting Committees. Their aim was to recruit a 'Sportsmen's One Thousand' – a battalion of members of sporting clubs and associations who would 'join together, train together and fight together'. This recruitment tactic had been tried earlier in the war in both Melbourne and in Sydney. The whole program was under the direction of the Melbourne barrister and Commonwealth Director General of Recruiting, Donald Mackinnon. In Melbourne, a meeting of the Sportsmen's Recruiting Committee was held at the rooms of the Victorian Cricket Association on 7 March 1917. Nine days later, twenty recruits signed up at a rowdy rally at the Melbourne Stadium after a night of boxing and vaudeville.

No branch of sport was neglected, with the enlistment and appointment as officers of two leading sportsmen in New South Wales – solicitor and footballer Les Seaborn and Sheffield Shield cricketer Austin Diamond – heading the campaign in Sydney.

Seaborn was a stocky forty-year-old. He had been a successful rugby winger and acquired the nickname Dodger playing club rugby. He went on to play at interstate level in 1907. He also had a strong military connection, having served with the Australian Rifles in 1899, and he had remained a member of the militia until he joined the AIF. Diamond, forty-three, was an electrical engineer with a disciplined and determined disposition. He had been a New South Wales batsman playing alongside Charlie Macartney and Tibby Cotter, and had captained the unofficial Australian tour to Fiji, Canada and America in 1913.

In Sydney, the Sportsmen's Battalion was launched at a well-attended meeting at the Town Hall on 3 April 1917 with the aim of recruiting 150 men initially for the unit, with Seaborn and Diamond leading them overseas. By the end of April 1917, the *Sydney Morning Herald* reported that the city was 'absolutely plastered' with appeals to 'Be a sport and enlist'. One rally, held on 4 May at the Sydney Stadium in Rushcutters Bay, featured free entertainment, including 'boxing exhibitions, wrestling displays, jiu-jitsu, blindfold boxing, fancy and speed skipping by ladies, bugle blowing competition for soldiers and sailors, singing by well-known vocalists, and several high-class vaudeville artistes'. Massed bands added to the carnival atmosphere.

The appeal to join the Sportsmen's Unit sought to frankly shame young men into joining the war effort, asking if they were 'content to let your best pal do your fighting, let your elder or younger brothers take part in the big scrap and fill your place?' Seaborn and the committee wrote:

> You can go with your own kind, the crowd of boys that love a good horse, the boys who like a good, rugged scrap, the boys who delight in rough and tumble game of footer, or who will go through blazes to do a thing for which they will gain little but the experience. These are the men Lieutenants Les Seaborn and Austin Diamond

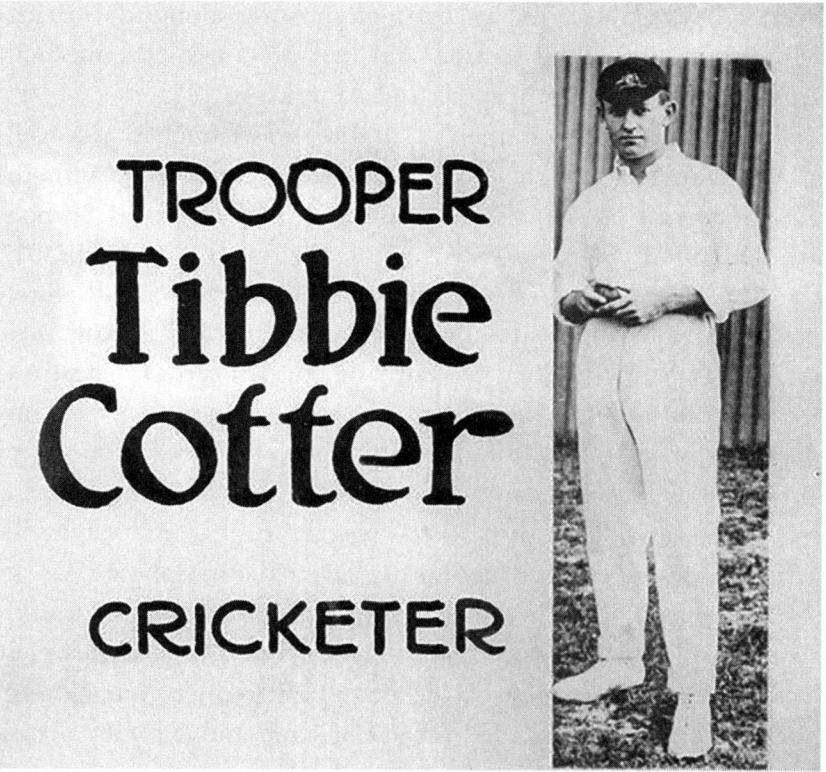

The Tibby Cotter recruitment lantern slide. AWM P04366.001.

are looking for — the real dinkum oil, 24 carat-all-the-way-through 'sports'.

The 150 men who enlisted in the Sportsmen's Unit were designated the 20th Reinforcements for the 19th (Sportsman's) Battalion and on 16 July 1917, full of optimism, they boarded the transport *Port Melbourne* and sailed out of Sydney Harbour to war. They left knowing they were a special group; each man having had his Attestation Papers marked 'Sportsmen's Unit' to set him apart from others. Not only that, but they also had notepads with its own letterhead. However, just a month after arriving in Britain, the unit lost Seaborn when he broke his arm badly playing sport and was hospitalised.

Prime Minister Billy Hughes put his case for a second conscription plebiscite. Focusing on sportsmen was one of Hughes's key messages, as he showed at an appeal in Sydney in July 1917, arguing that voluntarism was on trial, with Australia needing to find 7000 men per month 'or face eternal disgrace'. Australia's sportsmen had already established a magnificent war record, but there were many still out of khaki, he said, adding:

> Sportsmen of Australia, to you is given a great opportunity, upon you rests a heavy responsibility. As you have played the game in the past, so we ask you to play the greater game now. This is your day. Its success or failure rests with you. You are wanted to-day in the trenches far more than you were ever needed in the football or cricket oval. I ask you to be true to yourselves, and to prove yourselves worthy members of the great brotherhood of sport.

Hughes's appeal failed to turn public sentiment when the nation voted on 20 December 1917. Although the second plebiscite was less far-reaching than the question asked in 1916, eschewing full conscription of able-bodied men, the anti-conscription vote won by a larger margin than it had in the first vote. The rhetoric did not match the result, with less than 1 per cent of Australia's fighting force having been recruited via various Sportsmen's Battalions during the war.

10

PUT OUR SCORES ON THE BOARD!

In the small world that was Sydney's sporting scene in the early years of the twentieth century, the champion swimmer Cecil Healy came to know Les Seaborn. Cec, as he was known throughout Australia, was short and stocky with powerful arms and shoulders, and famed for brilliant finishes in the pool. He had developed the two-beat Australian crawl and was credited in 1904 with swimming the fastest time recorded for the 100 yards freestyle. He achieved Olympic glory at the 1912 Stockholm Olympics, winning gold in the 4 x 200-metre swimming relay.

But it was his Olympic silver in the men's 100-metre race that made the world take notice. Incredibly, the US team failed to turn up for the semi-finals due to confusion around the race start time, which was even more galling for them given the US team included race favourite Duke Kahanamoku. In what has been described as one of the greatest acts of sportsmanship in Olympic history, Healy refused to swim unless Duke was allowed to compete. The Olympic Committee relented and Kahanamoku competed and won the gold medal, later declaring that Healy was 'the true Olympic champion'.

Travelling overseas before the war, Healy began to understand the looming threat of Germany's growing military and industrial might. This prompted him to write in the Sydney *Sunday Times* in February 1913, warning of dangers he foresaw and doubting that the Olympic Games scheduled for Berlin in 1916 would happen.

> They seem to have a genius for detail, everything dovetails so completely. Nothing is out of place. It all prompts the thought that when the order is given for her army to march, GERMANY'S BATTALIONS WILL MOVE SWIFTLY AND SURELY, whithersoever they are directed, without hitch or hindrance. We had something to learn from them in the way of conducting sport, I thought, and on my return to Australia in 1907 I at once commenced to introduce some ideas I had picked up into my own little world of natation [swimming]. They were dubbed 'Healy's made-in-Germany schemes.'

The Berlin Games were duly cancelled with the outbreak of war. Enlisting in the AIF in September 1915 with the Army Service Corps, Cec Healy initially served behind the front line as a Company quartermaster sergeant in charge of stores in Egypt and France. A request to transfer to active service saw him sent to the infantry officer school at Cambridge University. There, he swam, rowed, boxed and played rugby. And then, on 1 June 1918, he was commissioned as an officer in the unit that seemed the most perfect fit imaginable – the 19th Battalion. He wrote to his family that he cherished 'the hope that I will be able to sell my life dearly and earn the respect of the men whom I command'. There, he was reunited with his mate Les Seaborn.

This must have cheered Seaborn immensely as he had been through a wretched time. His arm had taken several months to heal. Officially, he was part of the Training Brigade until 1 April 1918 – by which time his men had been transferred to France.

Worse still for Seaborn, the men of the 19th Battalion were placed as reinforcements into the 35th Battalion, another New South Wales unit. Seaborn was anxious to proceed to the Front. Frustratingly, while he convalesced, his men had fought their first major battle, suffering serious casualties – without him.

At least they had been kept together when, on 4 April, they went into battle at the village of Villers-Bretonneux in the Somme as the German spring offensive pushed to break the stalemate on the Western Front. The outcome for the Sportsmen's Unit was devastating: ten men killed and an unknown number of wounded out of the 150 men who had sailed from Sydney on 16 July 1917. During the fighting over the next few days, Austin Diamond was hospitalised after a gas attack near Hangard Wood, barely 2 kilometres to the south of where his fellow sportsmen men had been cut up in battle.

Clearly, the new sports recruits lacked battlefield experience. This stood in contrast to what Captain Walter Belford, of the 11th Battalion, observed at the start of 1918: that AIF veterans by now were no longer inexperienced and reckless soldiers but part of an Australian army infused with a new spirit. These veterans were battle-hardened at a time when there seemed to be no end to the war in sight. They accepted this with 'a fatalism that was peculiarly their own'.

> Most of the boys entered the line believing that it was most likely to be the last time in, not for the battalion, but for themselves. When diggers had seen their dearest 'cobbers' killed alongside them, they could not hope that they would always escape themselves, so they accepted the situation with a certain amount of stoicism that in no way interfered with their efficiency.

This was a state of mind that could not be gained easily: acceptance of an outcome that depended not on sporting prowess but indefinable situations where mortality was beyond individual control. Belford's men understood this.

Seaborn's arm finally recovered, and he rejoined the 19th Battalion in France in late July 1918, where he was able to catch up with his old mate Cec Healy. Within a month they were fighting at Mont Saint-Quentin, going into battle with the 19th Battalion and fellow New South Welshmen in the 20th and 17th Battalions. On 31 August Seaborn displayed exactly the kind of heroic gallantry he had been advocating at home during recruitment rallies. Having reached the objective, Seaborn suddenly found his position surrounded by Germans. In a few minutes nearly all his men became casualties. But with only six men and a Lewis gun left, Seaborn attacked and with sheer gallantry drove the enemy off, inflicting heavy casualties.

Seaborn was awarded the Military Cross for his action, but it was a subdued celebration as the attack had taken the life of Cec Healy two days before. While leading his platoon in clearing out German machine-gun posts in a field near Péronne, Healy was shot in the neck and chest and killed. On hearing of his death, his friends were devastated. Besides Seaborn, they included Syd Middleton, a fellow Olympian from the Stockholm Games and now a major. Middleton, a champion rower, had been Healy's commander and wrote to Healy's family: 'By Healy's death the world loses one of its greatest champions, one of its best men. Today, in the four years I have been at the front, I wept for the first time.'

Seaborn survived the battle unscathed, but a few weeks later, on 10 October 1918, he was gassed – barely one month before the end of the war. This left him with chronic lung problems for the next year or so, and he would spend months in hospital as part of his recovery.

As the Allies gained a decisive upper hand, having stopped the German spring offensive in March and April, there was time at last to take to the cricket fields of Britain, the summer having ushered in the hope that the war could finally be won before year's end. The first matches were between an England team and a side comprising players from the Dominions, in which Australians dominated the selections. In game one, played at Lord's on 29 June 1918 before a crowd of 12,000 spectators, the Dominions batted first, Eric Barbour again leading the side. Charlie Macartney, having been awarded the Meritorious Service Medal, scored 22 and Charlie Kelleway 30. Cyril Docker chipped in with 23 while Major A.G. 'Johnny' Moyes, a Sheffield Shield batsman for South Australia, scored 22 in a total of 166. Post-war, Moyes would make his name as an outstanding cricket commentator and analyst.

England's captain, 'Plum' Warner, was the best of the English, scoring 35 not out, in a team that also featured former England Test batsman C.B. Fry, of the Royal Navy Reserve. With England collapsing to be all out for 98, Macartney starred with the ball, taking 3–22, while Docker's pace was too much for the English, snaring 4–39 in the Dominions' victory. A second match followed a fortnight later, with England batting first and scoring 157. Although the Dominions collapsed to 8–34, time was called, and the match ended in a draw.

Back in France, AIF units prepared for the great Allied offensive launched east of Amiens on 8 August 1918. Camped at La Kreule near the deserted town of Hazebrouck after involvement in defensive operations in early July, the 11th Battalion's band found that sports days could be a trap for the unwary. The afternoon was hot and the bandsmen thirsty, and to cope they drank 'copious ambrosial draughts', as Captain Walter Belford described it. The musicians had barely recovered when they were ordered to attend a special dinner in the mess that evening for Captain Edward Brennan, a visiting doctor who had been at the Gallipoli landing. Belford described what happened next.

> They did their best, and painstakingly massacred some well-known tunes. Some more liquid refreshment was sent out in the hope of improving matters, but it was no good. One by

one the bandsmen deserted their posts, and finally there were only three players left, the bandmaster, the big drummer, and the trombonist. The others had vanished ... all the trombonist could do was to dribble into his instrument ... the residue had to remain on duty until [the toast to] the King was 'drunk'.

With American troops flooding into the Western Front, the 11th Battalion was encouraged to take up baseball among the troops. Belford saw the motivation behind this as a 'desire to promote "L'entente cordiale"'. Baseball gear was purchased 'and several attempts made to get the lads to play, but no one took seriously to the game'. Third Brigade athletics and swimming carnivals continued where possible – including one where a soldier competing in an underwater swimming race in late August 1918, just a few days after the Battle of Amiens, failed to surface. The unfortunate digger had survived the battlefield only to die through heart failure on a day of levity and relaxation with his mates.

As summer gave way to autumn and the nights grew longer, Belford listened to the nightingales and sedge warblers singing in the bushes and reeds alongside the river, while the rumble of guns was heard faint and far off. 'Australian leave was just starting in the battalion, and in the quiet of these lovely nights the wonderful thought that home was no longer an impossible dream came to cheer many of the boys.' By early October, the diggers' ranks were severely depleted due to heavy casualties and falling enlistments in Australia. After a request from Prime Minister Billy Hughes, they were withdrawn from the line after the AIF's final battle at Montbrehain, which claimed 430 Australian casualties.

By then, the AIF had achieved astonishing success in a series of momentous battles against the Germans. In July 1918, General Monash had secured a model victory at Le Hamel; in August, in what became known as a 'black day in the history of the German army', Australians and Canadians achieved an unprecedented breakthrough at Amiens, and that same month captured Chuignes Ridge, the main German position forward of the Somme. During this period, the AIF won recognition for their finest feat of arms in the war at Mont St Quentin, taking the hill and allowing capture of the town of Péronne, forcing a German retreat to the Hindenburg Line, their last line of defence. At Bellicourt, the Australians had broken through the Hundenburg Outpost Line, and along with the Americans they then broke the line at Bellenglise. Montbrehain was enough.

And then the war was over. Diggers, suddenly with more time on their hands and despite winter closing in and the weather deteriorating, devoted afternoons to sport. Inter-battalion matches were held. The mood was carefree as the Australians basked in the warmth of a grateful France.

With Germany's surrender on 11 November 1918, Sir John Monash, now knighted and commander of the Australian Corps, reflected on the role of sport in the battlefield performance of his troops. Before the war ended, he had been forced to protest to senior British civilian and military figures, including the chief of the Imperial General Staff, Sir Henry Wilson, regarding British recognition of the feats of his men being downplayed. Monash had warned that unless this was rectified, he would not hold himself responsible for the maintenance of their fighting spirit. 'I put it plainly that they are by nature and instinct sportsmen, and that they would refuse to go on playing any game in which their scores were not put up on the scoring-board.'

Monash expanded on his views in a foreword to a book by AIF chaplain George Cuttriss, *Over the Top with the Third Australian Division*, published as the war ended in 1918:

> It is precisely because the Australian is born with and develops in his national life the very instinct of discipline that he has been enabled to prove himself so successful a soldier. He obeys constituted authority because he knows that success depends upon his doing so, whether his

activities are devoted to the interests of his football team or his industrial organization or his regiment. He has an infinite capacity for 'team' work.

Over the Top was one of the first books on the Australian experience of the slaughter on the French battlefields, Cuttriss having been a chaplain to the Third Division for two years on the Western Front. Imbued with a fervent belief in 'muscular Christianity', Cuttriss asserted that the sporting instinct was so ingrained in the average Australian that amusement and athletics had become part and parcel of his life, and his efficiency as a fighting force increased as a consequence. Mirroring the sentiments of Bean and Ashmead-Bartlett, Cuttriss asserted that the Australian digger's 'well-knit, muscular frame, and cheerful, free-from-care disposition, and love for clean sport' was the envy of many. 'Australia has given to the world champions in almost every branch of sport, and the traditions which have been established on the football and cricket fields and in athletic circles in years preceding the war are being upheld and added to by her sons "somewhere in France".' Importantly, he caught the unique nature of how the Australians approached sport on the Western Front.

> Games appropriate to the season are played at the back of the lines. The ground selected for football or cricket may be shell-marked, and the materials used roughly made and incomplete. Football matches between different units have been as keenly contested on the muddy and broken fields of Belgium and France as those that have been played on the specially prepared grounds of the Homeland. The Australians have held their own against other units in both cricket and football.

Cuttriss could have added war. The war was now over; and there was a chance to celebrate. And sport was the way forward.

II

ALL DRESSED UP AND NOWHERE TO GO

The men on the Western Front were not alone in celebrating the end of the war. Two weeks earlier, on 30 October, war ended in the Middle East when the Ottoman Empire accepted the Armistice with the Allies at the port of Mudros on the island of Lemnos. This meant the release of several Australians who had become POWs of the Turks during the war. There had been nearly 200 captured, some seventy-six of them during the Gallipoli campaign and the remainder over the succeeding three years during the ongoing campaigns against the Ottomans. About a quarter died in captivity.

Sport was an important part of the Australians' experiences in captivity at the various camps, such as Hadji-Kiri in the Taurus Mountains of central Turkey. But they needed sports equipment. In letters to their families and the Australian Red Cross POW Department, which was responsible for the welfare and comfort of all Australian POWs during the war, they requested that footballs, boxing gloves and cricket gear be sent to the camps. Officers and men were allowed to play cricket matches against each other at one camp – on the proviso that the two teams did not speak to each other. The men surmised that the Turks probably feared the POWs might hatch an escape plan.

Among the POWs held by the Turks was Sergeant Maurice Delpratt, of the 5th Light Horse Regiment, who was taken prisoner in an attack on the Balkan Gun Pits at Gallipoli on 28 June 1915. Captured behind enemy lines, he was held at the Hadji-Kiri camp for the duration of the war. Delpratt wrote home frequently. In one letter in March 1918, he described a sports carnival organised by Allied POWs as part of Easter festivities. He outlined the events in which he had participated – the 100-yard dash, shot put and long jump – and proudly explained that he had beaten 'a big field of French and British competitors' to win the sprint race. He noted with some glee that he had placed second in the jumping and won the egg-and-spoon race.

Released after the Armistice, Delpratt made his back to Britain to join the problem confronting the AIF: with the Great War over, how were 180,000 Australian service men and women with 7000 dependants to be repatriated to Australia, demobilised and ushered back into civilian life? This epic task, which would take almost a year to complete, was given to Sir John Monash in November 1918. He believed that the men in whom a 'fighting morale' had been successfully implanted must now be supplanted with a 'reconstruction morale'.

At first, the men had difficulty comprehending the end of hostilities. There were 95,000 Australian troops still in France when the Armistice was signed on 11 November. In England, more camps were set up on Salisbury Plain to house war-weary troops, but this carried the risk that so many men living in close quarters with time on their hands was a potential time bomb. In the vacuum that the Armistice created, the 9th Battalion's Private Gerald Evans described hanging about 'all dressed up and nowhere to go'.

Discipline, out of the line, was not a strong suit for the AIF, with Australian soldiers ten times more likely to go absent without leave than the New Zealanders or Canadians. Yet with the maintenance of discipline and morale critical, sport became the means, essentially replacing military drills. In December 1918, the 1st Division moved into positions in Belgium to prepare for repatriation.

The task was momentous. Sports officers were appointed at all levels and committees formed to develop sports programs. Central to the planning at the highest level were Brigadier General Thomas Dodds, commandant of AIF Administrative Headquarters in London, and the champion sportsman Major Syd Middleton. Middleton had served through Gallipoli, Pozières and Flanders in the 17th and 19th Battalions. Summoned from France to Corps Headquarters in London, he mapped out an extensive program to introduce Army Championships. No time was lost in gathering the best Australian athletes together. Inter-platoon, inter-company, inter-battalion, inter-brigade, inter-division, inter-corps, and inter-army competitions in various sports were organised. The 3rd Battalion's War Book noted that 'as much sport as the weather permitted was engaged in, and representatives left the unit to compete in Divisional and Corps boxing and football teams'. Gerald Evans described regular games both within the 9th Battalion and against other units. 'There were some very good games of football played at Chatalet, between our boys and the Belgians. Our side won, then the next Sunday they imported some from Charleroi, but the diggers won again, so they had to get some from Brussels.'

But the need was wider than just within the AIF. After four years of war and the complete suspension of championship tournaments for that time, 1919 would see a remarkable boom in sport in Britain and France. On 6 January 1919, Middleton, along with representatives of other Dominion armies, met at the War Office in London. On the table was a plan for the inauguration of an Army Rugby Union competition to be played among Allied teams, and a cup to be presented by the King.

The AIF Sports Control Board's role was to encourage sport in all units and supervise organisation and selection of AIF representative teams for Inter-Army Championships. The Australian YMCA donated a trophy, the Australian Corps Sports Cup, with points awarded to divisions and corps troops in rugby, Australian Rules, cross-country running, and boxing. The winning team in each sport would be awarded six points, the others five, four, three, two and one according to where they were placed.

A Sports Section was established at AIF Headquarters. Teams were organised, with arrangements for housing near training facilities to allow selection trials. On New Year's Day 1919, the eight best rugby players nominated by each Australian Division gathered at a school in Belgium to begin a fortnight's training for a match against a French army team. On 19 January, the AIF team – dubbed the 'Trench Team' – travelled to Paris. On the offensive and dominating for most of the game, the Australians won 6–3.

The Corps Rugby Competition began in March, with a team from each of the five AIF divisions and one from the corps troops. Scattered around the countryside, each team was to play every other team, often on snow-covered or muddy fields. They travelled long distances in army wagons to these games – and always accompanied by a crowd of enthusiastic supporters. The 2nd Division's team went through the competition undefeated, scoring 96 points to 3 against, their line being crossed just once.

At the completion of the competition, the British Fourth Army, to which the Australian Corps was attached, invited the AIF to supply a team to represent it against the Second Army at Cologne. Winning 21–6, the Australians then played an additional match against a Royal Air Force (RAF) team, defeating them 41–0.

Separately, the Inter-Service and Dominion Forces Rugby Competition began on 1 March. After some training and trial games, an AIF team was selected to compete over six weeks. Competing for the King's Cup, it was the first time teams from the northern and southern hemispheres had played in a round-robin tournament – the competition thus pre-dating the Rugby World Cup by nearly sixty years.

Besides Australia, teams from New Zealand, Canada, South Africa, the British army and the RAF were involved. With Major Wally Matthews acting as manager, the AIF side contained eight internationals. Among them was the captain, Lieutenant Bill Watson, a celebrated Wallaby front-row forward. Other Wallabies included centre Dan Carroll – a lieutenant in the American army during the war – who would become the only two-time Olympic rugby gold medallist, in 1908 for Australia and in 1924 for America. Carroll had emigrated to the US after the 1908 Olympics and, as a serviceman in the US army, returned to play for the AIF in the King's Cup. Also in the team were Wallabies Lieutenant Bill Cody, Sergeant Dudley Suttor, Private Jimmy Clarken, Corporal Darb Hickey and Medical Officer Captain Jackie Beith.

In a tight 6–3 struggle, the AIF lost the opening game to the British on the stroke of full-time, but they bounced back in their next fixture and, with the forward pack dominant, secured an 8–5 win over South Africa. Next, a disjointed AIF were shocked to lose to the RAF, 7–3. Chastened, they atoned with a 38–0 thrashing of an outclassed Canada at Twickenham. A match against an undefeated New Zealand followed. With their opponents boasting several All Blacks, this would be as stern a test for the Australians then as it would remain down the decades. A crowd of more than 7000 people watched as the AIF Fifteen, again with their forward pack dominant, upset the New Zealanders 6–5, scoring two tries to one. Rumour at the time was that Jimmy Clarken engineered the victory, claiming: 'I know how to beat the New Zealanders!' In those days New Zealand was persisting with a two-man front row. His tactic was

The AIF rugby team defeated Canada 38–0 at Twickenham in March 1919.
AWM D00528.

to stick his head in between them and secure the loosehead prop for the AIF no matter which side the ball was put in. Not to be outdone, the New Zealanders went on to win the tournament and the King's Cup with a 9–3 victory over the British at Twickenham.

In his book on the AIF and sport played in 1918–19, *Soldiers and Sportsmen*, journalist Lieutenant George Goddard, a Western Front veteran, commented that at the outset of the competition the Australians had been criticised for rough play. But this criticism fell away as the tournament went on, and ultimately they were congratulated on the spirit in which they played their matches, adding that the presence of the four Dominion teams in the King's Cup was a splendid thing for rugby in Britain. As well, the AIF team played eleven tour matches around England and Wales. 'The game had suffered, along with nearly every other form of sport, from the inaction of the previous four years; but this great contest did more in a month to bring it back to its pre-war popularity than the ordinary club games would have done in a couple of seasons.'

In France, too, rugby was in danger of disappearing during the war years as soccer gained popularity as the game of choice at the front. The presence of Australians and New Zealanders playing rugby kept the game alive. Official matches were also organised between Australian and New Zealand divisions, such as the 1st Australian General Hospital and the New Zealand Bakery units, which met in Rouen in May 1916. A highlight was the contest for the 'Somme Cup' in April 1917 at the Vélodrome de Vincennes, Paris. More than 60,000 spectators came to watch the match between the French army team and the New Zealand 'War All Blacks', who won 40–0. Post-Armistice, the French once again faced the New Zealanders, along with Australians, Canadians, Welsh, British and Americans, thus confirming France's place in international rugby. These were critical months for the code in Europe, with the success of the international army teams competitions ensuring rugby maintained its profile.

With the conclusion of the King's Cup rugby tournament, the focus returned to the various sports played in the Australian Corps Sports Cup. Soccer always had enthusiastic followers, and they were alive and well in the Corps competition. Unlike the rugby teams, which were selected from the full division, soccer teams were drawn from units of battalion or equivalent strengths. A British unit that had been attached to the AIF for two years was chosen to represent the 2nd Division, and fully justified the selection by coming through the competition with an unbeaten record. The sobering reality, however, was that the soccer competition carried no points for the Corps Cup, which was won by 1st Division by half a point from the 5th. The consolation for the 2nd Division was a special silver cup that Corps HQ provided. In effect, this unfairly relegated the soccer competition to a second rung – an oddity in a part of the world where soccer was the dominant sport.

There was no such issue with Australian Rules, a sport of no consequence in Europe and Britain. Indeed, it even encouraged passionate debate among Australians. As Lieutenant George Goddard presciently observed:

> The relative merits of rugby, Australian Rules, and soccer were debated as keenly on the battlefields and in the back areas of France and Belgium as they ever were under the sunny skies of Australia. It was possible to make a good guess at the State from which a man hailed by the vehemence with which he supported a certain brand of football. The argument with the Kaiser was more easily settled than this one. The patronising manner in which a supporter of one particular game would ask another to 'come and see a real football match' was most amusing.

And keen interest there certainly was in the Australian Rules competition – which did carry points for the five divisions and the Corps troops towards the Corps Cup. The very large playing area required involved some delicate negotiation, but ultimately the 1st Division defeated the 2nd Division side to win the competition. The men had to make do with balls often made from scraps of leather while on the battlefield, so the VFL gifted footballs to teams in the Corps Australian Rules competition.

With the Corps Cup settled, the AIF turned its attention to the boxing ring and the Inter-Theatre of War Boxing Tournament at Aldershot. Among those competing was Sapper Harold Hardwick, who had served with No. 2 Signal Squadron in the Middle East. At the age of thirty, Hardwick had an extraordinary sporting career behind him. A schoolboy champion swimmer, he went on to win the New South Wales 100 yards freestyle title in 1907–08. Next season he won the state freestyle titles for the 100, 220 and 300 yards, and for the ¾-mile and 1-mile events.

In 1911, Hardwick represented Australasia at the Festival of Empire in London to celebrate the coronation of King George V, competing in swimming and boxing. Two days after winning the 100 yards Empire swimming title, and with little training, he stopped English champion William Hazell in the first round. Just an hour later he won the Empire heavyweight title, stopping his Canadian opponent in 2 minutes 35 seconds. While in England, he won the 100, 220 and 440 yards Amateur Swimming Association championships. Returning home in triumph, he was named 1911's 'Sportsman of Australia'. In the 1912 Olympic Games in Stockholm, he was a member of the Australasian team that won the 4 x 200-metre freestyle event in the unofficial record time of 10 minutes 11.6 seconds.

If this was not enough, this extraordinary athlete also played rugby union for New South Wales and in 1914 he won the state amateur heavyweight boxing championship. In 1915, he turned professional, winning four of his eight professional fights. One of his losses was a knockout at the hands of the legendary Les Darcy in the seventh round – after he had broken two of Darcy's teeth. The Armistice signed, Hardwick made his way from Egypt to England in April 1919 for the Inter-Theatre of War Boxing Tournament. Few in the AIF would have been surprised when he won the heavyweight boxing title – nor when he was chosen by the 400 competitors at the tournament as the 'Ideal Sportsman' of the British forces. The criteria for the award were:

- He must play the game for the sake of the game.
- He must play for his side, and not for himself.
- He must be a good loser and a good winner. He must be modest in victory and generous in defeat.
- He must accept all decisions in a proper spirit.

- He must be chivalrous towards a defeated opponent.
- He must be unselfish, and always ready to help others in every possible way to become proficient in sport.
- He must be a cheerful comrade.

These were the simple, idealistic moral standards that the Allied victors hoped would be reaffirmed to shape post-war society. After four years of brutality and grief, there was an overwhelming desire for a return to noble values, to re-establish the comfortable pre-war parameters that had determined society. The criteria for the award reflected this, drawing on the 'muscular Christianity' that was so influential in religious, political and military circles at the time. These men, aware of it or not, were the embodiment of these attitudes. The hall erupted in applause when Hardwick went forward to receive the trophy – an honour he highly prized.

12

A GOLDEN DECADE BEGINS

If Australia was conscious of the need after the Armistice to keep restless troops occupied, the Americans faced the same problem on a much larger scale: there were two million 'doughboys' of the American Expeditionary Forces (AEF) in Europe when the war ended. They, too, turned to sport, and the idea of a 'military Olympic Games' was born.

As the end of the war approached, American Elwood Stanley Brown, who had served in France as athletic director of the YMCA, proposed to US General Headquarters an athletic program for the demobilisation period. Brown contended that when intensive military training was suddenly stopped there would be 'no mental, moral or social program' adequate to fill the void. Sport again was the solution.

Underpinning Brown's analysis was a heavy dose of morality. Two years earlier, the American command had to deal with an epidemic of venereal disease among troops during a border conflict with Mexico. And the purported attractiveness of French women galvanised the authorities into action. As French sports historian Thierry Terret saw it, the Inter-Allied Games that followed were both cathartic and a means of diverting excess energy in more acceptable ways.

The idea of a military Inter-Allied Games was picked up by General John Pershing, Commander-in-Chief of the AEF in January 1919. Eighteen countries agreed to participate in a competition that would be exclusively for men – or, as Terret put it, 'a stage for masculinity' – with sports such as boxing, rugby and shooting that were seen as 'virile' and appropriately male. General Birdwood replied on behalf of the AIF that every effort would be made to send the most representative athletes of what he deemed 'warrior sportsmen'. With any reference to 'Olympic' carefully avoided, planning proceeded rapidly. Competitions would be held on the outskirts of Paris in the Bois de Vincennes, the centrepiece of which would be the Pershing Stadium, a new 25,000-seat arena the Americans built for the occasion.

Australia, relatively well advanced in its repatriation arrangements, decided to enter only sixty-three contestants in the track and field events, cross-country running, swimming, tennis, boxing, wrestling, tug-of-war, rowing and hand grenade throwing. Competing against Australia were the United States, Belgium, Canada, Czechoslovakia, France, Guatemala, Hedjaz (now part of Saudi Arabia and Oman), Italy, New Zealand, Portugal, Romania, Greece and Serbia. Britain had a low-key presence, with just one or two entries in the overall competition.

The Games would declare no one country the winner; rather, only the winners of each event would be recognised. The two-week meeting opened on a sunny Sunday afternoon, 22 June 1919, before a crowd of 90,000 spectators watching a grand parade of nearly 1500 athletes. The Australians were led by Captain Gordon Coghill, a successful amateur boxer from New South Wales and the AIF's contestant in the officers' heavyweight division. They wore blue and gold outfits with the rising sun emblazoned on their chests.

Coghill carried an oversized Australian flag and, Syd Middleton observed, the team, with the 'tug of war giants ... made a magnificent appearance'. They received a stirring reception from the French spectators during their progress around the arena, a great, approving cry of 'Les Australiens! Vive les Australiens!' echoing through the arena. Such a greeting was bettered only by that accorded to France's own athletes, Captain George Goddard observed.

After years of rough living, the Australians had the relative luxury of sharing two- or three-man tents, with comfortable beds and, as Syd Middleton noted, sheets and pillowslips, to boot! He added that they were sandwiched between the Greeks and Serbians.

> It was a wonderfully cosmopolitan and picturesque assemblage. When the various Athletes foregathered in the huge American YMCA in the evenings, the riot of colour, the comic-opera uniforms of the various southern European nations, and the wonderful appearance of general fitness and physical strength, was something not easily forgotten.

Hilariously, the Serbians sang snatches of grand opera, and while the Australians enjoyed the singing, it was decidedly unwelcome after 10 p.m. when sleep was the priority. It seemed that the Serbians were unconcerned about sleep and no one in the Australian lines spoke sufficient Serbian to explain the etiquette of sleep time, so a version of sign language was resorted to. 'After a shower of tent-pegs and mallets, they took the hint,' Goddard observed.

On their other side, 'the Greeks held wordy warfare until far into the night'. An annoyed Australian envoy, clad in pyjamas, 'gave vent to a magnificent flow in two languages – English and obscene – and finally convinced the swarthy gentlemen that it was time to shut up. Thereafter all was quiet,' Goddard added.

In keeping with the military nature of the Games, a bayonet competition was also considered as it had been part of the training for soldiers. However, the committee wisely rejected it because there 'could be no satisfactory manner of judging such a competition'. Indeed. But there was no such difficulty with another lethal military weapon – the hand grenade – and a contest for the longest throw was included. The weapon used was the French F1 defensive grenade, with a total loaded weight of 600 grams, 165 grams lighter than the Mills bomb that the Australians first used at Gallipoli. There was no restriction on the throwing method employed. Two Australians entered the contest but were outclassed by 'the giants from the United States', who took all three places. The winner, a US army chaplain, threw just shy of 75 metres, while the Australians – despite all the confidence that a cricket background was supposed to provide at Gallipoli – could not break 60 metres.

Swimming, which was held at the Lac St James, a lake in the Bois de Boulogne outside Paris, was expected to be an Australian strength at the Games, but here too they came up against an outstanding swimmer, Norman Ross from the US Air Service. He won the 100 metres backstroke, and the 100 metres, 400 metres, 800 metres and 1500 metres freestyle. He was given a standing ovation by the crowd and departed with a swag of trophies. At the Olympics the following year, he won three gold medals.

The Australian squad was led by Lieutenant Bill Longworth and included boxer Sapper Harold Hardwick in the 800-metre relay. The course for the swimming at the Lac St James was challenging, with competitors noting that a mouthful was sufficient to 'interfere seriously with the function of the human organs'. Despite these challenges, had Norman Ross not been there, Goddard believed, the AIF 'would certainly have cleaned up the whole of the prizes'.

As it was, they had to contend with seconds and thirds in most events, with Longworth – also a Stockholm Olympian –

coming second in the 400- and 800-metre events. However, honour was restored by Longworth, Hardwick, Ivan Stedman and Jack Dexter in winning the 800-metre relay race. Amid the delighted cheers of the spectators, the team won by 50 metres from the American team.

Tennis was another sport in which the Australians went into the Games with confidence, and with good reason. Already in 1919, the AIF players had shown consistent winning form. By the end of the year, they would have laid claim to sweeping most tennis championships before them. Even as the Inter-Allied Games were being planned, the AIF were making their mark in tennis.

At the Covered Courts Championship meeting at Queen's Club, London, the AIF entered a seven-man team, consisting of well-performed representative players. In the singles, armed with a powerful serve that rose from the wooden court surface with alarming speed, Australian Captain Gerald Patterson made it through to the final, where his opponent was an Englishman, Corporal Percy Davson. A master tactician who, in his profession as an architect, had supervised the laying of the courts at Queen's Club, Davson quickly worked out how to master Patterson's serve by meeting the ball as close to the floor as possible, with the face of his racquet almost parallel with the floor. By this means and keeping a stiff arm, he was able not only to return the serve but to get pace on the return, allowing him to wrong-foot Patterson as he rushed to the net. Davson won the match in three sets. To complete the tournament, the AIF's Gunner Randolph Lycett and Major Rodney Heath won the doubles.

The Inter-Allied tournament in Paris followed. On the hard surface, Patterson faltered, losing to both AIF Captain Pat O'Hara-Wood and the French champion, André Gobert, who in turn easily defeated O'Hara-Wood. However, Lycett and Wood were too strong for the Americans in the doubles, winning easily. Further success followed, with Australia defeating the

Americans in the team matches to emerge as the Allied Armies Championship winners.

In early June, with Wimbledon a month away, the left-handed Norman Brookes arrived in England from Australia to join the AIF team. Brookes, winner of Wimbledon and the Australian Open, had served as a non-combatant with the rank of lieutenant colonel. The Wimbledon tournament had not been held since 1914, which meant Brookes was the reigning men's singles titleholder, and would defend it. The resumption saw 128 entries to challenge him. But first there was the final, and on 3 July Gerald Patterson took centre court against his British opponent, Algernon Kingscote, who had no answer to the Australian's stroke power. He lost in fifty minutes.

The win meant Patterson qualified to meet Brookes in the challenge round four days later, the two Australians vying for the men's singles title. Brookes' form was unknown, but it soon became clear he was not the player he was in 1914. At the peak of his powers, Patterson won the title 6–3, 7–5, 6–2. To complete an Australian triumph for the tournament, O'Hara-Wood and Staff Sergeant Ron Thomas defeated Randolph Lycett and Rodney Heath in the doubles final.

The British press reflected the completeness of the Australian domination. Such headlines as 'England's Tennis Slump', 'Wimbledon Taken Over by Invaders', 'Colonial Domination', 'What of the Old Country?', 'Wonder-child of Australia Beats Our Best', and 'Little Talent to Hold Visiting Players' gave testimony to the Australian success. Another Wimbledon men's singles title followed for Patterson in 1922, and the Australian title in 1927 in a golden decade for Australian sport. The world began to take notice.

13

THE NOBLE ART

If diggers weren't scrapping on the football field or belting leather to the boundary, there was always another option: lacing on the gloves and stepping into the boxing ring. From the first transports that carried troops to war in 1914, boxing held a fascination that did not wane, whether on the ships or at the camps for men just out of the trenches. Not all the memories were positive, however, as George Goddard explained: 'Many of the less bellicose spirits remember with a feeling of horror the compulsory boxing bouts on board ship on the way to Egypt and France.' On such occasions the smaller, less practised men were in high demand as sparring partners. Unsurprisingly, compulsory boxing had its critics. For those voluntarily entering the ring, it was a different matter.

Within a fortnight of the signing of the Armistice, an Australian Corps Boxing Tournament was held at Abbeville, France. On the form shown there, a team was selected to fight in elimination trials with men from AIF depots. From these trials, an AIF team was chosen to contest the British Empire and American Services Boxing Tournament at London's Royal Albert Hall in December 1918. The British won the tournament, with the Americans second and the Australians sixth out of the nine teams.

A month before the Inter-Allied Games opened, and after a boxing tournament in April at Aldershot, England, Syd Middleton was far from confident about the chances of the AIF team.

> From what I saw of our boxing on the night of the finals, I am afraid we will be poorly represented in Paris; in fact, as the contests will be 10 rounds, I am much afraid our showing will be very poor, for an indifferent performer can manage to weather three rounds often enough, but the superiority of the good man is so marked in the longer contest.

Middleton either underestimated his team or was deliberately playing down expectations – not least about Private Albert 'Digger' Evans. Digger was there to prove a point and emerged as one of the star performers in the boxing ring. Yet his background was anything but promising. Hailing from Cobar in far western New South Wales, Digger was born in June 1895 and aspired to be a boxer from the age of seven. However, he had to contend with a series of debilitating breaks to his left arm from both football and a fall from a tree. Surgery followed, involving the removal of bone, leaving his left arm shorter than the right. Undeterred, he changed his stance to lead with his right hand, turning him into a southpaw. As a teenager, Digger began to build his boxing skills through sparring at the back of a Cobar hotel, for threepence a win. He did this on the quiet. 'My mother tried hard to get me to give up football; she said it was too rough. Had she known I was fighting there would have been ructions.' A blacksmith by trade, he would later assert that swinging the hammer made him tough.

In March 1916, he and some mates travelled the 300 kilometres from Cobar to Dubbo to enlist. Army records show

'Digger' Evans. AWM D00158.

that just shy of his twenty-first birthday, he was 1.6 metres tall and weighed 54 kilos. It was in camp at Dubbo that Digger had his first fight in the ring. Buoyed by the experience, he did not hesitate to jump in the ring again at the Liverpool barracks, winning an exhibition bout. More success followed on the troopship to Britain and, after reaching the AIF's Lark Hill Camp on Salisbury Plain, he went forty-five fights without defeat. Attached to the Australian Army Services Corps, Digger was transferred to the AIF camp at nearby Sutton Veny, where several more fights followed without loss.

Word of his performances caught the ear of an English boxing promoter and matchmaker, Charlie Lucas, who, on watching Digger in the ring, immediately saw his potential and arranged a six-round bout with a boxer in his stable. Despite giving away 4 kilos in weight, Digger happily agreed. On winning the contest, Digger was selected to fight in the Inter-Army Championships of the British Southern Command at Bristol. Again, he gave away weight to the Southern Command's lightweight champion, yet Digger was happy to get in the ring. 'We boxed four rounds,' he recalled, 'and the judges ordered another two rounds. The extra rounds having been completed, he [the British boxer] got the decision, in spite of the fact that he never landed a punch.' The loss aside, Digger was selected to represent the AIF in military tournaments in London, where he won first the bantamweight title and, shortly after, the featherweight title. Later he took part in an Anzac tournament at Hurdcott camp, Wiltshire, where, after six bouts in the one day, he won the bantamweight title.

With the Armistice signed, Charlie Lucas, who by now was Digger's manager, took him to London seeking professional fights and was matched with the champion Welsh boxer Jimmy Wilde, nicknamed 'the Mighty Atom', in the bantamweight division of the King's Trophy at the Albert Hall, in December 1918. It was a three-round contest watched by thousands of Australian troops cheering on the boy from Cobar. Digger had a

6-kilo weight advantage and knew he would need it against the British and world flyweight champion. He was 'extremely happy that it wasn't the other way about'. This was a major step up for Digger, who recalled to a biographer:

> I was asked if I feared the greatest little fighting machine the world has known, I laughed. What was there to fear? It was a privilege to meet Wilde. Opponents had to be in the first flight before being considered for matches with him. And looked at in that light, I suppose I should have felt honoured.

Wilde made the pace with a flurry of punches, but the will-o-the-wisp Digger jabbed, held and moved astutely around the ring.

> With my southpaw stance I expected to have Wilde wondering for half a round until he sized me up. My condition was good and three rounds was not far to go, and so I planned to set the pace and go flat out all the way. Wilde evidently figured on making an early start, as he whacked me a beauty on the nose that made me see stars. The claret started to flow. The Mighty Atom hit with terrific force. I went for him after that first punch and didn't allow him to get set for another. It was a sizzling affair. We unleashed more punches than are usually thrown in a short bout. The pace was on from start to finish and it had the packed hall thrilled with excitement. The cheering was deafening. In between rounds I could not hear what my seconds were saying.

All through the three rounds the Australian mob yelled and chanted, 'Dig! Dig! Dig!' They were convinced Evans had won, just as the Welsh battalions were as they broke into song. As the M.C. pronounced Wilde the winner, the Australians loudly voiced their protest. Digger recalled: 'I felt quite satisfied that I had made a good scrap of it with the world's premier midget. Naturally I was sorry the decision went against me, but my disappointment was short lived.' Some weeks later, Digger fought for the British Empire bantamweight title and won. He was now ready for the Inter-Allied Games, where he was selected to represent the AIF in boxing in the bantamweight division. He went into training with the rest of the AIF team in April 1919, *The Anzac Bulletin* disagreeing with Middleton's assessment by asserting that the AIF would send 'a really good team of boxers' to the Games.

As the official Games' history noted, from the start 'Australia's string of fighters loomed up strong on the fistic horizon'. America had a team of champions, while France had counted on winning, with entrants who were all veterans and promising contenders for honours. Belgium and Italy both entered strong teams.

The boxing ring stood in the middle of the open field at the Pershing Stadium. On day one, Digger Evans watched on as other members of the Australian team jabbed and weaved before thousands of spectators. The tournament was divided into two sections: officers and other ranks. Captain Gordon Coghill scored a knockout against his Royal Navy opponent in round one of their officers' heavyweight clash. Coghill next scored a points win over an officer of the Indian army. He entered the final as the favourite. His opponent, the AEF champion Bob Martin, had other ideas. Although described as a 'green' boxer, Martin led cleverly with three left jabs to the Australian's stomach, causing Coghill to lower his guard, which was what Martin wanted. The Australian led with his left and Martin's instantaneous counter, a right swing to the face, ended the bout and won the American the heavyweight title. The fight had lasted just one minute and thirty-six seconds. Sportsmanlike, Martin carried Coghill to his corner.

Trooper Tom Watson, 7th Light Horse, carried the AIF's colours in the lightweight championship final against American 'Benny' McNeil. Watson was regarded as one of the AIF's smartest boxers, possessing an agile ability to use his hands. Like McNeil, he hit hard. In the ring, there was little to choose between them, each calling into play 'all the resourcefulness at his command', according to the Games history, and the bout was a 'slashing affair' but 'not the wild-swinging fight of unskilled boxers'. There was little to choose between them, with both men giving and receiving considerable punishment. 'At the end, they stood arm-in-arm with broad smiles on battered faces and submitted to the photographic ordeal.' The judges gave McNeil a points victory, and Watson had to content himself with second place. Some of the Parisian dailies expressed their conviction that Watson had won.

When Digger Evans entered the ring, he did so with obvious confidence, which led observers to note 'his winning and cheerful smile'. Indeed, whenever he fought, the smile stayed – often to the chagrin of his opponents. Evans's closest battle was his elimination bout with 'Babe' Asher, the American bantamweight champion. The Games history commented that Asher hit harder than Evans, but Digger's cleverness kept the American out of range for the most part. Syd Middleton observed that he had lost none of his form against an opponent whom the Americans unhesitatingly rated the best they had in the division.

> From the fifth round onward Evans began to take the lead, and once he had established it, he maintained it. His footwork was wonderful, and he used both hands cleverly. The American had the advantage of height and reach and, as is the case with the whole of their team, he was trained to the minute. The bout went the full distance – ten rounds – and the decision went to Evans amid much acclamation from the few Australian spectators. It was a

good decision, and the Americans themselves recognised the justice of it.

In the final, Evans faced an Italian, Enea Marzzorati, in an evenly matched contest. But gradually Digger forged a lead, Goddard noting that the Italian was 'considerably worried by the superior speed and footwork' of the Australian. He 'could make no headway against the smiling Digger', and the judges awarded the verdict and championship to Evans on points after ten rounds.

The Games history commented that Evans was a 'decided favourite with the ring-side fans of all nations', adding that he was 'far and away the cleverest boxer in the tourney'. His punches may have lacked 'steam', but he made up for this by hitting almost at will, landing blows where he wanted to. His favourite trick was to wait for his opponent to lead and then step in with a fusillade of rights and lefts to the head or body. All his bouts were won on judges' decisions; all of them but one were by wide margins. Digger emerged as a 'smiling assassin' in the ring, his shortened left arm proving not to be a disadvantage and perhaps his unique southpaw stance disconcerting opponents.

As the Games ended, there was one boxing title still to be resolved, and until the final day it was shrouded in doubt. At stake was the light heavyweight title. In the training camp, Sapper John Pethybridge had been dubbed 'The Mesopotamian Terror', having been attached to the Anzac 1st Wireless Signal Squadron in Baghdad. He had won a heavyweight contest there, and had come to England for the army championships.

Pethyrbridge was not tall, standing at 1.72 metres, but what he lacked in height he made up for in bulk, weighing 90 kilos when he enlisted in July 1917. He was a fighter with a broad and muscular body, his arms heavily tattooed and, as his army medical history described him, his physical development 'powerful'. To Goddard, he was a 'rugged fighter of the hard-hitting type, with a great capacity for mopping up punishment as well as giving'.

His journey to the final was not without incident. In his first fight at the Games, Pethybridge faced Fernand Campagne of France. Overwhelmed by the Australian's avalanche of blows, the Frenchman was knocked out in the first round, sent to the canvas by a heavy swing to the body. In his second bout, the Australian met the American fighter Paul Norton, with both men standing toe to toe and trading blows in the first two rounds. Pethybridge shrugged off two heavy blows from Norton to his jaw. He was, it seemed, 'quite unperturbed'. Round three opened with the two raining heavy punches on each other, but then Norton fouled Pethybridge, who went down and was carried from the ring on a stretcher. Norton was disqualified and the fight awarded to Pethybridge, who was bedridden for several days, leaving the future of the final up in the air.

However, on the last day Pethybridge agreed to fight the other finalist, Italian Erminio Spalla, for the title. Sportingly, the Italians sent word to the Australian camp that they had no desire to press the matter in their favour and call upon a man to fight when he was not physically fit. The Australians thanked them but, as the Games were about to finish, did not want to leave the title unresolved. Although the official history described the ensuing fight as a 'slashing affair', it was quickly apparent to Goddard that Pethybridge had not recovered. 'The bout opened briskly with heavy exchanges. The Italian was a tall, strong man with a terrific punch, but not much style,' he wrote. The fight went the allotted ten rounds, and Spalla won on points – nonetheless the bout underscored Pethybridge's toughness.

Writing in *The Referee*, boxing correspondent W.F. Corbett noted that Gordon Coghill's loss should not have been unexpected as he had been badly wounded on the battlefield on three occasions. He then took aim at the Americans, pointing out that the Inter-Allied Games were not restricted to soldiers who had fought in the war, which advantaged some of the American boxers who had served only in 'home service'.

The Games used a scoring system for the boxing under which a nation was credited with 2 points for every bout won by its fighters. The nation whose fighter lost was credited with 1 point. The scoring included both preliminary and final bouts. With 20 points to its credit, by virtue of eight wins and four losses, the United States led the field in team scoring. Australia was second with 17 points, while Canada and France tied for third with 16 points each.

There was a similar outcome in the catch-as-catch-can wrestling, with Australians making it through to the finals in the featherweight, welterweight, middleweight and light heavyweight divisions but losing on each occasion to American opponents, and so on finishing second overall behind the Americans. The tug-of-war team fared worse. The eight-man team averaged around 90 kilos each. Their first match was against the Greeks, and they had no difficulty in winning in two quick pulls, lasting 45 seconds and 55 seconds. Buoyed by success, their confidence was high when they took on the much lighter Belgians. However, the Belgians were better coordinated, and their combined effort outdid the Australians in the first pull, winning in just over a minute. After this first defeat, the AIF team 'went all to pieces, and the splendid, combined work of the smaller men triumphed over the spasmodic, individual outbursts of their heavier opponents' in 2 minutes 43 seconds. However, the Belgians were too light to match 'the giants from America' in the final, who took out the title.

The Australian contingent was granted a few days' leave in Paris before returning to England. The teams disbanded and the men awaited repatriation. But the unique sporting season of 1919 was not yet over, and the Australian focus now turned to England in search of success.

14

THE AWESOME OARSMEN

The Inter-Allied Games in Paris had taken centre stage in late June and early July 1919, but across the English Channel the sporting landscape in Britain had been frenetic for several months – even as the 1918–19 Spanish flu epidemic ravaged the country, killing 228,000 people. Against this grim background, it was not just soccer and rugby that revived memories of pre-war sporting glory. Among the most anticipated contests was the 1919 Henley Peace Regatta. What unfolded became a legend in Australian and world rowing.

The regatta, held at Henley-on-Thames, got underway just a few days after the signing of the Versailles Peace Treaty in late June 1919. The focal point was the King's Cup, contested over a course 1 mile 550 yards [2112 metres] long. The AIF entered two crews in the heats. The first included Syd Middleton, who had been part of the winning eight at the 1912 Henley Royal Regatta.

Drawn out of a hat, the two AIF crews were pitted against one another on the second day of the regatta, with No. 1 Crew winning by three-quarters of a length in a time of 7:31. The other heats in the cup were between Canada and Oxford

University, New Zealand and Cambridge University, France and America. The Canadians rowed gamely, but Oxford University won by two lengths in 7:28. The American crew soon pulled ahead of the French in their heat and scored a comfortable win by three lengths in 7:40. Against the New Zealand team, Cambridge came on with a great spurt to win by three-quarters of a length in 7:17.

The draw for the second round resulted in the AIF No. 1 Crew facing Cambridge University, and Oxford University facing America. At the half-mile, the Australian boat was half a length in front, and led at the mile by nearly a length, going on to win by three-quarters of a length in 7:24. In the second semi-final heat the Oxford crew overhauled the Americans with a strong finish to win by a length and a quarter in 7:25.

The final between the AIF No. 1 Crew and Oxford University was held on the last day of the regatta. On the riverbank, the Sports Control Board had erected a spectator stand with a clear view of much of the course, including the finish line. Thousands of Australian soldiers had turned out in force to cheer on the AIF boat. As the crew members made their way to the Boat Enclosure, diggers rushed up to them clapping them on the back and wishing them good luck as they began stripping from their blue blazers and flannels to their rowing togs. The opportunity to devour free afternoon tea provided by the YMCA added to an already buoyant mood.

On a cold, grey and drizzly day, the Australian crew drew the outside position again, known as the Berks station. The crews got away to an even start. But the Australians were quicker to move and took the lead earlier than was expected, soon settling to a slower rate of striking than their opponents. As they turned the slight bend in the course the Australians swung into a line straight down the centre of the Thames. A full-throated cheer erupted from the Australians on the riverbank as the first distance marker showed the AIF crew to be half a length ahead.

The AIF No. 1 crew (right) defeat Cambridge University before going to win the King's Cup. AWM D00798.

Reaching Fawley near the halfway mark in 3:25, they had increased their lead to a full length and maintained that lead to the finish, winning in 7:07 – the fastest time recorded for the full course during the regatta. On the riverbank orderlies lifted legless diggers out of their wheelchairs and hoisted them onto their shoulders to catch the victorious Australians cross the finish line to win the gold cup.

A fortnight later, on 18 July, the Australians prepared to race again in the eights at the Inter-Allied Games in Paris. The course selected was on the River Seine over 1 mile 330 yards (about 1900 metres). There was a good stretch of water and plenty of room for three crews to row abreast. The entries for the eight-oar race consisted of crews from Czechoslovakia, Italy, Belgium, Australia, New Zealand, United States, Canada, Portugal and France, with Cambridge University as the representative of Britain.

The great interest of the regatta centred on the eights race. The Australian crew had altered considerably since its win at Henley. Middleton and Lieutenant Henry Hauenstein, the two Olympic oarsmen, who had supplied weight and experience, were not available, so two new men were brought in from No. 2 Crew. This meant there was little time to train as a crew and only two days to learn the course and polish their coordination.

Australia and New Zealand won their heats, as did the Cambridge University crew. The final took place under perfect conditions – smooth water and no wind – with the Australians drawing the central position. The three crews got away to an even start. When the crews settled down, Britain had a slight lead from Australia, with New Zealand dropping back. They rowed in this order to the halfway mark, where it was clear that the New Zealanders had fallen away, as a tight struggle developed between Australia and Britain. The two boats came dangerously close together, and the umpire warned the coxswains to pull out to avoid a foul. The crews were now rowing practically stroke for stroke and in the rush into the home straight Britain led by a few feet – a lead they maintained to win by a third of a length in a time of 6:26^{3}/s, with the New Zealanders a length behind the Australians.

As Australia was competing in the Inter-Allied Games, so too was an AIF rifle shooting team at Bisley, a Surrey village about 40 kilometres from London. The site of the National Rifle Association's (NRA) British national championships, Bisley was well known to Dominion marksmen, who competed there for the King's Prize, which, since 1860, has been widely regarded as one of the world's most prestigious prizes in fullbore target rifle shooting. During the war, its range was used as a school of musketry. The war over, the NRA now organised the Victory Bisley Meeting of 1919, the first shooting tournament at Bisley for five years. It was a natural attraction for Dominion troops and, ultimately, there would be around a thousand competitors.

Among the thirty-strong AIF team was Lance Corporal Wally Green, thirty-one, from Mount Gambier in South Australia. Green's war experience set him apart from the rest of the team: he had been a prisoner of war, captured by German forces at the Battle of Noreuil in northern France in April 1917. One of 3850 Australians taken prisoner by Germany in the war, he would remain a POW at Soltau, south of Hamburg, until repatriated in December 1918. Having been a member of the Australian team to compete at Bisley in 1913, Green volunteered to join the Diggers Team instead of immediately returning to Australia.

Normally, long rifles were used for the Bisley tournament, but they were in limited supply in early 1919 (although, with some excitement, forty were unearthed from the Tower of London – unsurprisingly, their condition was so poor they could not be used). Instead, practice began with the short magazine Lee-Enfield Mark III rifle – a weapon never intended for target shooting. While less accurate, it became the Australian weapon of choice during the war, and it also became the weapon for the King's Prize.

However, problems arose, not least because the ammunition in use for the championship left barrels badly nicked and the shooting erratic. Critics of the short rifle contended that any success was due to luck rather than skill. Staff Sergeant George Lee recalled much cursing about the short rifle, but he became even more aggrieved when he took his first shot at the 200 yards range and his rifle barrel exploded, pieces of it narrowly missing the Range Officer. Another AIF team member, Staff Sergeant Fred Harrison, was also critical of the decision to use it for the blue-ribbon event. He was the leading marksman in New South Wales and had competed at Bisley previously, commenting that given a short rifle of war manufacture with neither sighters nor slings, and with fixed, open sights, together with inferior ammunition, 'the Bisley King's of 1919 was nearer a gamble than a test of shooting ability'. Armourer Sergeant Stan Edwards, a triple King's Prize winner, agreed: 'Luck was a greater factor than science.'

Teams representing Britain, Australia, Canada, South Africa and New Zealand competed in the Kolapore Cup (donated in the nineteenth century by an Indian rajah), with Britain winning from Australia by six points. Australia was awarded the Colonial Prize, which carried prize money of £50. Mixed results for Australia continued with seconds in the Mackinnon Cup and Empire Trophy. Australia won the Martin's Cup with 833 points. An analysis of the Australians' placings in the various events showed that their shooting was very consistent throughout the whole meet. The Australians won four first prizes, several second prizes and three thirds, but the main trophy, the King's Prize, eluded them.

While the Victory Meeting was unique in opening competition to all past and present members of the British and Dominion forces, Fred Harrison saw the tournament as an anti-climax, with the shooting throughout much below the standard of pre-war Bisleys. Three weeks later, the team sailed for home. In 1927, Wally Green would win the Victoria King's Prize, but what was most impressive was his ability to surmount the debilitating effects of eighteen months as a POW to contribute to his country's results at the 1919 Bisley. Not only was he the highest-placed Australian in the King's Prize final, but he was the AIF's highest points scorer in the Empire Match, securing second place for Australia.

For Australia, the tournaments at Bisley, Paris, Henley and Wimbledon all provided varying degrees of success, but it was the Australian cricket team that put the final lustre on the extraordinary year in sport that was 1919.

15

A FIGHTING FORCE

First-class cricket the world over had been dormant for five years – the Sheffield Shield in Australia, the Currie Cup in South Africa and the County Championship in England had all been cancelled for the duration of the war. While there had been cricket during this time, with high-quality military matches between England and Australia at Lord's, by 1919 it was time to resume cricket more widely – and at the highest level.

As troops awaited repatriation on Salisbury Plain, they formed teams to compete in the local London league, but there was also a strong desire to resume Tests between Australia and England. The early discussion centred on a series of Victory Test matches between an Australian XI and an England XI, but several prominent Australian players, including Charlie Macartney and Eric Barbour, were adamant that they had been away from home for too long and returned to Australia. The English authorities refused to believe that Australia could field a representative combination to first-class standard and the idea was dropped.

As a stalemate loomed, the AIF Sports Control Board intervened, announcing the formation of the Australian Imperial Force Cricket Team. A tour was mapped out, with the board agreeing to financially support the players in their thirty-four matches, twenty-eight of which would be at first-class level. Local English clubs and county teams were keen to support the tour, in most cases allotting 50 per cent of the net proceeds of matches to the AIF. The program included matches against all the first-class counties, the Marylebone Cricket Club (MCC) and Oxford and Cambridge universities, as well as a tour of Scotland.

In March 1919, the various AIF camps were asked to send their best cricketers to Kennington Oval in London to show their mettle in several net sessions. With about a hundred men batting and bowling in the nets, the selection decisions fell to Lance Corporal Herbie Collins. Former England cricket captain Pelham 'Plum' Warner, who attended these sessions, was struck by one 'long streak' bowling with searing pace in the nets. Lieutenant Jack Gregory was an unknown, but so fast was his bowling that Plum Warner was impressed. The selectors decided to take a close look at this 'mystery man'. They would have known his cricketing heritage: his uncle, Dave Gregory, captained the Australians in the first ever Test match against England, in Melbourne in 1877. His brother, Ned Gregory, also played in the match, and his son, Syd Gregory, would represent Australia in Test cricket. Jack Gregory was poised to join them. 'We watched him for a while, and decided he might develop into a fair player,' Collins recalled.

When the team was selected, one notable name was missing: Jack Massie. If he had been fit, he would have been among the first selected. Massie was on leave from the army in London in the summer of 1917 when a journalist with the *Illustrated Sporting and Dramatic News* saw his bowling at Lord's. In his report, republished in Sydney in *The Referee*, he dismissed rumours about the impact that Massie's war wounds had had on his ability to bowl. Massie took 7–24. The correspondent felt privileged to have been there:

> It was a rare treat to get a front-row seat of a real bowler once again. I had it that Major R.J.A. Massie had been so badly wounded on Gallipoli that he would never bowl again. True, the fortune of war ordained that he should be shot through the left shoulder and lung, and he was, before the war, by far the best left-arm bowler in Australia ... he is the genuine article if ever I saw it.

Massie modestly put his performance down to his friend Plum Warner, captaining the other side, making the wrong decision at the toss on a wet wicket. 'Plum won the toss and batted. He should have sent us in really, but did not do so. It was a bowler's wicket.' Despite the praise heaped on him by the paper, Massie downplayed his effort, asserting that he had not been able to use the nice headwind on a helpful wicket.

> I am no bowler now, I am afraid, so I will have to go in for batting instead. As a matter of fact, I am no batsman either, but may make something of myself yet. My arm was a good bit better than it was last time although I did not bowl so well.

Massie went back to France, where he was again severely wounded on 3 February 1918. A solitary German bomb played havoc with a training exercise, with shrapnel badly damaging his left and right feet. He recovered to the extent that he could walk but, according to his military medical record, he could not run 'or go for violent exercise'. His combined injuries meant his first-class cricket career was over. Awarded the DSO and twice mentioned in despatches, he was promoted to lieutenant colonel and remained involved in sport for the AIF after the Armistice, working with his fellow Sydney sportsman Syd Middleton on the sports program in France. Massie came back to London to marry his fiancée in June 1919 and was a spectator when the four-month AIF cricket tour began.

The tour opened at Attleborough in Norfolk. A team raised by financier Lionel Robinson provided the opposition and included the elegant England left-handed batsman Frank Woolley and the all-rounder Johnny Douglas. That first match finished in a draw, but the Australians were soon into their stride, beating Essex by an innings. Against Cambridge University, they were even more dominant. Herbie Collins and captain Charlie Kelleway posted 165 for the first wicket, establishing a solid foundation for a declaration at a towering eight wickets for 650. Victory by an innings and 239 runs followed.

In the next match, against Middlesex at Lord's, the Australians had the best of a keenly fought draw. Collins made his first century of the tour with 127, while the leg spin of Sergeant Allie Lampard captured six wickets for 91 in the Middlesex first innings. As the Australians prepared to play Oxford University, they found themselves without a wicketkeeper. Collins recalled:

> The day before the match we were searching frantically for a 'keeper. Anybody would have done. Somebody told me – I think it was the licensee of the local inn – that a young fellow named Oldfield was in the town. This man remembered that he had heard Oldfield say that he kept wickets for a Glebe (Sydney) junior side before the war.

The Australians combed the town to find Oldfield, who reckoned he 'wouldn't be in the class of you chaps. Besides, I haven't got any togs.' Collins, not to be put off by the shy and nervous Oldfield, commented, 'We nearly had to kidnap him to get him to the ground. Meanwhile we rustled up togs.' The unknown was how Oldfield would cope with the pace of Gregory, who, according to Collins, was blossoming as a fast bowler of the 'destroyer' type.

We were all wondering what was going to happen when this inexperienced youth from Glebe stood up to him. We thought the only thing in his favour was that he said he 'liked wicket-keeping'. Gregory had a terrifying run as he pounded down to the wicket. I told young Oldfield that he had better stand well back. Oldfield, who had never seen Gregory, said nothing. The fast bowler's first ball was a ripper. Oldfield took it beautifully.

Oldfield took four catches during the match. After that, he shared the wicketkeeping with Ted Long, and later became the first-choice 'keeper on return to Australia. After the Oxford match, a draw followed against Surrey at The Oval, a game notable for the great English batsman Jack Hobbs scoring 205 not out, in a total of 344. The AIF responded with a massive 554 for seven, with centuries by Lampard and Major 'Nip' Pellew, and 96 by Gunner Johnny Taylor.

Although the runs flowed, and critics were starting to take notice of this nondescript AIF side, the Surrey match was overshadowed by a drama involving Kelleway. During a wicket inspection, a critical remark from the abrasive Kelleway offended a groundsman, who reported it to the Surrey committee. When they took a dim view of the incident, a tense meeting in the Australians' dressing room followed. In an extraordinary turn of events, the AIF commander, General Birdwood, approved Kelleway's sacking.

Collins was elected in his place and celebrated his first game as captain with a strong ten-wicket win against the MCC at Lord's. At Hove, in June, the match against Sussex was drawn, with slow left-armer Collins bagging eight wickets for the match. At Old Trafford, the Australians thrashed Lancashire by an innings and 157 runs, Collins scoring 103, with the left-arm medium pace of Stirling capturing 5–38 in Lancashire's first innings and leg spinner Lampard unplayable in their second with 9–41.

Against Yorkshire, the Australians needed 170 to win when the last-wicket pair of Gregory and Ted Long came together at nine for 116. They put on 54 to win the game. This was a match in which Gregory's sheer pace unsettled the Yorkshiremen and saw him take 6–91 in the first innings and 7–79 in the second. A draw against Hampshire followed before the Australians, in their twelfth match, finally tasted defeat at Lord's against the Gentlemen of England, captained by Plum Warner. Against the Gentlemen's 402, the Australians collapsed for 85. In the follow-on, they were dismissed for 184.

Playing Northamptonshire next, they won by 196 runs in a match notable for Gregory scoring 115, his maiden first-class century. In an outstanding bowling performance, he took eight wickets for the match. After a series of second-class matches, the team travelled to Leicester for a drawn match, marked by brilliant batting by Pellew with 187, Willis 156 not out and Collins 121 in a total of 5–551 declared. Next up, Derbyshire defeated the AIF by 36 runs. The Australians returned to winning form against Worcestershire, victorious by an innings and 203 runs. Gregory was fearsome, taking eleven wickets in the match. Pellew with 195 not out and Willis 129 not out, again shone with the bat.

Warwickshire were the next victims, the AIF winning by an innings and 38 runs, with Collins scoring 110 and taking 5–73. Another century to Willis, with a finely constructed innings of 130, came against Nottinghamshire at Trent Bridge as the Australians totalled 371. The county side responded with 391. In the second innings of the drawn match, Collins hit 118 to take him past 1000 runs for the season. He followed up with 95 in the next match, against Surrey at The Oval, but again the result was a draw that left the home crowd unhappy with the Australians, whom they accused of slow batting. Amid cheers, one angry spectator ran onto the field, argued with the umpires and pointed flamboyantly to the clock. Play continued, the

Australians no doubt wary of the presence of Jack Hobbs, who had scored a double-century against them a few weeks earlier.

Against Sussex at Hove, Carl Willis's purple patch continued, with 127 in a victory by an innings and 54 runs. In the Sussex first innings, Gregory was at his destructive best, taking 6–38 and Collins 4–47, which he followed up with 6–27 in the second innings. A three-day match against Kent at Canterbury that ended in a draw was notable for Gregory's seven-wicket haul in the first innings, and for Willis, 95, just missing out on another century.

A match against Essex followed, with Taylor scoring 146 in the AIF's second innings of 8–447, and Gregory bagging nine wickets for both innings in an easy Australian win by 309 runs. A two-day fixture against Gloucestershire was drawn, before the AIF faced Somerset at Taunton for an easy win in which seamer Charlie Winning and the orthodox left-arm spin of Collins did all the damage, Winning taking 6–30 and Collins 4–38. Collins followed up with 67 not out to give the Australians a 159-run lead. On the final day, Collins was near-unplayable, taking a career-best 8–31.

There were three final first-class three-day matches played in September, the first against a strong South of England XI, which included Test players Frank Woolley, Phil Mead, Arthur Gilligan and Jack White. The AIF dismissed the South for 183, Charlie Winning capturing 5–57. The AIF managed 162, Willis top-scoring with 54. The South were all out for 280 in their second innings, leaving the AIF 302 to win, but they could only make 179.

The South batted first in the second match, in Portsmouth, with Gregory using the rainy conditions to bag 6–42 as the South were dismissed for 104. For Collins, his 3–41 gave him the double of 1000 runs and 100 wickets in a season. Australia responded with 206, before the South collapsed again for 115, Winning snaring 5–30 as Australia won by ten wickets. The third and final match, against a representative English XI at Scarborough, was a different story as the Australians looked to finish the summer on a high note but instead were bowled out for a paltry 81. The English replied with 187, and Gregory, with his usual searing pace, took 7–83. The AIF hit back with a strong second innings of 296, with Willis, the team's highest run-scorer for the season, belting 96 – but not enough to save the Australians from a two-wicket defeat.

The AIF suffered just four defeats on tour, having won and drawn twelve each of the other twenty-four matches. As captain, Collins attributed the side's success to their unselfish play. The fact that every member of the team had been on active service made their victories all the more admirable. Jack Gregory, with his exhilarating pace and penetration, had emerged as a feared fast bowler.

In Sydney, the assessment of the *World's News* was that the team was not to be judged from the standard of an Australian Test eleven but, as the record showed, 'it was a real fighting force'. Apart from Gregory's bowling, the strength was collective rather than individual, with every batsman capable of scoring runs. At a farewell banquet in London, the English cricket administrator Lord Harris said the Australians had done better than they had probably ever anticipated, adding that the occasion was unique – 'an Eleven of cricketing soldiers'.

When the AIF cricketers finally arrived home in Australia – winning ten matches in South Africa en route – they played three final matches, the last being a satisfying win over New South Wales in Sydney. Jack Gregory and Bert Oldfield both earned their Test debut for Australia against England at the Sydney Cricket Ground in December 1920, playing alongside Charlie Macartney, Collins, Kelleway, Taylor and Pellew. They thrashed England by 377 runs. Just over a year later in Johannesburg, Jack Gregory scored the fastest century, measured by minutes, in Test cricket, reaching three figures in just seventy minutes.

For Oldfield it was especially satisfying to begin a Test career that had been threatened never to happen after he was found semiconscious and partially buried near Ypres in 1917. The attack left three of his comrades dead. These players knew that some 250 first-class cricketers had died in the war. But cricket had sustained them and so many others in the face of this horror, from the early match between the 1st and 3rd Australian Light Horse Brigades at Gallipoli, to makeshift 'Tests' on the Western Front and genteel games on the playing fields of Britain as the fighting raged on. A return to cricket – and normality – was something to be cherished.

The 1919 Imperial Force Rugby XV also stopped in South Africa on their way back to Australia. In Durban, they defeated Natal and arrived home to a hearty reception from the rugby community. The ranks of Wallabies who had gone to war had suffered grievously, with countless players either dead or injured. Of the estimated 5000 rugby players who enlisted, 500 were killed, including ten Wallabies, seventeen New South Wales Waratahs and three Queensland players. So heavy were the losses that some clubs folded, with the game wiped out in Queensland for more than a decade. From the 1913 Wallabies who had scored a historic 16–5 Test victory over the All Blacks, to give Australia its first Test victory on New Zealand soil, six did not return from the war. Gallipoli took two – Fred Thompson and Harold George. The other four – Bryan Hughes, Herbert Jones, Clarence 'Dos' Wallach and William 'Twit' Tasker – died on the Western Front.

Rugby in Australia was on its knees, and administrators determined that there was an urgent need to build on the success of the AIF team in Europe; indeed, they had defeated New Zealand, who were just as strong then as they would be a century later. A series of eight exhibition matches was arranged against New South Wales and Queensland, together with three games against an Australian team, plus some regional games.

In the first game, against the New South Wales team at the Sydney Sports Ground, a crowd of 10,000 watched as the AIF forwards dominated in a 42–14 victory. The *Sydney Morning Herald* commented that 'the Diggers thoroughly deserved the high reputation that had preceded them'. The AIF won all eight games on the tour, amassing 268 points to only 78 against them. Their success reinvigorated the game, ensuring that rugby union would not become another war casualty. Just as in cricket, the AIF rugby squad provided the nucleus of players for the New South Wales and Australian teams in international matches against New Zealand and South Africa throughout the 1920s.

While this was a time of rebuilding across Australia, the war's had consequences hit hard among many of the nation's returning sportsmen. Among them was Jack Massie, who looked back on a wrecked cricket career that should have seen him opening the bowling for Australia with Jack Gregory. Before the war, that was his destiny. Post-war, with that honour denied him, he wrote a book, *Bowling*, aimed at assisting coaches in schoolboy cricket.

He would go on to a successful business career, and take those skills to World War II, which in 1943 saw him appointed as chairman of the Ministry of Munitions in New South Wales. That same year tragedy struck with the death of his wife, and his son killed in action.

Before those deaths, however, he had to deal with another horrifying event involving his good mate and fellow cricketer, Dr Claude Tozer. They were first XI teammates at Shore School and Sydney University and made their debuts for New South Wales together against the touring South African team at the SCG in February 1911. After graduating as a doctor, and aware of the need for medicos on the frontline, Tozer enlisted in May 1915 and arrived at Anzac Cove three months later. Having survived typhoid, he moved to the Western Front where at Pozieres in July 1916 he suffered a severe gunshot wound which left him unconscious for two days. With shrapnel embedded in the right temporal lobe of his brain, doctors in London decided it was too dangerous to operate and left it there.

While convalescing in England, Tozer was promoted to major before returning to France in April 1917. In early September 1917 he was transferred to the 3rd Field Ambulance and later that month during the 3rd Battle of Ypres along Menin Road he was in charge of organising the evacuation of hundreds of wounded diggers. Under constant enemy shelling as he worked in the open, he disregarded his own safety to dress the wounds of casualties. For his courage he was awarded the Distinguished Service Order.

Promoted to chief medical officer, Tozer spent the rest of the war at the No 3 Australian General Hospital in Abbeville in the Somme where he was able to mix medical duties with time out for cricket. Playing nineteen matches for the hospital in 1918, he was their star batsman, compiling 405 runs at 135, including one century.

Returning to Australia, cricket became the one bright light in Tozer's life as he suffered the lingering effects of shell shock and the grief of his fiancée suddenly dying. He played for the Gordon Cricket Club and soon was selected again for the New South Wales team. Appointed state captain, he was on the verge of Test selection when he was shot and killed by his lover. Among the mourners at Tozer's burial at Waverley Cemetery in December 1920 were Austin Diamond and Jack Massie, both inconsolable.

Elsewhere, Robert Grieve returned to Melbourne, his Victoria Cross elevating him to a rare hero status in the eyes of the city. He went back to successfully playing sub-district cricket for Brighton. In 1925 he took part in a match to raise funds for the Returned Soldiers' Distress Fund. As Greg Growden pointed out in his book, *Cricketers at War*, many also saw it as a chance to celebrate the feats of Australian cricket's first VC recipient. Among the several Test stars of previous years who travelled to Melbourne for the match were three former Australian captains – Clem Hill, Monty Noble and Warwick Armstrong. They led the three cheers for Grieve.

Judy Masters, promoted sergeant by war's end, overcame his wounds to achieve sporting immortality as one of Australia's greatest ever soccer players. Having survived Gallipoli, and a shoulder wound at Pozières in July 1916, the end of the war saw him return home to marry his war bride. In the 1920s, he went on to represent Australia on twenty-two occasions, including six full international matches, for five of which he was captain. Playing centre forward in a match against England in Sydney in 1925, he stunned the visitors with a goal just ninety seconds after the kick-off. When he retired, he was acknowledged as Australia's finest soccer player and known as 'the Little Master'. Having played more than 400 games, his record showed he had never been cautioned.

Private Duncan Thompson, already a representative rugby league halfback when he enlisted in September 1916, was shot through the chest at Dernancourt in April 1918, and told he could never play sport again. Defying the medicos and known variously as 'One Lung' and 'The Wizard', he did, winning rugby league premierships with North Sydney in 1921 and 1922, and playing nine Tests between 1919 and 1924.

And then there was Nick Winter, who embarked for Egypt with reinforcements for the 7th Light Horse Regiment in October 1915 and was later posted to the Australian Army Service Corps as a driver. Arriving in France in June 1916, he was employed mainly in depot duties, where he had time for sport, especially athletics. Post-war, he was selected to represent Australia at the 1924 Paris Olympics in the triple jump. To the astonishment of the athletics world, he won gold when he cleared 15.525 metres (50 feet 11¼ inches), setting an Olympic record and breaking the world record, which had stood since 1911.

Men such as these, who had been through the war, etched their names in sporting history with remarkable achievements, but so many of their fellow World War I sportsmen did not have the chance to play their part in post-war sport, either not surviving the conflict or coming home with limbs lost or suffering psychological trauma. And that would be an ongoing story.

During these years, Charles Bean began his momentous task of writing the *Official History* of the war. He established himself at Tuggeranong Homestead, a mere 20 kilometres away from where the new temporary Parliament House would be built (Canberra had been designated as the national capital in 1913). Regular tennis matches took place on the ant-bed tennis court which Bean's staff had restored, and a concrete cricket pitch was laid down in an adjoining paddock. Along with his staff, returned servicemen, local graziers, farmhands, schoolteachers and schoolboys, Bean formed the Tuggeranong Twisters Cricket Club to play in a competition that stretched from the Tuggeranong Valley to surrounding towns and villages.

This was mirrored elsewhere in Australia, where local veterans were often found on the sportsfield, golf course, cricket pitch or tennis court. Most were still young and, hardened by military life, were keen to get involved in local competitions. Citing Wagga Wagga in the Riverina as an example, historian Ian Hodges notes that every week local sport was covered in detail, and every week the city's returned servicemen featured in stories about a recent match or one to come. This focus underlined the continuing association between sport and the AIF in the post-war years, not just in Wagga but across the nation. Importantly, it was an obvious means by which returned men could hold onto the comradeship that many soldiers felt was the brightest part of their wartime service.

Albert Jacka was the first Australian in the Great War to receive a VC. His physical prowess and skills as a boxer were central to his legendary status and his image was used in numerous recruiting posters, with the Sportsmen's 1000 drawing a direct link between sporting prowess and war.
(AWM ARTV05616)

A detachment of the Sportsmen's 1000 marched through the streets of Melbourne in October 1917 as the campaign for new recruits to go to the Western Front intensified the focus on the nation's sportsmen.

While Official Historian Charles Bean's photo made the cricket match at Gallipoli's Shell Green famous, his was not the only photo of the ruse to distract the Turks from the imminent departure of Allied troops. Padre Thomas Bennett, 22nd Battalion AIF, was a keen photographer and also captured the game at Shell Green with this hand-coloured lantern slide. *(Padre TP Bennett collection, State Library of Victoria)*

On 28 May 2001, the Australian cricket team visited Gallipoli and re-enacted the game at Shell Green while on their way to England for their Ashes-winning tour. *(Hamish Blair, Getty Images/ ALLSPORT)*

Private Joseph MacMaster, 2nd Battalion AIF, snapped an unidentified Australian Army Nursing Service Sister as she stood at the wicket during a pause in the cricket. Although the location is not stated, it is likely to be the Australian convalescent home at the Al Hayat Hotel, Helouan, Egypt, where MacMaster was sent to recover in July 1915 after suffering a gunshot wound at Gallipoli in April. *(AWM P04752.001)*

Corporal Frank Beattie Davidson, 56th Battalion AIF, handcrafted this rough cricket bat from a silver birch branch. It was used at cricket matches held at Bussy-lès-Daours in France by 5 and 6 Platoons, B Company, 11–15 June 1918. *(AWM RELAWM01048)*

Diggers in slouch hats crowded onto the beach at Gaza, Palestine, in July 1942 to witness a surf carnival march past. More than 70 per cent of the active, eligible members of the Surf Life Saving Association of Australia volunteered to serve with Australia's forces abroad in World War II.

Trainees of the Australian Women's Army Service Officers Training School in World War II waiting to go onto the tennis court for a doubles match during their recreation sports period. *(AWM 065150)*

Early in World War II, Australian soldiers based in England play a game of cricket on a muddy pitch with a makeshift wicket and a considerable degree of enthusiasm.

While one of their number kept a look-out above for enemy planes these Australians played a game of cricket in the ruins of a Tobruk street. Standing on the balcony is believed to be Gunner Harold Smart Pullman, 2/5 Australian Heavy Anti-Aircraft Battery.

With their eyes on the target, Sergeant Lorna Bieber and Corporal Ronda Cabot take aim during an archery competition in Brisbane in February 1945. *(AWM 087803)*

During the AIF 9th Division's voyage home to Australia from the Middle East in February 1943, nurses from the Voluntary Aid Detachment took part in a 'horse race' on the sun deck of the *Nieuw Amsterdam*. *(AWM 050326)*

Sisters of the Australian Army Nursing Service relax with a game of deck quoits on the troopship bringing the AIF 7th Division home from the Middle East in early 1942.
(AWM 011863/30)

At Fawkner Park in Melbourne's South Yarra in January 1944, Lieutenant Colonel Kathleen Best of the Australian Army Medical Women's Service was run out in a game of cricket between officers and other ranks. The wicketkeeper was Corporal J Scott.

Major William Roach of Pennant Hills, NSW – part of the Engineers team who came second in the diving championships at the Annual British Commonwealth Force Korea Swimming Carnival. *(AWM SWEJ0048)*

An elevated view of the German POW and internment camp, Stalag 383. A large group of POWs are assembled around the camp swimming pool, which was also the camp firefighting reservoir. In the foreground a few prisoners are playing volleyball. *(AWM P02070.002)*

Commanding Officer Lieutenant Colonel Frederick Gallagher 'Black Jack' Galleghan *(back to camera, right)* and other officers survey troops playing tunnelball aboard the *Johan van Oldenbarnevelt*, en route to Singapore, 1941. *(AWM P02569.058)*

LEFT: While he waited in Malaya for the Japanese attack, Warrant Officer Scott Heywood donned the pads and wrote home, 'The one of me in my cricket gear is worth enlarging, I think.' *(Courtesy Doug Heywood)*

BELOW: Flight Lieutenant George Archer's handmade golf ball from Stalag Luft III, a German POW camp. *(Author photo)*

Royal Australian Navy Quartermaster Gunner Joey Donovan *(right)* spars with Leading Seaman Ken Needham on the deck of destroyer escort HMAS *Parramatta* during the international five nations exercise, code-named Bersatu Padu ('Unite'), in 1970. *(AWM NAVYM0601/02)*

With Australians prominent, riders push off in a bicycle race between Kure and Hiroshima, Japan, in November 1947. Adelaide rider Lieutenant AM McDonough, of the Britcom Base Workshops, leads the way. *(AWM 145070)*

In the Hiroshima to Kure 18-mile marathon relay in November 1952, Corporal CE Fry took over from Captain Claude Smeal in a leg of the race. *(AWM 148219)*

Captain Claude Smeal *(right)* was captain-coach of the Britcom signals regiment team competing in the Hiroshima to Kure 18-mile marathon relay and is seen here receiving the winner's trophy in November 1952. Three months earlier, Smeal represented Australia in the Marathon at the Helsinki Olympic Games. *(AWM 148220)*

Australians and South Africans adopt a novel approach to discussing Test cricket tactics – with bullets as stumps and rocks as field placements – at a Korean airfield during the Korean War. *(Courtesy South African High Commission)*

Korean War photographer Lloyd Brown, of Melbourne's *Herald* and *Weekly Times* newspapers, captured this spontaneous game of cricket in a Korean village in 1950, with tank barrel included in the bottom left of the frame. *(AWM P04858.025)*

Members of 8 Platoon, C Company, 5 RAR snatched a brief respite from operations for a game of volleyball in the company lines at Nui Dat in January 1967. During the Vietnam War, a volleyball court was set up in most platoon lines and used as recreation in between operations and patrols outside the wire. *(Photograph by Private Doug Bishop)*

Troops from 1 RAR grabbed this opportunity for a game of touch footy in Vietnam. *(Courtesy Phil Anderson)*

Australian Army engineers from the 1st Mentoring and Reconstruction Task Force play a game of cricket on a dusty pitch in southern Afghanistan in May 2009. *(CPL Ricky Fuller, courtesy Australian Department of Defence)*

An Australian soldier takes the ball past an Iraqi defender during a friendly soccer match between the Overwatch Battle Group (West)-3 and the Iraqi Army in July 2007. The grim determination of the Australians was matched by the toughness of the Iraqis, many of whom played in bare feet on a rock-hard desert pitch, and resulted in a 3–3 draw. *(Captain Michael Brooke, courtesy Australian Department of Defence)*

ABOVE: Royal Australian Air Force aviator, Aircraftman Matthew Smith *(right)* and the Essendon team observe a minute's silence as part of the annual Anzac Day 2025 ceremony at the Melbourne Cricket Ground ahead of an AFL match between the Bombers and the Collingwood Magpies.
(CPL Michael Currie, courtesy Australian Department of Defence)

LEFT: The Northern Territory ADF and Police, Fire and Emergency Services women's teams compete during the ANZAC Shield game in Darwin in May 2025. The annual Shield series includes two AFL games between men's and women's sides from the relevant services.
(CPL Madhur Chitnis, courtesy Australian Department of Defence)

At RAAF Base Amberley, Queensland, in October 2016, air force teams competed in a Tug of War competition, pulling a C-17A Globemaster heavy transport aircraft. The 128-tonne transport provides a logistics backbone for ADF operations, allowing Australia to rapidly deploy troops, supplies, combat vehicles, heavy equipment and helicopters anywhere in the world.
(CPL Brenton Kwaterski, courtesy Australian Department of Defence)

The ADF has been represented at the Invictus Games since they were first held in 2014, and partnered with Invictus Australia to send 33 competitors and their family and friends to the Games held in Vancouver, Canada, in February 2025. More than 500 competitors from 23 nations took part in the week-long event. *(WOFF Ricky Fuller, courtesy Australian Department of Defence)*

World War II

16

THE OLD AND THE NEW

As the Wallabies arrived in the English port city of Plymouth on 2 September 1939, the uneasy European peace of the previous twenty years was about to shatter and the players' dreams of sporting glory would end. Just a day later, they heard the radio broadcast of British Prime Minister Neville Chamberlain telling the world that as Hitler had failed to respond to British demands to leave Poland, Britain was now at war with Germany. The consequences were quick. In Australia later that same day, Prime Minister Robert Menzies declared that as Britain had declared war on Germany, Australia was now also at war with the Third Reich.

The ramifications for Australia were immediate and deep, but for the Wallabies listening to Chamberlain from the Grand Hotel at Torquay, they were personal. From a planned twenty-eight-match, four-Test tour, their hopes for what would be the high point of their sporting careers were dashed. The tour was to last ten months, and after matches in Britain and Ireland the team was scheduled to play two Tests against France and, as it happened, one against Germany, which was seeking to replace France as the dominant rugby nation on continental Europe.

From there, the Wallabies were to tour Canada and the United States and, on the way home, play two Tests in New Zealand against the All Blacks. With Europe now at war, tour manager Dr Wally Matthews, a World War I veteran who had represented New South Wales pre-1914 and managed the AIF rugby team which toured England, Scotland, Wales and France at the war's end, was disconsolate. Matthews described fighting back tears on leaving a meeting with the English Rugby Football Union at Twickenham. The decision had been made that the tour was over without a game being played. Matthews knew he had to tell the team that they must return to Australia immediately. In his diary, he wrote: 'Stood in the middle of the empty ground on the first day of the war.' To revive spirits, a team photograph was organised at a rugby ground opposite the team's Torquay hotel. Matthews recorded the moment: 'A lovely study, the boys looked grand. Sad to think there is to be no play.'

Victorian Nicky Barr, the team's hooker, noted the 'air of depression, and more strongly, even resentment' among the players. 'We were asked to fill sandbags and protect The Grand [Hotel]. The feelings must have been incredibly strong because the beach disappeared in one day, there was no sand left.' The mood was grim as they then helped build an air-raid shelter before visiting Buckingham Palace to meet the King, thence to Twickenham so they at least could say they had been to the ground. There, they were greeted by empty benches and piles of air-raid precautions equipment.

Nicky Barr had been chosen in the Australian team over Eddie Bonis, recognised as the Prince of Hookers throughout the rugby world. Experts predicted that he would develop into one of the greatest union players of all time. But he would never play a Test and would represent Australia only once. With war declared, Barr tried to enlist to fight for England, but the rules forbade it. Two weeks after their arrival in England, the

Wallabies boarded their ship back to Australia, ending what became known as 'The Tour That Never Was'.

A game was arranged on the way home in Bombay so that players who had not done so could say they had played for Australia. The tour over, Matthews told the players: 'We have one job in front of us now ... to return and get into Australian uniforms without delay.' Most of them would, including Nicky Barr, Stan Bisset and Cecil Ramalli, a scrum half who was Australia's first Aboriginal and Asian Wallaby. Some would finish the war with injuries that stopped them from playing rugby ever again; some would never recover from the horrors of their experiences; and some would die while serving, among them Kenelm 'Mac' Ramsay, Jack Turnbull, Jack McDonald, Mick Clifford and Winston 'Blow' Ide.

The aborted rugby tour came with Australia unprepared for war. In the twenty years since World War I, Australia's armed services had fallen to their lowest ebb through austerity and retrenchment. A new volunteer army, the Second AIF, was hurriedly formed as provisions of the *Defence Act* precluded the five existing Militia divisions from serving overseas. On 15 September 1939, Menzies announced the formation of the new expeditionary force. It would comprise 20,000 troops and consist of one infantry division and auxiliary units. Thus the 6th Division, the first division formed within the Second AIF, was raised on 28 September 1939. Commanded by Lieutenant General Thomas Blamey, the division initially consisted of the 16th, 17th and 18th Brigades, each established with four infantry battalions. A few weeks later, Menzies announced the reintroduction of conscription for home defence service effective 1 January 1940. Unmarried men turning twenty-one in the year ending 30 June 1940 would be drafted into the Militia.

The onset of war brought to the fore the new generation of military leaders who had graduated from the Royal Military College Duntroon in Canberra, among them Donald Jackson, born in 1915, and Frank Hassett, born in 1918. They were mates, Jackson a year senior to Hassett. The son of a railway yard manager, Frank Hassett began his course in March 1935, aged sixteen. By his third year at RMC, he was excelling academically and proving himself an able athlete and boxer, later captaining the rugby XV, where he was a prolific try-scoring winger. Like Hassett, Don Jackson excelled in rugby union. At the close of the 1938 season the Australian Rugby Union approached Army Headquarters informally requesting that Hassett and Jackson be stationed in a rugby-playing city during the following year as they were being considered for the planned 1939/40 tour of the United Kingdom, Canada and the United States. But both were moved to Darwin and neither handled a football in 1939.

A farewell march through the streets of Sydney marked the Second AIF's final week before the troops sailed to war. On 4 January 1940 a crowd estimated at up to 500,000 people came to cheer them on their way. The *Sydney Morning Herald* commented: 'The long khaki columns thrilled the heart of Sydney as it has not been thrilled for a quarter of a century, since that still Spring day in 1914 when the First AIF marched through the same streets on its way to Anzac and imperishable glory.' So straight were the lines of the troops stretching over nearly 2 kilometres that they 'could have been measured with a ruler'. As a company of troops marked time outside a hotel in Elizabeth Street, 'a well-known Sydney artist dashed through the crowds with foaming jugs of beer. The troops could hardly be blamed for not refusing this attention.'

A charity cricket match between former internationals who had been members of the First AIF and a scratch team drawn from the Second AIF followed at Trumper Park, Paddington. Despite having no experience with the gloves, Don Jackson kept wickets for the new AIF, while for the old, the by-now legendary Test wicketkeeper Bert Oldfield was behind the stumps. On the field alongside him were other legends: Herbie Collins, Charlie

Macartney, Charlie Kelleway, Johnny Moyes, Bill Trenerry, Eric Bull, Johnny Taylor and Charlie Winning, with others in the grandstand.

Between wars, in 1927, Macartney and Oldfield had taken an Australian team on tour to Singapore and Malaya during a brief upsurge in the popularity of cricket there, little knowing that a few years later a grim chapter in the history of the Australian Defence Force would take place there. That day was now closer as they took the field at Trumper Park.

The First AIF made 7–246, with Macartney top-scoring with 81. The Second AIF could only manage 230 runs, of which twenty-year-old Basil Holmes 'Jika' Travers made 67. This was no surprise because at both school and Sydney University he had excelled academically as well as in cricket and football. In its account of the match, The Sydney *Sun* observed that the First AIF's attack did not contain 'any heavy artillery'. The report continued: 'Charlie Macartney, carrying a few extra pounds to the wicket, sent down a few overs with the deft action of a Mills bomb thrower, but the balls did not explode when they hit the pitch.' Nonetheless, he still finished with 3–38, while Johnny Moyes took 3–69. Despite their lack of practice, the combined guile of the First AIF proved too much for the young army cricketers, whose fielding was disappointing and whose bowling lacked in penetration. After the match, First AIF team captain Herbie Collins said there was 'sufficient material in the Second AIF cricket team to make a team equally as efficient as the original AIF team'. Bert Oldfield, who organised the day, presented Don Jackson with an autographed bail 'to mark my keeping without a bye'.

In its match coverage, the *Sydney Morning Herald* concluded that the old AIF players 'gave their younger opponents a lesson which may be used on a sterner field. Lighter thatched, heavier-girthed, with the elasticity of youth departed, the veterans contrived to outplay the younger men.' Johnny Taylor and 'Hammy' Love had had a merry time, while the tall and bespectacled Charlie Kelleway batted in characteristic style. 'There may be many stiff and sore limbs today and a few bruised shins among the "boys of the old brigade", but none will deny that it was worth it all.'

The paper added that in the spirit of the match, Charlie Macartney had informed the Governor-General that *he* was 'Governor-General' – his old nickname with the crowds – long before Lord Gowrie arrived in Australia. Macartney had 'batted in exhilarating fashion ... playing shots that left the onlookers gasping with admiration – and himself for breath. He also showed that he is still a cunning bowler.' The paper noted that Macartney was still serving as a non-commissioned officer in the army Records Section.

The match over, Lord Gowrie had moved to the centre of the oval and gripped the hands of two private soldiers and led the singing of 'Auld Lang Syne'. 'It was an amazing scene, and its significance was not lost on onlookers.' The day finished with Herbie Collins calling for three cheers from his men for their successors of 1940. Six days later, on 10 January 1940, a convoy of ten ships steamed out of Sydney Harbour, taking most of the 6th Division to Palestine. There, they would complete their training before joining the British Expeditionary Force in France. At least, that was the plan.

17

TOUT JUSTE

After five weeks at sea, the troops of the 6th Division were aching for a beer and a good time in the bars of Cairo when they arrived in Egypt in mid-February 1940. Instead, they were told they were going to Camp Julis near Gaza in Palestine, 350 kilometres away, with a daily beer ration of two pints each. Julis was just one of the eight major campsites chosen for the Australians in Palestine, spread out along the length of the Gaza Road, running north to south through Palestine. Julis was intended to be home for four major units and one company. The site at Qastina was put aside for five major units, as were Beit Jirja and Gaza Road. Three units were to be assigned to Barbara (Kilo 54) with another four at Deir Suneid, north of Gaza. A large Australian hospital of 600 beds was to be based at Gaza Ridge, with several billets for other units in Gaza itself.

Two months later, the troops at Julis prepared for the twenty-fifth anniversary of Anzac Day – the first time in twenty-two years that Australian troops would commemorate the occasion overseas. Services were held in Palestine throughout the morning, with a Dawn Service at the Gaza War Cemetery, another at Jerusalem and others at the various camps. If that

Anzac Day was a poignant reminder of exploits and sacrifices of Australians in the Middle East in World War I, the Australians also had a more immediate contest in their thoughts: three days after the Anzac commemorations an AIF Rugby First XV was to play the French at Beirut. Les Marsouins were the champion team of the French army in the Levant and the Australians knew they faced a tough battle.

Among the men selected were noted inter-service players Captain Frank Hassett (2/3rd Battalion), Captain Don Jackson (2/1st Battalion), Lieutenant Basil Holmes 'Jika' Travers (2/2nd Battalion), who would later represent England, his brother Lieutenant Bill Travers (2/1st Battalion), a New South Wales representative, and Melbourne surgeon Captain Edward 'Weary' Dunlop (Australian Army Medical Corps). Weary had enlisted in the 6th Division on 13 November 1939, and a month later was posted to the Australian Overseas Base Headquarters in Jerusalem. There, he was appointed acting assistant director of medical services. Weary was also an Australian rugby international, having played for the Wallabies at the age of twenty-five in their defeat of the All Blacks in 1932. He was a speedy, hardworking lock.

Cheekily, the French flew in five internationals on military duty from France to strengthen their XV. Honour was at stake. A crowd of more than 7000 spectators came to Beirut stadium to watch the match. Jika Travers was appointed the Australian captain and before kick-off met his French counterpart to toss and decide the length of playing time. Unknown to the French, the AIF had staged matches in the lead-up to the contest to pick their strongest team: firstly, the 2/1st Battalion team defeated the 2/2nd Battalion 8–3 on 17 March. A game between the Julis and Qastina camps followed and then a Possibles versus Probables match was staged to narrow final selections.

Wanting the French to believe they were not match-fit, Jika suggested short halves. The French responded that this was an international and halves of less than thirty minutes was unthinkable. A bemused Jika replied that if this was the way the French saw it, the AIF would be prepared to play forty or fifty minutes a half. They settled on fifty-minute sessions.

The AIF were under strict instructions not to retaliate or play rough, and the French exploited the situation to the full. The partisan crowd gave the French as much help as they could, upsetting AIF goal kicks by swaying in unison behind the posts for all their attempts. At half-time, the Australians were given the green light to play vigorously – within the rules. They did. Don Jackson, playing breakaway, relished the opportunity.

> The match became a joy as I crash-tackled half and five-eighth as they touched the ball and saw the inner backs begin to flinch and dispose of the ball wildly. It was not long before a large French forward sought to reduce this problem by running up in full view to kick me on the side of the head. There upon our own Goliath advanced to pick the miscreant up at the waist from behind and threw him over his head to the ground. The new victim lay on his back kicking the ground with his heels and bellowing. The referee reached the scene, and no melee developed; on the other hand, Senegalese, Algerians and Moroccans on the hill began to climb the fence seeking vengeance.
>
> At this point I was able to get up, and with more of a sense of the ridiculous than any inspiration, went over to our convulsed opponent on the sand to pat him on the head in a fatherly way and put the ball on his chest. This put the crowd in a huge humour and the colonial forces returned to their side of the fence, and what is more, began to see us in a new light. The French team began to tire half an hour before the end and lost three men with broken bones.

In a letter to his family, Bill Travers noted that the French 'all talk too much on the field' – a characteristic that his brother Jika turned to advantage after the Australians' winger, Lieutenant Richard Featherstonhaugh, had made a fine dash down the wing only to be stopped on the line by the fullback.

> A breach for hands in the ruck by the full back gave a free kick on their line. But wait – they are all arguing like hell about something. It appears our winger put his foot out about the 25-yard line and the French line umpire had not put his flag up. The whole team stops and curses the line umpire; one of them picks up the ball and kicks it as hard as he can at the poor fellow scoring a bull's eye in his tummy. In the meantime, Jika picks up the ball and drops a short kick and scores a try. When the Marsouins realise what has happened they are dumbfounded, but a try it was and as the referee told me after 'tout juste'.

The AIF won 11–5. That night the Australians went to one of the city's cabarets, the Kit Kat, to celebrate their victory. Entertained by French officers, Don Jackson made the most of the champagne. 'When the cabaret began, we joined in the delightful pastime of firing corks at the scantily dressed showgirls close by, claiming any hits on specific parts of the anatomy.'

The rugby victory was the high point of the AIF's sports experience since their arrival. Amid the usual field exercises, it was not the only involvement in sport. The 2/1st Battalion War Diary shows that the unit's soccer team twice played the Beersheba Police, drawing nil-all at Julis and winning 2–1 in the return match at Beersheba. Besides soccer and rugby, the Palestine Athletic Association, an affiliate of the Olympic Federation, also invited the AIF to compete in track and field athletics and boxing, along with British and French teams, thus ensuring a high standard. Phil O'Brien, a private in the Petrol

Company, Army Service Corps, settled in at Camp Barbara, near Gaza, with cricket and boxing high on the agenda — including a challenge from rugby league players to Australian Rules players for a hybrid game.

> The Queenslanders formed a rugby league team and challenged the Aussie rules players to a game. We had a few games, but the rule book had to be thrown out the window, or, rather, into the desert. I doubt if we ever made any converts to rugby league. During this period, I was extremely fit. I remember one Saturday I played a scratch game of rugby league in the morning, then four quarters of Aussie Rules in the afternoon and boxed in a tournament that night.

This was the Phoney War, the period in which no significant military action occurred in Western Europe. The Phoney War came to an end in April, when German troops invaded Norway, and then on 10 May Germany attacked France, Belgium, the Netherlands and Luxembourg. With the French surrender on 22 June, Germany controlled Continental Europe. Life in the Middle East began to change as the North African Campaign began in earnest — but not without some last official sports events. General Blamey, echoing his World War I AIF predecessor in the region, General Harry Chauvel, announced that an AIF race meeting would be held at the New Flemington Track at Barbara. The meeting was set for the first Saturday in September 1940. Referencing racecourses in Australia, the race program, mostly over five and six furlongs, comprised the Caulfield Plate, the Randwick Cup, the Hobart Stakes, the Morphetville Plate, the Perth Stakes, the Doomben Newmarket Cup and the Victoria Racing Club Trophy.

Two days later, the *Sydney Morning Herald*'s war correspondent reported that a crowd of 20,000 gathered for the meeting, which had been 'the sole topic of conversation among the troops for days'. A proper course was marked off and a totalisator set up, and several former registered bookmakers now in khaki called the odds.

> Arabs from many miles around, to whom any form of horse racing is meat and drink, swarmed in on horses, camels, and afoot. There were, dark-faced sheikhs from the desert, with curved silver swords at their sides and daggers in their belts, wealthy landowners, businessmen from the towns, wearing European lounge suits and red fezzes, and hundreds of fellahin from the surrounding farms and villages. It was one of the few racing occasions when picking the winners with a pin was as good a method as any because the horses were all country bred Arabs and there was no guide to form. There was, of course, the usual supply of 'good oil' acquired from Arabs by devious methods, but most punters preferred to trust their own judgment after seeing the horses in the saddling paddock. It was an assembly comprising the pick of the country's horseflesh, but the Arab jockeys were an unpredictable quantity. Though wearing the familiar bright colours of the Victorian [sic] Racing Club, they rode without boots or saddles and with whips held high like sabres in old-time cavalry charges. However, they had the crowd on its toes with some good finishes.

The race meeting was not the only diversionary activity in Gaza. From the troops' arrival, swimming had been popular. Although the beaches were good, channels and strong currents made the eastern Mediterranean surf dangerous, leading to a few drownings. This led to a surf life saving club being established at Gaza. There were plenty of men to run it as more than 70 per cent of the active, eligible members of the Surf Life Saving Association of Australia had volunteered to serve, and that October a surf carnival was held. As a large, flag-waving crowd of local people and Australian troops looked on, bronzed diggers competed in beach and surf races, with a march past that clearly reflected the influence and style of military marches. In peacetime this influence would continue.

One of those involved was Lance Corporal Dave McErlane, a lifesaver with the South Curl Curl Life Saving Club in Sydney, who went on to help his R & R team to victory.

Although the bulk of the Australian force was based in the Middle East, elements of the Second AIF were in Britain throughout the war, and between June and December 1940 around 8000 Australian soldiers organised into two infantry brigades and supporting units were also sent there. During this time, war correspondent Kenneth Slessor watched as troops tried to resolve the matter of which football code was best. The match was between the 'impossibles' and the 'improbables', but Slessor thought it might better have been called 'singlets over' versus 'singlets under', since the players all wore regulation dark blue army sweaters and had arranged their singlets in this way to distinguish between the teams. The match was a willing affair, Slessor's report noting that all ranks were 'levelled in the mud'.

> After a good deal of preliminary argument and expostulation during which New South Welshmen and Queenslanders came to blows with Victorians and South Australians in defence of their rival codes, it was agreed to play Australian rules. Several hardened rugby enthusiasts left immediately with sneers on their faces while a group of soccer partisans watched gloomily. However, despite the players' lack of recent training, the game was fast and exciting and the 'improbables' won by a margin of 11 points. It was a curious mixture of all four Australian codes since the rugby diehards stubbornly insisted on tackling and the soccer players on dribbling.

In readiness for the fighting ahead, the newly formed 7th Division AIF embarked for the Middle East to join their Second AIF comrades in October 1940. The 6th Division fought their first major land battle when they joined other Allied troops against Italian forces at the town of Bardia, on the coast of Libya. On 3–5 January 1941, the Italian positions were attacked and Bardia was captured. More than 40,000 Italians were taken prisoner. Three weeks later, after advancing west along the Libyan coast, the 6th Division captured Tobruk from Italian troops and the town became a garrison for the Australian and British forces.

There was more opposition, however, at the ancient Libyan desert fortress of Giarabub. A few days before the garrison fell on 21 March 1941, men of A Company, 2/9th Battalion, organised a game of cricket to while away the time, with Bren guns mounted on a nearby hill for anti-aircraft protection. With the game underway, A Company's officers were busy studying the Italian positions in the south-east and planning the attack. Major Fred Howard, HQ, watched the match before sunset:

> Tobruk and Benghazi saw many a scratch game in their time, but no eleven, I venture, had quite so fantastic a setting as that which played amid the sand dunes of the escarpment north of Giarabub. In a hollow surrounded by an immense horizon of nothingness, half-naked figures with a makeshift bat, a tennis ball and a petrol tin wicket seemed to give a netherworld parody of all earthly pleasures. But, squatting in the outfield in a battle-dress already stained and torn, the padre gave to the scene the benison of a civilised enthusiasm.

By April, Germany's Afrika Korps, under the command of Field Marshal Erwin Rommel had begun to cut off and surround Tobruk. For eight months, from April to December 1941,

Tobruk was besieged, with some 3000 Australian troops killed or injured.

It was not just the desert that challenged the Australians. In the mountains of Lebanon the 1st Australian Ski Corps School was opened, operating from December 1941 to May 1942 at a ski resort at an altitude of 1900 metres. With the Australian command realising the need for some form of mobile infantry in snow country, the school aimed to train 160 ski troops for each Australian Division in the Middle East. The aim was to train them to undertake reconnaissance and raiding patrols and general intelligence work in the otherwise almost impassable conditions of the Syrian winter.

Heading the school was Major Robert Savage, a signals officer who was also an accomplished skier. A staff of ten, including some of Australia's best skiers, aided by skiers including British Olympic competitor Major James Riddell, were brought together to provide expert tuition. Two courses, each of about fifty students, were trained, with about half emerging as competent skiers. Japan's entry into the war and changing priorities in North Africa meant that the Australian ski experiment was short-lived. Although the school was closed after only three months, and its staff returned to their units, its legacy was seen post-war, with a surge in the numbers of keen skiers back in Australia. The return of the Australian ski troops undoubtedly helped to stimulate this sudden increase, as did the large numbers of refugees arriving in Australia from European countries where skiing was well established.

Elsewhere in North Africa, there was no diminution in the desire for sport among the Australian and New Zealand troops stationed there. This could take various guises, as Captain Chas Daintree, a member of the 2/13th Battalion, 20th Brigade, witnessed. Leaving Palestine for Cairo en route to the Western Desert, he pulled into Cairo in the late afternoon for an overnight stop, before pushing on westwards to overtake the main body of the Brigade. In Cairo he and his fellow officers decided to treat themselves to a touch of luxury, thinking it would probably be their last taste of high living for some time. They checked into the smart Continental-Savoy Hotel. After dinner they were sitting in the large palm court entrance foyer when a group of young New Zealand officers entered, obviously having a wild night on the town. More Kiwis from a different unit followed. According to Daintree:

> [A]s if signalled by a referee's whistle, and accompanied by much shouting and shoving, they immediately locked together in a rugby scrum. This behaviour seemed to be accepted as normal by guests and waiters alike, who simply moved themselves back from the melee and went about their business or watched the contest from the sidelines with varying degrees of disinterest. One officer, evidently not a rugby enthusiast, wearing the glazed look of a stunned mullet, provided the light entertainment by shuffling round the perimeter, lifting the potted palms from their stands and dropping them on the marble tiles, where they burst with predictable results.
>
> Meanwhile, one pack of 'forwards', having gained the upper hand, had pushed their opponents to the top of the front steps, down which the entire scrum then collapsed in total disorder, ending in a noisy shambles on the footpath. They didn't reappear and the whole show lasted only a few minutes ... I've no doubt that the two units concerned would be presented with the bill for damages in due course.

At Tobruk, a more notable event occurred on 30 July 1941 when teams representing the Australian 20th Infantry Brigade and the British 107th Royal Horse Artillery Regiment took to the field at the 'Tobruk Cricket Ground' for a cricket match. The 2/4th

Australian General Hospital's Lieutenant Rupert Goodman recalled that, at the time, 'things got a bit quieter'. The problem, he said, was finding a flat area of ground. There was also the added danger of unexploded ordnance. 'You had to get an area where if you hit a ball somewhere you'd have to make sure you'd pick up the ball and didn't pick up something else. But we had a cricket match.' A big square near where the hospital was located was chosen to be flattened out.

Coir matting was laid down for the pitch, and while tricky, it was less of a concern than the outfield, which bore ample evidence of the damage wrought by 9-inch shells. A unique set of rules governed play, giving a tongue-in-cheek collective finger to the danger inherent in the siege. The match was scheduled to start at 1400 hours.

> **Hours of play:** Play to be continuous, except by interference by air raids, until 1800 hrs. Play will NOT rpt NOT, cease during shell-fire.
> **Refreshments:** All players will supply own beer. Rum issue, before and after match, is being arranged by Manager.
> **Dress:** Shirt, shorts, long socks and shoes (if available), hats F.S. (or bareheaded). ITI helmets or other fancy headgear will NOT be worn. Umpires will wear white coats (if available) and will carry loaded rifle with fixed bayonets. Tin hats to be used (on head only) by wicket-keeper, if desired.
> **Umpires:** One umpire to be supplied by each side. Unbiased umpires preferred but these may be changed if things are going against team concerned. Remarks to umpires on receipt of adverse decisions to be confined to those words used during dive-bomber attacks.
> **Weapons:** All players will be searched for concealed weapons before start of play. All weapons found, other

than S.T. grenades, Mills bombs, and revolvers, will be confiscated (this does NOT apply to the umpires).
Additional rules: Any other rules may be added or deleted as a majority of players, umpires or onlookers think fit.
Medical: Manager will make medical arrangements and have ambulance in attendance. A parade of stiff (muscle) players will be held at 0900 hrs, 31 July 41.

Nicky Barr, a member of the ill-fated 1939 Wallaby tour, by now was also on his way to the Middle East, with No. 3 Squadron Royal Australian Air Force (RAAF). Before leaving Australia, he had captained the RAAF rugby team, sparking folklore of the day Air Force met Army. With the bell about to ring, a free kick was awarded to Air Force on their own goal line. With the RAAF side leading by a point, under the rules of rugby all Barr had to do was kick the ball into touch and the game was over. But not according to his standards – if Army could beat him, Army could have the chance. Twice he put the ball into the air. Twice Army failed. In the Middle East, Barr's chivalry soon came to the fore in combat.

On 11 January 1942, flying a Tomahawk at El Agheila, he went to the rescue of a downed pilot escorting Blenheim bombers that were attacking Rommel's advance base. In the scrap that followed he shot down his first enemy fighter, a Messerschmitt Bf 109. But there was another German fighter following, and Nicky was in his sights. As cannon fire raked his fighter, he dived low to gain speed. He was skimming along just above the ground when the plane was flung half over on its back. Anti-aircraft guns had caught him, and as his propeller hit the ground, he crashed beside Allied motors and tanks in battle. Nicky was pulled from his aircraft and jumped into a slit trench. When the engagement was over, an ambulance took him back to his squadron.

Later that year, on 26 June, six days after Rommel's capture of Tobruk, Barr was leading four planes on reconnaissance when, after downing an enemy fighter, he himself was shot down and captured. Badly burned in the crash, he was taken POW and spent the next five months in hospital in Italy. He would escape later in the war, with a record of twelve aerial victories behind him. Meanwhile, half a world away, some of Nicky's teammates from the '39 tour were among thousands of Australians who were also being tested by a different opponent.

18

AN END TO THE GOOD TIMES

If ever Australian troops sailed into an oasis of complacency and British assurances of invincibility, it was in February 1941 when the 8th Division, four RAAF squadrons and eight warships sailed off to defend Singapore and Malaya from the advancing Japanese. Britain had reaffirmed its promise to Australia in 1937 that in the event of conflict in the Asia-Pacific, it would send a powerful fleet to Singapore. Churchill believed Singapore to be an invulnerable fortress. The naval base, with its guns pointing out to sea, was protected from attack by water, while to the north the dense cover of jungle of the Malay Peninsula, along with the poor roads, was considered an effective barrier. The idea of an overland invasion down the Malay Peninsula was ridiculed.

But as the Japanese Imperial Army was cutting a swathe through Asia, the fear grew that Malaya and Singapore would soon be under attack. Stationed in Singapore and Malaya in readiness to defend the peninsula were about 80,000 Australian, Canadian, Indian, Malayan and British troops. General Officer Commanding Australian Forces in Malaya, Major General Gordon Bennett, was there to welcome the Australian force:

'The tension here now is grave, our enemies may count their men in millions, we measure ours in spirit and determination.'

For the next ten months, training for war began in earnest in Malaya. Echoing Monash, Bennett strongly believed sport was important for fitness and morale, to the point that playing sport supplanted ceremonial drills and parades. Sport became a natural diversion and with British troops aplenty close by, cricket and rugby were logical choices for old rivals. The Australians tended to appoint the most experienced cricketers as team captains, while the British followed a more hierarchical structure, with team captains generally being the most senior officers.

The Malayan cricket season began on 1 March, just two weeks after the 8th Division arrived in country. The RAAF having been stationed in Malaya since the previous August, the airmen were well placed to join the local competitions from the start. On the first weekend of competition, the RAAF played Fort Canning, a team that comprised senior British officers and other ranks. The Australians scored an easy victory, scoring 211 and bowling Fort Canning out for 108. Captaining the Australians was twenty-five-year-old Corporal Alan Barnes, No. 1 Squadron RAAF, a handy club cricketer for the champion Sydney club Mosman. Barnes, who with 66 was the highest scorer, was joined by three other Australians who also retired not out. The AIF joined the competition soon after, enjoying the multi-racial nature of the local teams they played with – something in which they were encouraged, according to Russell Braddon, a gunner in the 2/15th Field Regiment. Braddon would achieve post-war fame for his books about the Malayan campaign. 'Between the Malays and ourselves there sprang up a jovial familiarity,' he wrote, which was exemplified by the mutual greeting 'Hullo Joe' accompanied by a thumbs-up.

When Captain Ben Barnett, 8th Division Signals, arrived in Malaya in August 1941, the local cricket season was coming to an end. Fair-haired, bronzed and blue-eyed, the thirty-three-year-old Barnett was not just the archetypal Australian of the Anzac myth but also a sporting hero. Pre-war, he was Australia's Test wicketkeeper, having succeeded the legendary Bert Oldfield. Barnett had been wicketkeeper on the drawn 1938 Ashes tour of England, scoring 46 in the innings defeat in the fifth Test.

Quiet in manner, Barnett was popular and respected and relished a new challenge. A 'Test' match was arranged, and Barnett, captaining the Australian side, led his team to victory by seven wickets. 'Ben Barnett showed all his old touch behind the sticks,' Lieutenant Colonel Charles Kappe would later recall of the match. In the last game of the season, a combined AIF/RAAF team took on the Singapore Cricket Club, and while Barnett's performance behind the stumps was described by the *Straits Times* as 'polished', the Australians were defeated, managing only a score of 137 all out to lose by 30 runs. Barnett managed just 5, bowled by a ball that kept low, while Alan Barnes compiled a 'particularly pleasing' 33.

As with cricket, rivalry between Australia and Britain in rugby union flourished in Malaya. Because rugby was not popular in Malaya, the main contests were inter-regimental, state-based and with the traditional rivals, England. The Australians had quite a line-up of first-class players. A public exhibition match in mid-1941 between 'New South Wales' and 'Queensland' in Seremban where the AIF was stationed, included former and future state and international players. The New South Wales side had the likes of Cec Ramalli, John Fuller and Roger Cornforth. From Queensland were Phillip 'Blow' Ide, Burnett 'Chappie' Schulte, William 'Bill' Gannon and Vaux Nicholson. Queensland won 11–7.

In early November 1941, the AIF took to the field against the British army for a rugby union 'Test' match. Replete with state and international players, the Australians trounced the British 21–0. The *Straits Times* reported that the AIF were 'immeasurably superior to their opponents in every department

AIF troops playing cricket in Malaya. AWM 00996.

of the game', and except for seven minutes over the duration of the game, 'there was only one team in the picture'. Despite desperate resistance from the British, the Australians 'towered head and shoulders above them in dash, initiative and tactical skill'. The paper continued that Ramalli and Schulte, stand-off and scrum half respectively, were the mainspring of their side's success, and that Ramalli was the best player on the field but only just, for Schulte took a lot of beating. Ramalli had 'zig-zagged through the Army defence' to score a second try. A week later, Ramalli engineered a 'fine victory' by a Singapore–Johore side over the British army, 16–10. According to the *Straits Times*:

> Ramalli's play put him head and shoulders above any other man on the field. His elusiveness had almost a magical quality about it – he seemed to slip through the pack like quicksilver – while superb is the only word to describe the way he positioned himself. He was the

inspiration of every three-quarter break-through. He was there to take the ball over. He was always there.

Meeting once more on 22 November, the AIF again emerged victorious over the British army 'after a herculean struggle' to win 6–3. 'Ramalli gave his usual magnificent performance. Playing at the base of the scrum he was the source of every dangerous movement by the Australians and backed up his threes superbly. Again he distinguished himself by his dazzling breaks through.'

Around the same time, Warrant Officer Scott Heywood, Australian Army Service Corps, far from being an international, but a natural sportsman who had been reared in Victoria on Australian Rules, was happy to play rugby. 'I played my first game of rugby today and was I short of a gallop,' Scott wrote home. If it wasn't football, he also strapped on the pads for cricket, noting that matches in the various sports were well attended. 'You wouldn't think there is a war on, would you?' he wrote, adding, 'The hand shakes when I put it out for my pay.'

Besides rugby and cricket, troops from the southern states focused on Australian Rules. In late 1941, the Australian 13th General Hospital, established at Tampoi in Johore Bahru, organised matches between members of the hospital and surrounding units. Posted to the hospital, Corporal Lex Arthurson thought it said something about Australian Rules football when men, 'thousands of miles from the action which enthrals players and spectators alike in Southern Australia, would form teams for competition in Malaya'. Of one match he wrote:

> The game was played on the palace padang [playing field] of the Sultan of Johore ... As a football match it was a memorable joke. The rain came down ceaselessly that afternoon and the game was played to the accompaniment of the Sultan's band. Refreshments were available from

white-coated stewards all afternoon by a nod or a gesture from the players. The Sultan was not present at the game but evidently left orders not to spare the expense. Far more whiskies and gin squashes were served than was good for the game. The score didn't matter, and the game was played in good spirits!

The 'good spirits' were not to last. Malaya's defenders were forced to make do with inadequate armour and aircraft as Britain's best and most modern arms and equipment were committed to Europe for the war against Nazi Germany and Fascist Italy. They were ill-prepared when, early on the morning of 8 December 1941, Japanese troops landed at Kota Bharu, on the Thai border in north-east Malaya. A British squadron was mobilised to bomb the Japanese invasion convoy while No. 1 Squadron RAAF scrambled six Hudson bombers in a desperate attempt to hold the enemy. Flying through intense anti-aircraft fire to attack with bombs and guns, the Hudson crews were the first Allied airmen to strike a blow against Japan and sank the first Japanese merchant ship of the Pacific War. But this success was short-lived.

In the follow-up attack on Kota Bharu, the Japanese destroyed most of the RAAF's Hudson bombers, forcing No. 1 Squadron to withdraw south. Japanese Zero fighters attacked No. 21 Squadron RAAF, destroying seven Buffalo fighters on the ground. Their tactic of bombing British airbases quickly nullified the RAF's ability to either retaliate or protect troops on the ground.

For the British, the early signs of imminent disaster came with the sinking of the battleship HMS *Repulse* and battlecruiser HMS *Prince of Wales*, in less than two and a half hours on 10 December. Scrambled too late to help, 453 Squadron RAAF's pilots arrived on the scene in time to see the last Japanese aircraft disappearing over the horizon and the *Prince of Wales* beneath the surface, taking with it 327 sailors to join the 513 who had already died on the *Repulse*. The loss of the 'Gibraltar of the East' was fast approaching.

The Japanese attack was part of a massive land, sea and air onslaught that included the Philippines, Hong Kong and Pearl Harbor, the latter bringing the United States into the Pacific War. Once the Japanese forces landed in Malaya, they advanced rapidly inland, south towards Singapore. The Allied forces, including the Australians, fought doggedly over the next two months, but by 30 January 1942, the Japanese army had advanced to the Straits of Johore at the southern tip of Malaya. The weary Australian, Indian and British troops made their way over the Causeway joining Malaya to Singapore Island. On 1 February, after the last man had crossed, engineers blew up sections of the Causeway to isolate the island. It was to no avail.

19

THE CHANGI TESTS

At 8.30 p.m. on 15 February 1942, and without warning, an eerie silence fell over Singapore city. Orders came from divisional headquarters to cease fire. Incredulous and angry men heard the news that the Allied forces had surrendered to the Japanese after a campaign that had left 1800 Australian troops dead, and 15,000 among 80,000 Allied prisoners of the Japanese. The next day, the Allies faced a humiliating 30-kilometre march to Changi, through crowds of victorious Japanese soldiers and stunned civilians. Diggers who had proudly marched off to war were faced with the unimaginable – indefinite captivity. Now officially POWs, a new culture emerged – one of captivity with new rules, restrictions and deprivations.

The Australians were encamped at Selarang Barracks on the vast Changi peninsula, with large open grassy areas beyond the barracks, bordered by barbed wire on one side and the sea on the other. The much larger contingent of British POWs was close by in Roberts Barracks. Unlike other Japanese POW camps in Asia, the Australian and British POWs had relative freedom. The day-to-day running of the camp was left to their military commanders, and an immediate priority was restoration of military hierarchy and discipline.

As described in earlier chapters, the military had faced this problem before, at the end of World War I; their solution was to turn to sport. Now the situation was different: the war was still in full swing, but the need for the maintenance of order and discipline was the same. Again, the answer was sport. Crucial in a POW world, sport generated a sense of group solidarity. At another level, whether for player or spectator, sport helped counter the humiliation of surrender by restoring a sense of manhood. Within days, the men enthusiastically took up various sports, providing a means of maintaining fitness and a diversion from boredom. A structure quickly emerged, with officers in charge of various sports. Competitions began with cricket, and other sports followed throughout 1942: rugby, basketball, baseball and finally Australian Rules football.

Immediately after the fall of Singapore, the Australians salvaged sporting equipment out of deserted bulk stores, carrying it with them into captivity. What wasn't scrounged was ingeniously manufactured using whatever materials that could be found. Cricket balls, for instance, were made from scraps of black and white cotton, wound around a hard centre. One AIF officer commented: 'The balls used would not have passed international standards, but the uncertainty of their flight added to the fun and had even the best bats groping and prodding in an endeavour to hit the ball. It was hit though.'

Later in 1942, the Australian Comforts Fund began providing the POWs amenities that included precious equipment such as rugby and Australian Rules balls, cricket sets and basketball paraphernalia. 'Smiles appeared everywhere, and much serious training commenced,' according to Lex Arthurson. With the British POWs nearby, rivalry was inevitably revived in rugby and cricket.

On another level, cricket represented an immediate reassertion of the culture of both nations that, even in captivity, would not be dimmed. The game stood as a stark contrast with the Japanese, for whom sport was largely seen through a lens of martial arts. They did not comprehend the depth of attachment to the game, or the deep cultural attachment that the Australians and British had with cricket. Within two months of the surrender, in April 1942, the first cricket 'Test' between the old rivals was played.

Led by Captain Ben Barnett, Australia won this first match. Although he was the Australian Test wicketkeeper before the war, Barnett did not keep wicket but fancied himself as a slow leg-break bowler. Barnett then took the AIF team 'on tour' playing 'Tests' against various British units within the vast Changi area. Continuing through 1942, the Australians won most of the games they played, always in front of enthusiastic spectators. Private Mike Hubert, British army, watched a cricket match in August 1942 between the AIF and a team of British officers, in which the Australians, with a score of 8–177, defeated their opponents 175 all out.

> I had the extreme pleasure of seeing the famous Test Match Cricketer B.A. Barnett. He batted splendidly for 30 minutes and scored 50 odd and stumped 4 and caught 1. Later I heard him give an excellent lecture on 2 different evenings about cricket and social events in his two tours to England in 1934 and 1938; a picture of the many pleasant social activities and how the 10 Test Matches went. He spoke of Cricket in Australia and ended with a marvellous tribute to Don Bradman who he regretted to state was not likely to ever play cricket again. He was a delightful speaker, entertaining and witty.

Barnett's pre-war cricketing exploits became a popular lecture topic with his fellow POWs. It was not unusual for him to speak before some 3000 POWs at a time. Hubert was not alone in his admiration of Barnett's batting prowess. A member of Barnett's 'Australian XI' team, Corporal Guy Baker, AIF 27th Brigade, saw him as the natural choice as captain. Baker, who pre-war played with the Sydney club Balmain, was impressed by Barnett's batting, his driving often causing the bowler to lose his line and length. 'It was always good to come out after him as the batsmen could always make a few runs,' he said in one post-war interview. British POW Sergeant Ron Wilkinson recalled that once Barnett came to the crease, the British knew they had no chance. He added that the Australians were a 'good outfit', having amazing strength and endurance.

A cheekily provocative note Barnett sent to Colonel T.A.R. Scott, British 11th Division Signals, heightened the rivalry: 'Would you like to try and beat us at cricket next Sunday 30 August? I think it about time somebody downed us ...' To Barnett's chagrin, the Colonel's team won by one run. Honour at stake, a three-match 'Test' series followed. To those at Changi, this was the equivalent of an Ashes series between the two countries. In this spirit, the matches were dubbed the Sydney, Brisbane and Melbourne Tests, reflecting what would have been the England Ashes tour itinerary of Australia in 1940/41 had there not been a war. This was the alternative Ashes, and no less important.

The first was the 'Sydney' match, played on 20 September 1942. With all the formality of the real contest, the two captains, Ben Barnett and Lieutenant Dick Curtis, stood on the clay pitch, tossed a coin and shook hands. Post-war, Curtis recalled:

> The surroundings may have been unusual, but it was serious stuff. I'd played village cricket here in Norfolk and had always dreamed of playing for England against Australia. Well, every lad does. It was the first day of the first Test match and we were representing our country.

> Not on a stretch of rough earth with a marl wicket in Changi, but a perfect pitch at the Sydney Cricket Ground.

The match was hard fought and watched by an enthusiastic crowd of more than a thousand men. England won by one run: 107 to 106. The 'Brisbane' match followed three weeks later, on 11 October. British medical officer Dr Charles Huxtable watched on as the two teams battled it out on the *padang*. He concluded that the prowess of Barnett was the difference in Australia's win. 'He is a pleasant player to watch, both wicket keeping and batting.' Huxtable also began a popular series of talks on Test cricket, which enthralled those attending, British and Australian alike, in particular his account of the 1938 Ashes series.

With a break to the third and final 'Test' match, a match of another kind was played. On 24 November, Private Frank Day, 1st Field Bakery, noted in his diary: 'Big cricket match of cripples [*sic*] today, one armed and one legged and men with plasters.' The match meant much to the Bendigo baker, twenty-five, who had had his left leg amputated, reaffirming that the many men left disabled by the lost battles to save Malaya and Singapore were not forgotten by their mates in the sports program.

Sergeant Jack Croft, 2/15th Field Regiment, also noted these matches, attending one in the days after Christmas a few weeks later: 'Went over to the Convalescent Depot this afternoon and watched the Hoppies [the limbless soldiers] play cricket. The Other Ranks played the Officers. It is wonderful how these poor chaps have adapted themselves; batting with one arm, and one with one leg also fielding and bowling.'

In January 1943, the third and final 'Melbourne' match was played, with Barnett captaining the AIF side and Sergeant Geoffrey Edrich, a Lancashire cricketer and member of the famous Edrich cricketing clan, captaining 'England'. The two captains were idolised by their respective country's spectators, giving a few hours reprieve from the reality of life in the camp.

Among the spectators was Jack Croft, who noted that Australia won the match, scoring 154 runs to England's 152. Fifty-four years later, a member of the 'England' team, Private Cyril Bix, echoed the thoughts of Dick Curtis when he described the joy he felt. For that moment, 'We were prisoners no longer. It was a Test match between England and Australia. We forgot everything else.'

This was to be the last 'Changi Ashes Test' series, with cricket afterwards played in desultory fashion until the end of the war. The weakened state of the men precluded any serious play. Diseases such as beri-beri, dysentery and outbreaks of typhus and cholera spread through the camp. The diet was wholly inadequate, consisting mostly of rice with a very small weekly meat ration. Concurrently throughout 1942, thousands of the fitter men were sent as slave labour to work on the Burma–Thailand railway. Ben Barnett was one of them.

Towards the end of 1942 other sports, including boxing, continued sporadically. Preparing for a festival, the Japanese extended invitations to camps three, four and five to participate. Jack Croft wrote:

> They erected a boxing ring, and an inter-camp boxing match was arranged. We received quite a few entries from our camp, they were our permanent guards, cooks, water duty men etc. Some of the fights were very good and our camp won the point score. The winner of each bout was presented with 3 bottles of beer, 1 tin of pineapple, 1 tin of meat and vegetable stew and 3 bottles of cordial by the Japanese. All the boxers received something. The spectators, of which I was one, were supplied with cold tea (no sugar).

Besides boxing, Croft witnessed a rugby league 'international' between Australia and England, which Australia won 21–nil.

Boxing was popular with the AIF throughout WWII as seen here at the Ravenshoe military camp, Queensland, in December 1944 when Private J Taylor fought to a draw with Private J Leddy. AWM 085311.

But Croft also noted less mainstream competitive events. 'Big Frog Derby on tonight, some thirty-odd entries and all well-trained frogs. I can hear the bookmakers calling the odds as I write.' He explained that the amphibians were placed under a biscuit tin in the centre of a ring about five yards in diameter. When the tin was lifted, the first frog over the length of the circle was declared the winner. That night a frog called Snow White was favourite. Sent out at 2–1, Snow White won, leaping in ahead of Mickey Mouse, the second favourite at 5–1. 'These frog races have certainly caught on and there is more enthusiasm over them than any other sport,' Croft explained, adding that on one night there were a hundred entries.

> There are any amount of bookmakers and the betting is very spirited. The entrance fee is 20 cents, and each heat has about 10 entries. The owner of the winning frog takes the 20 cents. The Japanese guards were among the spectators and seemed just as excited as the rest of us.

As ever when gambling was involved with Australians, skulduggery was never far away. 'One owner was disqualified for six weeks. His frog was examined, and a pin was found in his colours bent up so that when the frog sat down it would prick him and set him in motion. The frog's name was Victory.'

Ironically, 'Victory' now seemed an elusive goal for those in Changi. Indeed, there had been a sporting event a year earlier that, in retrospect, gave a sense of foreboding, unimaginable at the time. On 21 September 1941, the AIF played the Japanese Baseball Club in Singapore, losing 6–4. The *Straits Times* commented that the Australians 'looked good in hitting but were unable to keep up to the Japanese fielding'. They had been outplayed not just in that match, but in the war.

20

NOT JUST A DIVERSION – A LIFELINE

Early on, kicking a football around informally called to mind the comforting familiarity of home. And as the weeks went by, Australian Rules became the most popular football code the Australians played at Changi. It gave them an outlet for their outrage and powerlessness at their status as POWs and at their military leaders, whom many blamed for the surrender. The play has often been described as rougher than the game back home. A clearly different game from the rugby union and soccer favoured by the British, Aussie Rules gave the Australians an opportunity to own and express a national identity.

Private Jim Makeham, of the 2/9th Field Ambulance, caught the mood of the time: 'As if by magic someone produced a football. At first the lads were able only to indulge in kick-for-kick between buildings on the hard bitumen surfaces. Then someone suggested getting a competition going.' However, there was concern that the diet on which the men were living 'was far from sufficient to engage in such a strenuous exercise'. A mere 2 ounces (50–60 grams) of meat was the weekly allowance.

Despite the inadequate diet, there was strong demand for a competition, and this led to the formation of the Changi

Football League, with some 600 men registering interest in playing Australian Rules. The POWs created a 'footy' oval in the no-man's land between Selarang and Roberts Barracks. Thirty-foot-long poles were fashioned out of rubber trees as goal and behind posts.

The six 'clubs' in the newly minted 'Changi premiership' were appropriately named: Melbourne, Richmond, Essendon, Carlton, Geelong and St Kilda. With about 15,000 Australian POWs to select from, some outstanding VFL players emerged. The organisers were well credentialled: Wilfred 'Chicken' Smallhorn, the 1933 Brownlow Medal winner, cricketer Ben Barnett (who as a schoolboy had captained Scotch College's Aussie Rules team), Private Les Green, 2/9th Field Ambulance, and Warrant Officer Roy Fox, 13th Australian General Hospital. Sergeant Peter Chitty (a former St Kilda league player) was a consultant. As in the VFL, each team had a committee and office-bearers to enforce the rules and formalities. Umpires were given control, with charges reported and heard by a three-man tribunal.

To the men confined to their hospital beds, the games provided a new interest and were the subject of much discussion, not to mention avid betting on the side. Jim Makeham concluded that it may have been a 'long way from the MCG [Melbourne Cricket Ground], but at heart these lads kept the spirit of the old game going'. Chosen to play for Geelong, Private Lou Daily (2/4th Machine Gun Battalion) approached Peter Chitty to join him. With sufficient inducement – three bowls of rice and the offer of captaincy – Chitty accepted.

Each team would play each of the other teams twice in the coming weeks. The two teams lowest on the points ladder were eliminated, leaving Essendon, Richmond, Carlton and Collingwood to contest the play-offs for a spot in the Grand Final. In the end, Richmond and Carlton won through to the Grand Final on 17 October 1942, with Carlton the strong favourite. Ben Barnett and 'Chicken' Smallhorn were the match umpires, with the game restricted to two twenty-minute halves, due to the weakened state of the men and the tropical heat.

They may have been weakened but honour was at stake, which meant the game 'was played like a battle with considerable aggression from both sides'. With the lead changing several times, coordinated attacks resulted in aggressive counterattacks, forcing players to draw on all their physical strength. Richmond finally won 10.9 (69) to Carlton's 6.8 (44).

The competition proved so popular among the men that further games were organised after the Grand Final, leading to an extended season. However, by 19 January 1943, the hospital authorities put a ban on Changi football because of the scarce resources available to treat the alarming rate of injuries. The season over, Geelong was undefeated, with one more win than Richmond. While Geelong claimed to have won the premiership, Richmond countered by pointing to their Grand Final victory. The competition was over, but to many it remained unresolved – an anticlimactic end to football at Changi.

Against the background of these competing claims, it was agreed that two 'representative' games be played in January to finally end the season. A fifteen-man-a-side game between the Australian General Hospital (AGH) staff and Selarang Barracks was set down for Friday, 22 January. Ben Barnett agreed to ditch his bat to play forward for Selarang, with Peter Chitty playing half-forward. Despite these two notables playing for Selarang, the AGH team won the game.

But it was still not over. Just two days later, the biggest game of the season was set down to be played between Victoria and 'The Rest', which comprised players from every other state. Chitty was selected as captain of Victoria. Lou Daily, who pre-war had played for both Geelong in the VFL and Subiaco in the West Australian Football League, captained 'The Rest'. The season, of course, could not end without the presentation of a medal equivalent to the Brownlow for the season's best and fairest.

The night before the match, and in keeping with VFL protocol, Smallhorn and Fox counted the medal votes behind closed doors. As they did so, there was feverish betting on the outcome. The bookies who had set up at Changi were sweating on the outcome as the big bets flowed in. It was not necessarily only money: besides cash, gambling currency included clothes, daily rice rations, wallets and watches.

Before play began next day, and with all due reverence, the Changi Brownlow medal for 'best and fairest' for the season was awarded. The medal has been variously described as fashioned from a piece of a metal from a downed Japanese aircraft wing or more likely from an old soccer medallion recrafted and engraved with 'Geelong FC'. On the reverse side was engraved the winner's name. Lou Daily garnered thirteen votes, but Peter Chitty with twenty-four votes was the winner.

With 'Chicken' Smallhorn umpiring, thousands of POWs and guards watched the match as the players fought not just their opponents but the enervating heat and the ongoing effects of the poor diet. As with the games played during the extended season, the match was restricted to two halves of twenty minutes. Despite this, the play was intense, with the lead swinging between the two sides until finally the Victorians won, 14.9 (93) to 10.5 (65). The end of match signalled that, finally, the Australian Rules season at Changi was over. Captain Norman Morrison, 2/29th Battalion, commented: 'King football did not reign very long, for two reasons. The boots were wearing out faster than they could be repaired, and the injuries were eating up medical supplies which must be reserved for more serious illnesses. Naturally everyone thought the excuses were flimsy.'

While Australian Rules was overall the most popular football game for the Australians at Changi, of the two rugby codes, rugby league emerged as preferred for both players and spectators – this despite rugby union being the official game of the AIF and, as they had shown in Syria against the French, played with serious intent. League was regarded as more the game of 'ordinary' Australians, as opposed to union, which belonged more to the 'upper classes' – those who had been brought up in the 'muscular Christianity' ethos of the elite private schools in Australia and Britain – and hence was played more by officers and doctors.

After the disastrous capitulation in Malaya and Singapore, POW military commanders undoubtedly felt they were in no position to insist on rugby union, given the level of discontent among the troops. In this environment, it was noteworthy just how many union players converted to league at Changi. For some former international rugby union players, it made perfect sense to switch to rugby league: mateship and team spirit trumped previous code loyalties.

A rugby league competition was set up in the latter half of 1942. By this time, several former rugby union internationals, including Cec Ramalli and 'Blow' Ide, had been sent to the Burma–Thailand railway in May 1942 amid mounting pressure from the Japanese to complete the railway line. A pivotal figure in the change was representative rugby union player Captain Burnett 'Chappie' Schulte, of the 2/10th Field Regiment, who had played halfback for Queensland between 1936 and 1939. At Changi he converted to league and played a key role in organising the competition.

The popularity of league among the Australian POWs, did not go unnoticed by British union players. Several British medical staff members switched to league. Although it took the medics some time to master the differences, they entered the Australian competition and began to win an occasional game. But as with Australian rules, the rugby league competition ceased from January 1943.

While the Australians preferred Australian Rules and rugby league, the British played soccer. They had a well-patronised league in which the Australians put up a team, but they were no match for the British. Throughout 1943, the Japanese guards watched these soccer games and began playing informally among themselves. Rules against fraternisation largely prevented games with the guards.

With the end of the Australian Rules and rugby league competitions, there was a vacuum for sport. Led by the versatile Ben Barnett, the Australians set up a baseball competition at Changi in late 1942. Earlier in the year, American POWs had been imprisoned at Changi following Japanese naval victories. On 28 February 1942, the Imperial Japanese Navy sank HMAS *Perth*, the USS *Houston* and the Dutch destroyer HNLMS *Evertsen* in the Battle of Sunda Strait during a ferocious night fight that left more than a thousand Australian and American sailors dead.

Among the survivors from the *Perth* was Chief Petty Officer Vic Duncan, who after abandoning the sinking ship, climbed onto a raft, to be joined shortly after by another shipmate. In the dark, Vic recognised him as Petty Officer Tom Johnson. 'He shot up on the raft. We had played deck hockey together and as we recognised each other we shook hands and congratulated each other on getting this far.' They had been members of the same deck hockey team – the traditional naval game always played at a fast and furious pace, with no offside rule and physically roughhouse.

Along with 307 men from the *Perth*, 368 sailors from the *Houston* also became POWs, firstly in Java and later, in 1942, at Changi. The Americans soon were playing baseball and invigorated the competition. The Australians, however, did surprisingly well against the Americans. Sergeant Jack Croft was a spectator to the clashes in late December 1942 when the AIF won four of five games, with Ben Barnett playing an important part in the wins. Croft rated Barnett a 'very good cricketer, excellent Australian rules footballer, good baseballer and over the average boxer'. Another spectator, Private Frank Day, thought it was 'funny to hear the way the Yanks and Aussies chip one another'.

Basketball, too, was popular and given further impetus by the American POWs. Private Bill Flowers, 2/9th Field Ambulance, related how he and three other Australian basketball enthusiasts sat down with the commander of the *Houston*, Captain Miles Barrett, to discuss how the rules of the game could be modified to suit the unique conditions at Changi. A level piece of ground, free from stones and pebbles, could suffice as a court. Accustomed to going barefoot, the POWs' feet were quite tough and could withstand imperfect surfaces. Coconut palms were used as posts, with ring and backboard made from what they had at hand.

Although football and cricket had largely stopped, basketball continued in 1943–44, despite constant disruption to the teams with the debilitating effects of sickness and men moving away to join working parties. In June 1944, all POWs from Changi were moved to Changi Gaol, a few kilometres away — a very different proposition to the relatively freedom of Selarang Barracks. The gaol was four stories high, 400 metres long by 100 metres wide. Throughout the period it was used for POWs, it housed between 4000 and 10,000 men — this, a gaol that before the war housed just 800 prisoners.

By this time, basketball had a taken on new lease of life with the formation of the Changi Basketball Association and a competition comprising ten teams using a basketball court just outside the wire. The competition ran for four months from November 1944. The highlight was the Grand Final: USA v Hospital A on 11 February 1945. After a tentative start by the Australians, the game was just five minutes old when the heavens opened and the match was called off for several hours. On return to the court, the contest was tight, and it was not until the final whistle that the Australians were sure they had won.

According to Bill Flowers, 'such was the noise of the barracking from the spectators, including some guards who had turned up to watch the spectacle, that it could be heard from deep within the gaol'. Reflecting on his participation in basketball as a POW, Flowers said he was often called a fool for practising and playing basketball, 'but I think my involvement had great psychological benefit ... yes, it was worth all the pain'.

The Grand Final was the last game to be played. The Japanese banned all sports at Changi, along with concerts and plays. The end of the Pacific War was another six months away.

21

MATES

In January 1943, en route from a POW camp in Java to an unknown destination, the surgeon 'Weary' Dunlop, by now promoted lieutenant colonel, and his 900-strong 'Dunlop Force', made a brief stopover at Changi. Sparks flew from the start. Dunlop's men arrived, as he put it, 'in filthy and sweat-stained rags', many of them bootless and hatless. The commanding officer AIF Singapore, Lieutenant Colonel Frederick 'Blackjack' Galleghan, a stickler for propriety, labelled them the 'Java rabble' from the 7th Division. This and other slights did not endear Dunlop and Galleghan to each other. Dunlop resented the officers 'all beautifully dressed ... swaggering along with their canes' when compared with his own 'stained and crumpled appearance'. And Galleghan resented Dunlop's forthright and less than respectful manner.

In the short transit of Dunlop Force at Changi, the British sports organiser Lieutenant Hamish Cameron-Smith, aware of Dunlop's reputation as a former Wallaby, set up a rugby union match to take advantage of his brief presence. With Dunlop to captain the Southern Area squad, a trial match was organised to decide who would be in Dunlop's squad against the Hospital team.

The ground was close to the sea, which gave Dunlop – his own health, like that of his men, already precarious – the opportunity to dash into the water every so often as his diarrhoea dictated. In the main match a few days later, the Hospital team, comprised largely of British doctors, won 12–8, with Weary scoring all the points for the Southern Area team. 'Enjoyable,' said Weary.

After thirteen days of relative comfort at Changi, Weary and his 'ragged bunch' were transported by the Japanese to Thailand as labour to help construct the Burma–Thailand railway between the administrative centre of Thanbyuzayat in southern Burma, and the town of Ban Pong near Bangkok in Thailand. Ultimately, 13,000 Australians would be forced into slave labour, of whom nearly 2650 died, as the Japanese set about building the 420-kilometre line. All told, there were more than 60,000 Allied POWs on the railway, including British, Dutch and Americans, as well as 200,000 Asian labourers. All but 50 kilometres of the route was across rugged terrain, covered in dense, malarial jungle. It would require building more than 600 bridges, as well as hundreds of viaducts, embankments and cuttings. The railway's purpose was to facilitate the Japanese goal of invading India.

A member of Dunlop's 'ragged bunch', Private Tom Uren, recalled: 'We had no idea of the hell ahead of us.' A professional boxer before the war, Uren was challenged to an exhibition bout at Changi. He had earned respect as a heavyweight, and his reputation preceded him. As a nineteen-year-old in 1940, he had fought for the Australian Heavyweight Championship against Billy Britt. Already in the army when he fought Britt, Uren had been given leave for the title fight. In the sixth round he knocked the more experienced Britt to the canvas but lost on a technical knockout in the next round. Uren's reputation spread.

A British POW, keen to make a name for himself as a boxer, challenged Uren in what was to be an exhibition match. According to Uren:

> During the first two rounds he hit me with everything, a lot of which was illegal. Not having much energy, I played it cool for the first two rounds, but in the third I gave it everything I had ... I really belted the hell out of him in the last round. I only wanted an exhibition match, but he wanted to make a reputation overnight. So, I went after him. That's the other side of Tommy Uren. I have a gentle side, but by Christ there is also a tough side.

The raw-boned Uren had left school at thirteen to get what work he could during the Depression. Growing up in the Sydney suburb of Harbord, he learned to box, became a surf lifesaver and a rugby league forward for Manly-Warringah. He applied to join the army in May 1939 and was accepted soon after war broke out. He served as a private in the 2/4th Machine Gun Battalion before being captured. Now a POW, Uren soon recognised the leadership qualities of his commander, Weary Dunlop.

After leaving Changi, the 'Java rabble' were loaded into a railway truck bound for the Konyu River camp on the Burma–Thailand railway. There, the appalling conditions, poor diet and brutal treatment by guards took a terrible toll. Uren was profoundly influenced by Dunlop, who fought to improve the situation of his men.

> In our camp the officers and medical orderlies paid the greater proportion of their allowance into a central fund. The men who worked did likewise. We were living by the principle of the fit looking after the sick, the young looking after the old, and the strong looking after the weak. A few months after we arrived at Hintok Road camp a part of British H Force arrived. They were about 400 strong. As a temporary arrangement they had tents. The officers selected the best, the non-commissioned officers the next best and the men got the dregs. Soon after they arrived, the

wet season set in, bringing with it cholera and dysentery. Six weeks later only 50 men marched out of that camp, and of that number only about 25 survived. Only a creek separated our camps, but on one side the law of the jungle prevailed and on the other the principles of socialism.

This spirit, Uren believed, was fundamental to their survival, which he attributed to Dunlop's leadership. While military hierarchy is fundamental to the military conduct of war, in POW camps like those along the railway, egalitarianism led to both a greater sense of group solidarity and increased survival. 'I developed enormously as a collectivist during those tortuous three and a half years as a prisoner of war.' Uren took these basic principles into his life post-war, and they continued to guide him through life. He later became a member of Parliament, deputy leader of the Australian Labor Party and a minister in the governments of Gough Whitlam and Bob Hawke.

Another member of 'Dunlop Force', Chief Petty Officer Ray Parkin, who had survived the sinking of HMAS *Perth*, was similarly affected by Dunlop's extraordinary leadership:

The men would do anything for him and are proud to be with him. I am sure it is his presence which holds this body of men from moral decay in bitter circumstances which they can only meet with emotion rather than reason ... This selflessness, this smile, command more from the men than an army of officers each waving a Manual of Military Law.

As the various groups of diggers arrived in Burma in preparation for the construction of the railway, there was a determination to keep alive the sporting spirit displayed at Changi. A quasi-Sheffield Shield series was arranged, with cricketers chosen to represent their home state. Soccer and Australian Rules football followed, although monsoonal rain began to play havoc with the grounds. Sport along the railway was rarely possible, given the deteriorating physical state of the prisoners and the need to conserve energy for the back-breaking work. But that did not stop the Japanese command from sometimes, bizarrely, using POWs to construct sporting facilities for their personal use. Lieutenant Colonel Tom Hamilton, commanding officer of 2/4th Casualty Clearing Station, and a senior AIF medical officer with 'A' Force, noted one such occurrence at Thanbyuzayat in May 1943. The Japanese officer in command, Lieutenant Colonel Nagatomo Yoshitada, had the 'light sick' driven out to make a football field and a tennis court at his headquarters. 'He and his officers, with perhaps half a dozen POWs, used the tennis court quite a lot,' according to Hamilton.

Somehow, the men always ensured that the Melbourne Cup was celebrated as best they could. Run on the first Tuesday in November each year at Flemington Racecourse, the Melbourne Cup is commonly billed as 'the race that stops a nation'. The tradition is so well embedded in the Australian psyche that wherever they were in the world, Australian troops would mark the event. In camps along the Burma–Thailand railway, the race would be celebrated in one way or another depending on the physical state of the prisoners and the forbearance of the Japanese guards.

In Tavoy POW camp in Burma on Tuesday, 3 November 1942, to the great surprise of the Australians, the Japanese commander decreed a holiday to allow the POWs to stage a simulated running of the cup. He even produced a 'cup' made from a highly polished coconut shell with brass handles. A 75-metre track was laid out on the soccer ground. The race entailed larger-framed men carrying smaller 'jockeys' in a race. 'Horses' and 'jockeys' were appropriately attired in whatever they could find to fit the part. 'Bookmakers' were busy – the currency being mostly cheroots.

There were nineteen starters as the race began at 3 p.m., amid great hilarity. The favourite on the day ran clear of the pack to much excitement among the spectators, but then lost his footing, fell and was overtaken by an outsider named Sweet Potato, with odds of 100 to 1, who won by 'a toe'. That night a Cup Ball was held, with a prize for the best female impersonator – a private who came as the actress Greta Garbo.

A year on, and further along the railway, the men were wrung out and a good deal weaker and sicker than the previous November. Yet they needed something to lift their spirits and reconnect with the culture that had shaped their lives. It was now 1943 and the diggers again improvised the running of the Cup on the traditional first Tuesday in November. In a letter that could not be sent and would not be read until years later, Warrant Officer Scott Heywood wrote glowingly to his wife: 'We could imagine we were home … we had a good time and several good laughs. Thank goodness we can still raise a laugh.'

Before the war, Heywood had been a cricketer, a tennis player and an enthusiastic member of the local Australian Rules team. As a good Stawell citizen, he ran in in the Stawell Cup Gift Carnival, notching up a series of fourth-place finishes. He had a commitment to keeping physically fit, and this now became even more important. Taken prisoner at the fall of Singapore, he was at Changi for only a few months before being shipped to Burma. Working on the railway was hard enough, but as the Japanese deadline for the railway to be completed grew tighter, the hours of work increased, as did the expectations of output. Heywood began to look at the work through a different lens. The more effort he put in, the more muscular he would become, despite the meagre rations. Digging, he told himself, in a useful reframe, would make him more attractive to his wife when he finally arrived home.

In April 1943, just weeks after winning the Changi Brownlow, Corporal Peter Chitty was transported to the railway where he found Private Jim Downie so ill with malaria that he could barely walk. With the men forced to begin a long march through the thick jungle, Chitty, slung his arm around Downie's waist and started down the path. As the days wore on, Downie's condition worsened, but Chitty was determined to get him to hospital and hoisted him and both their packs across his shoulders and carried on. Despite Chitty's care for his mate, Downie died in mid-May. After the war, Chitty was awarded the British Empire Medal, but it was his Brownlow medal that he said he treasured most of all.

In 1944, and the railway completed, Weary Dunlop was working at Nakom Paton in Thailand. This was a huge POW hospital camp designed to take 10,000 sick and broken survivors of the railway. The POWs, under the medical care of military doctors such as Dunlop, began to take stock of their situation. The previous eighteen months had been almost unendurable and many of their comrades had not survived. Again, sport became an antidote to a seemingly hopeless situation. As the men's diet improved, they began to resume sports of all kinds.

Later, Dunlop would reflect that it was a matter of ultimate pride to him that the Australians out-worked, out-suffered and out-lived every other national group on the railway.

> Now that I think is beyond question, and the Japanese recognised it. But the trouble was that if you were sinewy, indestructible, if you were a good workman, you got sent back and back and back on these terrible tasks with utterly inadequate food. You could see these magnificently strong men with great hearts who slowly went to pieces and died.

On Christmas Day 1944, Weary Dunlop participated in a 'race meeting'. Given his large build, he was, naturally, to be a 'horse' with a lighter-framed 'jockey'. While he was 193 centimetres tall, his weight had dropped from 91 kilos to 67 kilos. Having lost the first race of the day after drawing the outside of the stony track and tearing open his foot, he was determined to redeem himself in the final event – 'The Grand National'. This was a steeplechase that included water jumps, a bamboo fence, an attap palm hurdle and a double fence of bamboo. Being the only 'horse' to clear the water jump cleanly, and with his foot well bandaged, he won the race, celebrating with a 'cup' or two, derived from rice distillate.

Just five days later, Dunlop, the former Wallaby, was surprised to be asked to captain a cricket 'Test' match: England versus Australia. A tennis ball, a single wicket and a 16-metre pitch comprised the set-up, with the usual team of eleven men reduced to eight per side. When Dunlop came out to bat, he was greeted by a hushed silence – because an 'international' was at the wicket, albeit for rugby. 'We got the father of a hiding, licked by four wickets, an innings and about 60 runs. I ingloriously just broke my duck each innings …' Dunlop wrote in his diary.

Athletics, soccer, softball and swimming were also popular, and with food more plentiful, sport in all its manifestations became integral in keeping up morale for players and spectators. Even Japanese and Korean guards participated from time to time. Work did not stop, however. During this time, two bridges across the River Kwai were built with POW labour.

Sportsmen's experiences fighting the Japanese took various forms. One of the Australians from the ill-fated 1939 Wallaby touring team to England was Corporal Kenelm 'Mac' Ramsay, a versatile rugby forward, who had scored the only try for the Wallabies in the last pre-war Bledisloe Cup Test against the All Blacks. A member of the 1st Independent Company of commandos sent to New Ireland in 1941, Ramsay was stranded on the island after the Japanese invaded in January 1942. His company's orders were to retreat south and stage guerilla attacks, but Ramsay's little escape craft was spotted, strafed and bombed.

The survivors were interned at Rabaul, then put aboard the transport *Montevideo Maru*. En route to the Chinese island of Hainan, the ship was attacked by the submarine USS *Sturgeon*, the captain unaware that Allied POWs were on board. For the majority trapped in the hold, the end was horrific as they were scalded and choked by oil, flames and seawater. Mac Ramsay was among the victims of Australia's greatest maritime catastrophe, in which 1053 Australians died. In team biographical notes for the 1939 tour, he was described as 'the perfect team man'.

A few weeks later, his '39 Wallaby teammate Captain Stan Bisset, also a talented forward, arrived in New Guinea. He had already served in Syria with the 2/14th Battalion, with elder brother Hal. Both were excellent marksmen. From Port Moresby, the Bissets went with the battalion to the Kokoda Track to relieve the 39th Battalion, which had been fighting the Japanese for weeks and were holding out at Isurava. When Hal was mortally wounded in the fighting, Stan stayed with him for six hours before his brother died in his arms. In May 1944, Stan, who was awarded the Military Cross for his valour, was on his honeymoon, staying at Clifton Gardens Hotel in Sydney. While there, he ran into the ex-president of the Victorian Rugby Union, now a brigadier, who asked if he would play in a charity rugby match between the AIF and New South Wales at the Sydney Cricket Ground, and two days later for the Combined Services team, against New South Wales for a second time. Stan assumed he wouldn't be able to get leave. The brigadier had no such concern.

Short of fitness, Stan began a fortnight of skipping to get into condition for the June holiday weekend games, only to wake up one morning and read in the Sydney *Daily Telegraph*, 'Army captain goes into training on his honeymoon.' The story went on to reveal that guests at the Clifton Gardens Hotel were complaining about the skipping noises coming from upstairs. Stan was not deterred. 'We played at the Sydney Cricket

Ground, and we had five of the team of '39 in the AIF side and we beat New South Wales comfortably. It was a great game.' More than ten thousand spectators saw the AIF win 30–19 with the forwards, led by Bisset, dominating the line-outs and scrums. Forty-eight hours later, however, New South Wales defeated the Combined Services team 20–11.

While Stan went back to the war, another of his former teammates from the '39 tour, Winston 'Blow' Ide, a bombardier in the 2/10th Field Regiment, was ordered onto the *Rakuyu Maru* after his time on the Burma–Thailand railway. On 12 September 1944, in a convoy of transports taking POWs to Japan, the *Rakuyu Maru* was mistakenly attacked by American submarines and torpedoed by the USS *Sealion*. Ide was last seen by one of his mates, who called out to him to swim over to the safety of a raft. Ide shouted back that he was okay, but as 'some of the boys had been hurt', he would 'stick by them for while'. He was never seen again. A total of 1559 Australian and British prisoners perished.

22

THE DEMON

Keith 'Bluey' Truscott had changed. War does that. A champion footballer, and sometime cricketer, he had decided to enlist after playing a leading, aggressive role in the Melbourne Demons' 1939 VFL Grand Final victory over Collingwood. Football, and four seasons with the Demons, was one thing; war was another. And for someone as independent and adventurous as Bluey, the idea of being a pilot was irresistible.

With a shock of red hair, it was natural and quintessentially Australian that he would be given the nickname Bluey. He had grown up in Depression-era Australia when the awe-inspiring deeds of aviators like Charles Kingsford Smith and Bert Hinkler appeared in the weekly magazines that boys of his generation devoured. The stories gave them hope, something to dream about, even during the post–World War I years when the frequent sight of maimed survivors of the war was vivid proof of the horrors and slaughter of the Western Front.

Born in Melbourne in 1916, Bluey was an outstanding all-round sportsman at Melbourne High School, captaining both the football and cricket teams. He applied to join the RAAF just three months after he helped Melbourne win the '39 premiership.

Interviewed for enlistment on 5 January 1940, he began pilot training on 22 July 1940. Already a popular sportsman, his decision to enlist created a massive publicity storm. Amid feverish focus on the war effort, Bluey, with his boyish good looks, was regarded by the public as 'the prototype of Australian flying men', according to renowned aviation writer Stanley Brogden, who added: 'Every man in Australia felt that "Bluey" was part of him, but much bigger.'

Under the Empire Air Training Scheme – designed to overcome the British Empire's aircrew shortage to fight Nazi Germany – Truscott undertook the Initial Training Course before moving on to No. 3 Elementary Flying Training School, Essendon, on 22 August 1940 for his first flight. His sharp mental and physical qualities impressed his superiors, who regarded him as a 'very good type' and possessing 'determination and fighting spirit'. In the air, however, he struggled in the cockpit of the notoriously temperamental de Havilland Tiger Moth. Along with a 'tendency to roughness', his instructors were not impressed with his flying skills, rating him 'rather unsteady generally', 'heavy' on the controls, 'in doubt all the time' and 'apt to do anything silly at any time'. His reactions seemed 'very slow or else he thinks unnecessarily over what he is doing'. At the same time, the RAAF gave him leave to play in the 1940 VFL Grand Final. Despite having missed eleven games, he kicked a goal to help the Demons to yet another premiership, defeating Richmond 107–68.

His main flying instructor was aviator Roy Goon, a Chinese Australian from Ballarat who had flown as a volunteer fighter pilot with the Chinese in the Second Sino–Japanese War in 1937. Returning to Australia, and intent on defending the nation, his initial attempts to join the RAAF were rejected due to the *Defence Act* excluding individuals substantially not of European origin or descent. Finally, in July 1940, after the intervention of the Minister for Air and Civil Aviation, James Fairbairn, he became the first Chinese Australian commissioned into the RAAF. He would go on to command No. 83 Squadron RAAF but his initial focus was to train hundreds of pilots, with Bluey Truscott among his earliest. Roy Goon quickly assessed that while Bluey required some nursing through, his greatest problems were that his landings were 'bumpy' and that his 'judgement of height during landings' was poor. Over time however, he saw Bluey as a pilot who could handle an aircraft extremely well at altitude. At his final test on 16 October 1940, Bluey was described as 'average', eventually earning his wings, despite his many dodgy landings.

Arriving in Canada for advanced training under the Empire Air Training Scheme, Bluey was commissioned in February 1941, sent to Britain and joined No. 452 Squadron as a foundation member. The squadron saw heavy action from the outset, engaging in fierce dogfights, patrols and nerve-racking escort missions over the English Channel and occupied France. Flying a Spitfire, in August he shot down his first enemy aircraft, a Messerschmitt Bf 109E, and within three months his tally had risen to at least eleven German aircraft. His indifferent start as a student pilot notwithstanding, he was awarded the Distinguished Flying Cross and made a flight commander. Later, he was awarded a bar to his DFC with the citation: 'Skilful courageous fighter pilot ... Throughout [has] shown fine fighting spirit.'

Bluey by now was the best known pilot in the RAAF, and his fame spread, resulting in a fundraising drive. Redheaded Britons 'bought' their hero a personalised Spitfire. Fittingly, he named it 'Gingerbread'. In Australia he rapidly became a war hero. Just before Christmas 1941, the services' newspaper, *Army News*, reported that Truscott – 'one of Victoria's leading athletes' before the war – was the Australian Spitfire Squadron's "topscorer" against Nazi planes. He has shot down eleven "certains" and three "probables" and damaged two others.'

In January 1942, congratulatory messages flooded in from sporting associates when he was promoted Acting Squadron

Leader. Truscott sent his own message to Frank 'Checker' Hughes, the Melbourne Football Club's coach, expressing his hope to be back for Melbourne's 'fourth successive premiership'. As ever, he joked about the war in sporting terms: 'The Huns have black and white crosses on their, planes. Well, I ask you. If it's not natural for a fellow with red and blue [Melbourne's colours] on his Spitfire to knock over things coloured black and white [Collingwood's colours]?'

Within weeks, the Japanese bombing of Darwin on 19 February 1942 prompted the reassignment of Australian pilots to the Pacific theatre. On his return, the *Argus* described Bluey as 'the leading Australian aviator of the present generation'. His wartime exploits, on top of his football deeds, meant he was now idolised. But the spotlight embarrassed him.

Nothing could hold him back from another game of football. He was given the honour of leading his old club, the Melbourne Demons, onto the ground against Richmond at Punt Road on 16 May 1942. As he burst through the gate, three girls threw rose petals on his head and a crowd of 20,000 spectators gave him a rousing reception. By the second quarter, he was struggling; his lack of fitness was telling. He complained to Richmond's George Smeaton, 'Making it a bit hot, aren't you? Might give a bloke a kick.' Smeaton, a Navy man, replied, 'If I go any slower, I'll be crawling after you on my hands and knees.' Later, Bluey managed a goal after Richmond skipper Jack Dyer dropped a mark. Given his respect for Truscott, Dyer was likely to have fumbled the ball deliberately. As a mark of respect, Dyer raised Truscott's arm. At the final siren, men, women and children jumped the fence to swarm towards him. Melbourne lost the game by 79 points, but that seemed incidental; in the mood of the day the match was an opportunity to welcome home a hero.

Bluey later bumped into a former schoolteacher of his, the Test cricketer and former Australian captain Bill Woodfull, who asked if he had enjoyed the game. Shaking his head,

Bluey deadpanned: 'No. It's too dangerous.' Amid the wartime uncertainties of 1942, Bluey's return brought back memories of more carefree days and lifted Melbourne's mood, however briefly. Cricketer and pilot Ian Johnson later wrote that Bluey had done 'the craziest things but survived them all to enjoy the hard drinking, hard living life that was typical of all pilots who strove to hide their straining nerves behind the artificial superficiality that drink provided'.

In July 1942, Truscott joined No. 76 Squadron RAAF, flying Kittyhawks, which was redeployed to Milne Bay, on the eastern tip of Papua New Guinea. Arriving shortly before the Japanese incursions, there was great concern about whether the airfields at Milne Bay could be held. Along with No. 77 Squadron RAAF, 76 Squadron served throughout the weeks of the Milne Bay battle in constant rain, heavy mist and low clouds. The mountainous terrain, slippery runways and heavy anti-aircraft fire added to the danger. By August, Truscott had been appointed Squadron Leader, the previous leader having been killed in action. His tally rose to sixteen enemy aircraft destroyed, along with three probables and three damaged. The Battle of Milne Bay, fought from August to September, was a turning point in the Pacific War. Australian forces repelled the Japanese from the area, making Port Moresby safer from Japanese invasion.

Bluey and 76 Squadron headed south for a rest, depleted of men and planes. Based at Exmouth Gulf, on the West Australian coast, the squadron ran training exercises and escorted US Catalina flying boats into the bay after being out on patrol over the Indian Ocean. According to Truscott's biographer, Ivan Southall, on 28 March 1943 Bluey was performing a mock raid as he escorted a Catalina into Rest Bay. 'The sea was calm, that glassy evening stillness they had noticed so often, with the haze lying over it, with that subtlety and serenity of tone which denied the eye its judgement and even deceived the eye with its

RAAF Squadron Leader 'Bluey' Truscott discusses Australian Rules with American GIs in Melbourne in May 1942 after his return to Australia. AWM 012319.

Bluey Truscott DFC getting some batting practice at Strauss Airfield, Northern Territory, shortly before he was killed in March 1943. AWM NWA0037.

mirages and its fleeting shadows.' Bluey misjudged the altitude and plunged into the sea. Bluey Truscott packed a lot into his twenty-seven years and was a legend in his short lifetime. His was a life of comradeship, on the football field and in Spitfires and Kittyhawks. Individually, men like Bluey were daring and skilled, but it was in a team that they triumphed.

For the Melbourne Demons, the death of Bluey Truscott deepened the mourning that had befallen the club. The war had already seen the death of another of its greatest players, Ron Barassi senior, who had played with Bluey in the 1940 Grand Final victory. Having enlisted two months earlier, in October he sailed for North Africa with the 7th Division Supply Column, Australian Army Service Corps. Ten months later during fighting at Tobruk, Barassi died of wounds on 31 July 1941, the first VFL footballer to die in the war.

Another of Bluey's teammates in the 1939 and '40 Grand Final victories was ruckman Harold Ball. Two months before the match, he enlisted in the army as a private with the 2/9th Field Ambulance, Australian Army Medical Corps. In February 1941, he sailed for Singapore and Malaya. Before long, Ball, who celebrated his twenty-first birthday in May, was playing football, captaining an Australian Rules side drawn from the Army Medical Corps. In one match against the RAAF, Ball's AIF side won by four goals.

As the security situation deteriorated, Ball wrote to his brother in Victoria, attempting to reassure him: 'don't worry there's not a bullet made that can travel as fast as I can'. But bravado was not enough to save him from Japanese attack on 8 February 1942. A day later, Ball's unit was overwhelmed with the task of evacuating the many wounded to a dressing station, 'Hill 80'. Ball and three others were ordered to evacuate but soon after were taken prisoner. Three months later, a working party of Australian POWs found the bodies of the four men. They had all been tortured by the Japanese before being executed. The identity discs on one of the bodies whose wrists were tightly bound by wire belonged to Harold Ball.

Syd Anderson was a teammate of Truscott, Barassi and Ball, and played in the Demons' 1939, 1940 and 1941 premiership teams. Enlisting in December 1941, he joined the RAAF. Initially posted to Goodenough Island, he also flew from Wewak, at one stage the site of a large Japanese airbase. A flying officer with No. 100 Squadron, Anderson was part of a raid over Rabaul on the morning of 20 May 1944 when the Beaufort bomber in which he was navigator was hit. Forced to ditch into the sea, the crew scrambled onto a dinghy and made for shore but were cut down by machine-gun fire. Only one of the crew survived. Anderson died instantly. By war's end, the conflict had claimed the lives of fifty-seven VFL players – on top of the ninety-five lost in World War I.

Word spread quickly among Australian troops overseas that Bluey Truscott had died. On 29 March 1943, just two days after Bluey's death, Australian POWs at Stalag 383 in Germany started what would become a yearly event, a game between 'Eastralia' and 'Westralia', with the West winning 10.8 (68) to 8.19 (67). Journalist Roland Le Folet Hoffman, a POW at the camp, summed up the shock over Bluey's death: 'The game was dedicated to "Bluey" Truscott, whose brilliant star, with tragic splendour, flared across the sky as a symbol of sportsmanship in its best traditions.'

23

KRIEGIES

Perc Rodda was twenty-two, married and a newly qualified accountant in Adelaide when he went to enlist in the RAAF in late 1940. The medical examination was going well until the doctor showed him a book with coloured spots and asked Rodda what he saw. He was not impressed, telling Rodda, 'Stiff cheese, old lad, you can't go into aircrew because you're as colour blind as they come.' Having already been rejected by the navy because of his colour blindness, Rodda worried that he would not be able to serve at all. But his accountancy skills were urgently needed, and he enlisted in the RAAF as a paymaster.

In June 1943, Rodda, now a sergeant, arrived at No. 460 Squadron RAAF at Binbrook, Lincolnshire. Morale on the base was low, and he vowed to do something about it. Elected secretary of the Sergeants' Mess, he discovered that there had been pilfering from the till. He approached the station commander, Group Captain Hughie Edwards, VC, with his concerns. It was the start of a firm friendship between the two cricket enthusiasts. According to Rodda, Edwards told him:

'Well, I know all about flying and very obviously you don't, but then equally obviously you would know that I wouldn't know much about administration whereas you do. I want you and I to work together for the benefit of the Australians on the station because there is trouble.' I said, yes, I was aware that there was trouble. I hadn't got to the bottom of it but I would. He said, 'What we'll do is we'll start this cricket business off with an inter-squadron match. You can start getting a decent side together to challenge in the [local] competition.'

A competitive team was formed. The lanky Rodda was a fast bowler, and Edwards, despite continuing problems with a severe leg injury from a 1938 crash, proved to be a useful off-spin bowler, even though he had to shuffle up to the crease to bowl. Rodda soon discovered that the men regarded Edwards as 'God' and would follow him anywhere.

Genial and unassuming, 460 Squadron pilot Flight Lieutenant Bob Henderson was a handy cricketer, who with his teammate Corporal Alan Barnes, now a POW in Singapore, had helped his club team, Mosman, win the 1939 Sydney competition before he enlisted in the RAAF. Later in the war he would be selected in the Australian Services side, along with players such as Lindsay Hassett, who had served with the Second AIF in the Middle East and New Guinea, and the legendary all-rounder Keith Miller, a Mosquito pilot. Like his teammates, twenty-six-year-old Henderson was in awe of Miller's precocious batting and bowling talents – and of his cavalier, rebellious streak. 'I was roomed with him quite frequently to try and keep him from going over the edge, but that was impossible, of course. He was [a] wild man, yes. He was a very fine fellow, nevertheless, Keith.'

In mid-1943 Henderson was selected in the RAAF cricket team to play an England eleven at Lords. The Australians could only manage 100 runs after Sir Pelham Warner's team scored

201. A report of the match in the *Sydney Morning Herald* noted that despite the loss, Keith Miller, a flying officer, had given 'a delightful display of cutting and driving in making 45'.

The match coincided with operations of Bomber Command and the United States Army Air Force in the Ruhr Valley, and the major port city of Hamburg, in July and August 1943. Henderson had requested to be pulled out of the match so he could take part in the raids. Hughie Edwards, however, insisted that he play. 'So, I went.' Henderson had a good game, being the last Australian batsman dismissed.

His buoyant mood was shattered when he arrived back from Lord's to be confronted by the news that on return from the raid on Hamburg there was a plane missing from his squadron. 'While I was away, a sprog crew was short a bomb aimer and a wireless operator for the first raid and my two boys volunteered to go.' In that raid, a stream of 791 aircraft dropped 2284 tons of bombs on Hamburg in fifty minutes. Those two crew members were among the airmen who did not return. On his return, the news shook Henderson badly.

Two months before the Hamburg raid, thirteen Australians flew in Operation Chastise, the raid in which Bomber Command's No. 617 Squadron RAF set out to destroy three strongly protected dams in the Ruhr valley, the industrial heartland of Germany. The squadron's secret weapon in its attack on the Möhne, Eder and Sorpe dams on the night of 16/17 May 1943 was the innovative bouncing bomb. The bombs successfully breached the Möhne and the Eder, while the Sorpe was damaged but not destroyed. Of the 133 aircrew that took part, fifty-three men were killed and three became prisoners of war. Australian Flying Officer Tony Burcher, a rear gunner, was one of them.

After his Lancaster was hit by gunfire, Burcher bailed out, fracturing his spine on impact. Captured three days later, he was treated for his injured back and sent to Stalag Luft III, at Sagan (now Zagan, Poland), 160 kilometres south-east of Berlin – a German POW camp for airmen. Burcher would spend the rest of the war at Stalag Luft III amid its maze of barbed wire and grey buildings. A few months later, he was joined by another Australian in Bomber Command, Flight Lieutenant George Archer, also from Sydney. While it is not clear if they ever met, the chances are they did, especially through the sport played at the POW camp.

Like Burcher, Archer was among the 1476 RAAF airmen, mostly in Bomber Command, shot down over Germany who became prisoners of the Germans in the war. They were '*Kriegsgefangeners*' – war prisoners – to the Germans, but among themselves they were 'Kriegies', who were imprisoned in more than forty major camps, from Lithuania to the Rhine. In all, nearly 8600 Australians became POWs under the German and Italian regimes. Most of the AIF personnel were captured either in the North African desert campaign or in the chaos of the withdrawal from Greece and Crete.

Archer and Burcher were among 351 Australians who were confined in Stalag Luft III between its opening in April 1942 and evacuation in January 1945. A clerk from Sydney, Archer enlisted, aged twenty-three, on 22 July 1940, under the Empire Air Training Scheme. He completed flight crew training in Canada, before finally being attached to No. 158 Squadron RAF at Eastmoor in England. Two years after he joined the RAAF, on the night of 21/22 July 1942, he was the observer in a Halifax II bomber – one of 291 aircraft headed to the German steel production town of Duisburg. The raid was Archer's seventeenth operation, and the Halifax carried two 4000-pound bombs.

The night was moonless when a German Messerschmitt Bf 110 struck, its lethal gunfire raking the Halifax. The fuselage, and port and starboard engines burst into flames. With two of the crew dead, the Halifax dived rapidly. The pilot, Flying Officer Frank Hardy, fought to control the stricken bomber, thereby enabling Archer and the surviving crew members to bail out. Hardy crash-landed the plane outside the farming village of Schoonrevoerd, near Utrecht in the Netherlands, emerging badly hurt but alive. Archer, too, survived, rescued by two Dutchmen, who promptly handed him over to the Germans. His journey to Stalag Luft III began.

Archer couldn't help but notice the role sport played in helping keep the internees sane. Competitions in rugby, soccer, tennis and basketball sprang up. A sports day was held in June 1944, featuring athletes from Britain, Canada, New Zealand, South Africa and Australia. During a freezing European winter, Australians played ice hockey against the Canadians when an enterprising POW serendipitously flooded the compound. The two nations faced off in soccer, drawing 1-all, but Australia had the best of the rugby, defeating Canada 10–5 in November 1944.

Half a dozen cricket teams played on a concrete pitch that the POWs poured, with the Red Cross providing a few bats and six-stitchers. In two 'Tests' in 1944, Australia defeated England by five wickets in the first, and by 19 runs in the second, but lost to 'The Rest', according to 460 Squadron's Flight Lieutenant Arthur Schrock, 'by some runs'. One of Archer's jobs was to maintain the bats, which he did by rubbing the willow with oil from sardine cans. As the games went on, danger from the guards was never far away. Shortly after 460 Squadron Flight Lieutenant Harry Train arrived at Stalag Luft III, three cricket balls were hit outside the warning wire 'and one of the Goons [guards] took a shot at one of our chaps ... who attempted to retrieve one'.

In early 1943, captured RAF pilot Sydney Smith opened a Red Cross parcel to discover a five-iron golf club. He carved some nearby pine into a sphere and wound it with wool and cotton before layering it with cloth and stitching it together to produce the first golf ball manufactured at Stalag Luft III. Another captured RAF pilot, Pat Ward-Thomas, a keen golfer, joined the action.

They began by hitting stones between the huts, sparking interest from other would-be golfers at the camp. In time, the Sagan Golf Club was established, with a nine-hole par-3 golf course laid out. George Archer helped with its development. 'The area we had for nine holes was about 800 yards. The greens were just raked sand,' he explained in an ABC Radio interview in April 1993. They were roughly 8 to 10 yards in diameter, with shallow banks around them. The sandy surfaces, carefully smoothed, were true and fast for putting, especially when watered, with the longest hole about 150 yards. The course offered 'everything to be desired by lovers of the game – fairways midst pines and potato patches – greens of velvet smoothness', wrote Arthur Schrock. Competitions and exhibitions soon drew crowds, much to the bemusement of the German guards, who had little interest in golf.

RAF fighter pilot Oliver Green recalled that the warning trip wire that ran around the course created an additional hazard for the golfer because if his ball lay in forbidden territory, he could not retrieve it. 'He not only lost the ball and a stroke but also faced the harsher penalty of having to make another ball.' The alternative, of course, was to try to retrieve the ball and be shot.

The Red Cross supplied more clubs, as did the POWs by making crude clubs out of scrap timber. The heads were made by melting down and moulding watering cans, and silver paper from cigarette packs. Stealing their hut stovepipes drew a swift response from the guards. A growing interest in golf demanded an ongoing supply of balls. George Archer was ready. He started with two pieces of leather, each cut in a figure-of-eight pattern from old footballs or army boots. Inside was a small dob of solder from a tobacco tin, tightly wound with much thread. They may have looked like miniature brown baseballs, but they were in fact golf balls that Archer made to stringent specifications laid down by the Royal & Ancient Golf Club in St Andrews, Scotland, weighing 1.62 ounces (45.93 grams) and being 1.68 inches (4.27 centimetres) in diameter.

In the summer of 1943, a thirty-six-hole foursomes challenge was held, one team comprising two low-handicap British airmen, and the second a former Scottish schoolboy champion, and a Tasmanian, Bombardier Bill Sampson, who was no slouch with a mashie, having won a Kingston Beach Golf Club, Hobart, tournament in 1936 at the age of seventeen. Sampson, of the 2/1st Anti-tank Regiment, and his partner won the foursomes two up with a hole to play, to become Sagan Golf Club champions.

To the Germans, the POWs seemed content, occupied with golf and other sport in the camp.

According to MI9, a branch of Britain's Secret Service that helped Allied military personnel evade capture and assisted in their escape, Stalag Luft III was one of the most secure German prison camps. It was built on loose, sandy soil which would be difficult to tunnel into. The camp was surrounded by a double fence with manned guard towers, spotlights and razor wire, and seismographs were installed to pick up movement. It was also assumed that because the POW huts were 50 to 100 metres from the perimeter wire, tunnelling would be out of the question.

Undeterred, an elaborate plan was hatched in the camp. The feint was both creative and ingenious, happening right under the noses of the watchtower guards, with the golf course providing cover. Through the summer of 1943, four men walked each day through the canteen carrying a wooden vaulting horse, made from timber supplied by the guards ostensibly to make props for plays. The horse was always carried to the same spot near the eighth tee, about 18 metres from the wire wall that surrounded the camp. The horse, 1.5 metres long by 1 metre wide and 1.4 metres high, was placed over a carefully hidden entrance to an escape tunnel under construction. To increase its credibility while in place, a group of men vaulted the horse.

The ruse involved one or two airmen clinging to hooks on the inside of the horse as it was carried to the concealed opening.

Once in position, they would climb down about 150 centimetres and day by day extend the tunnel, lining it with plywood panels from Red Cross crates as they went. They not only dug out the tunnel but also dragged back the yellowy sand by bowl and string to the bottom of the shaft, shoved it into bags then pulled it to the surface. The sand then would be stuffed into socks inside the trouser legs of men, who would nonchalantly allow the sand to trickle down their leg as they walked around the area, mixing it with the darker topsoil around the golf course.

Once done for the day, the entrance would be carefully concealed to blend in with the surrounding soil. According to Archer, the demands of the exercise sessions on the horse posed their own problems as jumping over the horse for an extended period was physically tiring and the time grew longer as the tunnel lengthened. 'I can assure you that jumping over a horse four feet high and impressing the German guards ... was not that easy.' The horse was then carried back to the canteen building and stored each night.

While there was a roster of POW diggers, there were three main diggers from the RAF – Lieutenant Michael Codner, Flight Lieutenant Eric Williams and Flight Lieutenant Oliver Philpot – who would make their escape first. Their goal was a tunnel more than 30 metres in length that passed underneath the camp's walls. George Archer took his turn as one of the diggers, using a trowel and his hands. 'You wouldn't want to have claustrophobia. The whole time you were in there did you have this feeling, "I can be caught any moment".' All the while, guards were in the watchtower, just metres away, looking down on the POWs as they jumped over the wooden horse, golfers active on the course and footballers playing nearby. Archer was slated to be number seven to escape.

By the beginning of October, with the tunnel past the wire, the escapees decided on a time when there was no moon at month's end. On 29 October 1943, the three RAF airmen broke out just after 6 p.m. Philpot reached the port of Danzig in a day, stowed away on a Swedish ship and reached Stockholm, in neutral Sweden, a few days later. Meanwhile, Williams and Codner travelled to the port of Stettin and stowed away on a Danish ship. All three were repatriated back to Britain, ultimately becoming the only men to make successful 'home runs' from Stalag Luft III's East Compound. The escape became known as the Wooden Horse.

The Great Escape took place five months later in March 1944 from Stalag Luft III's North Compound. Of the seventy-six POWs who escaped, only three made it to freedom, and fifty were captured and shot; the rest were captured and reimprisoned. These two breakouts were seminal events in the history of POWs in Germany in World War II. They underlined the mood of defiance among Allied airmen, and gave a clear message to the Germans that though may be prisoners, they had not given up.

After the Wooden Horse escape, guards flooded the tunnel to prevent further escapes. Immediately associating the tunnel with the golf course as a ruse to hide escape preparations, the guards threatened to permanently shut down the golf course. They eventually relented and the course was reopened. And George Archer continued making his golf balls – just one remaining with his family in the post-war years as a powerful reminder of just what those tiny balls meant to the men in the camp. The making of golf balls, with the knowledge of the critical part they would play in an escape attempt, gave the men not just hope but a purpose.

Even if escape was not the end result, sport was there to keep the men fit and take their minds off their predicament. This was the reality not just at Stalag Luft III but also at other stalags. Forced to work in agriculture, forestry and industry, the men found sport helped to make their predicament tolerable. A magazine entitled *One Year*, produced with the assistance of the Prisoners of War Aid of the YMCA, in Geneva, between 1942 and 1944, contended that the memories of sporting activities would stand among 'the brighter moments of an otherwise drab, monotonous exile'.

At Stalag 383 at Hohenfels, Bavaria, a small contingent of 500 Australian commissioned and non-commissioned officers shared the camp with up to 7000 British, American, Canadian, New Zealand and South African POWs. They played a range of games, including rugby league, rugby union, soccer, basketball, baseball, boxing, wrestling, hockey, softball, swimming, volleyball, water polo, golf, and a variety of athletics events. An Australian Rules football league was set up, comprising teams named after native Australian animals, including the Kangaroos, Emus, Kookaburras, Wallabies, Snakes and Goannas. Committees were formed for each sport, along with coaches, trainers and managers. There were even swimming carnivals, which were held in a large tank of fire-fighting water. A camp sports store was established, while a team of masseurs attended to competitors and others constructed infrastructure such as football posts and a cricket pitch. Old stables were turned into training facilities and boxing arenas so that sport could be pursued even when the weather outside made outdoor sports impossible.

Above all, it was cricket that energised the British and Dominion POWs at Stalag 383. This was especially so in August–September 1943, when a triangular tournament between Australia, England and New Zealand was played. The outcome of the series was recorded in a unique book of cartoons, decorations and illuminated scorecards, the *Ersatz Ashes*, compiled by POWs Jim Welch and Jim Davies. The series was played on a rolled pitch that was described as 'venomously corrugated' that also 'haunted bowlers in their sleep'. A large green field of lush clover looked good at first but was actually a sloping surface, honeycombed with ruts and intersecting furrows, which bode ill for the fieldsmen.

In the first match, Australia defeated New Zealand by ten wickets, the cartoon for which featured a kangaroo in pads and carrying a bat looking back at a tearful kiwi bird being consoled by a lion promising to 'make him smile on other side of his face!' Hope sprang eternal, and that was not to be, with Australia defeating England by 198 runs in the next match. The result was reversed in the following game, with the English defeating Australia by ten wickets. When Australia defeated New Zealand in the next match by an innings and 55 runs, the Kiwis promised to 'show these big shots a thing or two when rugby starts'. Rain brought the series to an end, with one of the book's cartoons showing a padded-up batsman deep in water lamenting, 'Are we decadent or sissy – or what? Why was the Test series abandoned because of a bit of rain?'

That same summer, at Stalag 344 at Lamsdorf (now Lambowice in Poland), another triangular 'Test' series between Australia, New Zealand and England was played. Australia was captained by Warrant Officer Glen 'Pat' Ferrero, who had been captured in the Middle East in August 1942, after his Wellington bomber experienced engine failure, forcing him to bail out. With a reputation as a fine fighting batsman with South Melbourne before he enlisted, Ferrero had been teammates with Lindsay Hassett and Keith Miller. In the final against New Zealand, Ferrero scored 46 to lead Australia to a victory by four wickets and 150 runs.

After the series finished, Private Frank O'Brien, an amputee who was a mate of Ferrero's, returned to Australia under an arrangement with Germany for invalid servicemen to be repatriated. He described how the 'vociferous barracking of Digger supporters' helped Australia to victory. So keen was the barracking, O'Brien said, that 'the majority of the Australian supporters had sore throats for days after'. He went on: 'As in the good old days, the English team failed to relish the Aussies-style of verbal encouragement and disparagement.'

It was not only in cricket that families in Australia heard sporting news that gave them cause for hope. A few months

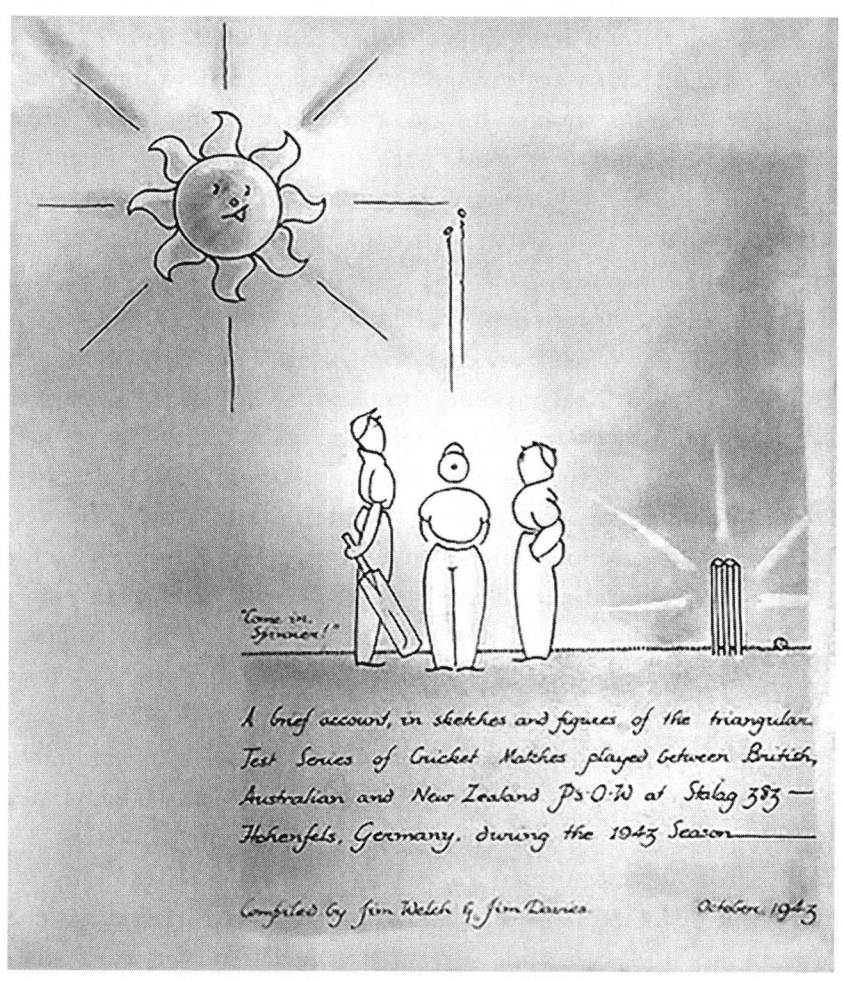

The 'Ersatz Ashes' written and illustrated by Jim Welch and Jim Davies while at Stalag 383, Hohenfels.

earlier, Private Roy Bailey, 2/5th Battalion, was part of an all-Australian boxing team from Stalag 7A, Moosburg, selected to meet a British POW team. The night of the tournament, a neighbour of Roy's father, Joe Bailey, in Fitzroy, Melbourne, rushed in to tell him that fights were being broadcast on shortwave radio from Germany. Tuning in, Joe Bailey nearly fell off his chair when he heard that his son was the next competitor. According to the *Sporting Globe*, young Roy 'licked the tar' off his opponent.

There was no prouder man in Fitzroy than Joe Bailey that night.

24

PLAYING FOR AUSTRALIA!

It probably helped Sister Jess Doyle that her maternal uncle was Jack Gregory and she had learned a bit of cricket from the World War I veteran who became Australia's great Test all-rounder in the 1920s. Now she was at war and had the chance to put those skills to use in a women's cricket match at the Palembang POW camp on the island of Sumatra. Jess Doyle was one of thirty-two Australian Army Nursing Service sisters attached to the 2/10th Australian General Hospital AIF who had survived the evacuation of Singapore as the Japanese conquered the island.

Of 130 who were evacuated, sixty-five had been aboard the coastal steamer *Vyner Brooke*, which left Singapore on 12 February 1942, only to be sunk off Bangka Island by Japanese bombers two days later. Eleven of the nurses were lost at sea and twenty-one were tortured, raped and then machine-gunned to death on Bangka Island's Radji beach by Japanese soldiers as they overran Sumatra.

Jess Doyle washed ashore elsewhere on Bangka Island and either found her own way to the nearby town of Muntok or was taken there by Japanese troops. Soon she was joined by more of her colleagues who had survived the sinking, among them Iole

Harper and Betty Jeffrey, who had become lost in a mangrove forest. Like Jess Doyle, Iole came from a cricketing family, being the daughter of a former West Australian leg-break bowler Walter Harper, who played for the state in 1908–09.

Around ten days later another nurse arrived – Sister Vivian Bullwinkel, the only survivor of the horrific beach massacre. They were about to endure three and a half years of captivity under the Japanese in civilian internment camps, alongside Dutch and British women, at Bangka Island, followed by internment at Palembang, Muntok, and finally Lubuklinggau in south-west Sumatra. The camp conditions in Sumatra for the women POWs were no better than elsewhere in South-East Asia for the tens of thousands of Allied troops maltreated by the Japanese. Among the handful of Australian women who were internees in Sumatra, Jess Doyle and Betty Jeffrey helped keep spirits up.

Noted for her outgoing and bubbly nature, Jess was always good for a story, many of which were directed against herself and the Gregorys, who were prominent in Sydney's sporting circles, especially cricket. Years later, Sister Wilma Oram (née Young) recalled that, during their incarceration, Betty Jeffrey was ever helpful, inspiring and full of fun when things were grim. 'I recall on one Melbourne Cup Day in the camp, Betty found an old bag, slung it over her shoulder and called the odds. A lovely light-hearted moment when we were all hungry.' And hungry they were in their grossly overcrowded huts, with the guards treating them contemptuously at mealtimes. Wilma Oram recalled how the 'Japs would bring in a piece of meat, and throw it on the ground, put a foot on it and carve it up with a bayonet.' In April 1944, Jeffrey wrote in her diary that she was 'so hungry I could hardly walk'.

By then, dysentery was rife, and there was typhoid in the camps. Hunger and illness had ravaged their bodies, leaving them emaciated and grossly underweight, but that couldn't stop them organising a cricket match in Palembang in mid-1944 after Dutch women in the camp wanted to know more about the game. Betty Jeffrey recorded the moment in her diary in September that year.

> With a worn-out tennis ball, packing case for a bat and a kerosene tin for stumps, we went at it and had a lot of fun. We had some talent, Jess Doyle being the niece of a very well-known Australian test player and Iole [Harper] the daughter of a former interstate bowler, so the standard should have been good. It was terribly funny. We had Jap guards fielding those sixers we hit over the top of the dormitories and so outside the camp. They thoroughly enjoyed themselves. Jess and Iole were the two heroines of the match. Jess top scoring and being a wizard at fielding and catching people out, like her Uncle Jack. Iole took the bowling honours, she was about the only person who could bowl *on* the wicket! None of us think Don Bradman and company will miss anything in the way of a Test player during our sojourn here, but we did have a most amusing day, even if we didn't impress the Dutch very much.

Despite the Dutch being left underwhelmed, the match clearly lifted spirits so much that a cricket match against the English women in the camp was seriously contemplated. 'We decided to have a Test match England versus Australia, but somehow we have never played that Test. I'm sorry, for I'll never get another opportunity to play cricket for Australia,' lamented Jeffrey. Given the women's progressively weakened state and illnesses, playing cricket that day was an achievement in itself. It seems, however, it was destined to be a one-off, as the less physically demanding activities such as concerts, mahjong and bridge were as much as they could muster in that last long year of their captivity.

25

BLACK MAGIC

It took Allied troops three months to win the Battle of the Beachheads – Buna, Gona and Sanananda – on Papua New Guinea's north coast before the Japanese were finally routed in late January 1943. The battle cost the lives of 1300 Australians and a thousand Americans as more than six thousand Japanese fought to the death. It was the single most costly battle for Australians in the South-West Pacific. The Allies began establishing large bases to support air and naval operations, as well as major offensive ground operations slated to begin in earnest later in 1943. The garrisons soon grew into small, bustling cities with, of course, recreation needs.

At Buna, which had been the main enemy base for the advance along the Kokoda Track, the Australians played inter-company softball and volleyball, as well as matches against American teams in their area. An unexpected find were the work horses that the Japanese left behind. With the Australian love of punting never far away, this was an opportunity too good to ignore. Australian units claimed the horses roaming free and established the Soptua Racing Club. Later that year, on 9 October 1943, the first race meeting was held, with most of the jockeys coming from the ranks of Australian troops and only a few Americans taking the reins.

That changed after Australian amenities officers discovered that American units also had many 'strange horses and mules' and urged their allies to participate in future race meetings. While not regular events, these races drew large crowds. Australian nurse Captain Mona Goldsmith of the 2/11th Field Hospital recalled that races were the 'outstanding social events of the area'.

Not that there were many such opportunities in the Allied campaigns in the South-West Pacific. But Australian and American military leaders knew the importance of maintaining morale as troop numbers swelled and the fighting dragged on. Among early events in 1943 were a series of swimming carnivals held in Port Moresby's seawater swimming pool, which attracted hundreds of participants and thousands of spectators. The events were open to 'both men and women of the Allied services'.

But there were cultural issues around sport, with the Americans showing little interest in cricket, rugby or soccer, and Australians disinterested in baseball. There were also difficulties in grading and clearing large areas for football fields and cricket pitches – although not on the island of Bougainville, to where Jika Travers, after his exploits against the French in rugby at Beirut earlier in the war, was posted in late 1944. For Travers, according to the *Australian Dictionary of Biography*, manliness was grounded in 'contest and courage in war and sport' and while on Bougainville, when there was a lull in the fighting, he played cricket on a 'cleared patch in the middle of the jungle' that Americans had cleared for baseball. On one occasion, a bemused Travers described the reaction of a group of bewildered GIs watching the Australians play cricket.

> The day is hot and the Australians are enjoying this change from the monotony of the jungle. Around the

ground there are gathered many American soldiers of all ranks, who are watching the cricket with a look of despair, or of boredom, or of genuine puzzlement. Every now and then they discuss some event with great waving of arms, but never with any apparent conclusion. Suddenly one of the G.I.s detaches himself from one of the groups and walks over to two Australian officers. 'Say, bud,' says the G.I., 'what is the object of this game?' The two Australians are absolutely flabbergasted that someone exists who cannot follow the game of cricket. But on the other hand, they are both hard put to explain the purpose of this game to the G.I. After several minutes of hard thinking they suggest that the purpose of the game is to score more runs than the other team.

Ultimately, shared sporting activities drew the most participants and largest audiences in the unique environment of war in Papua New Guinea and the wider South-West Pacific. Since 1943, Port Moresby had become the major hub of Allied sport – especially boxing. By late 1942, RAAF personnel were organising boxing tournaments there, with Americans in the area invited to take part. As American forces took on a greater role in the war, interest in boxing increased within a few months. Two new stadiums opened, one of which could seat up to 8000 spectators.

As with international professional boxing at the time, African American boxers soon dominated Port Moresby's boxing scene. Betting on the outcome was common. A letter to the *Sporting Globe* noted that the Americans thought 'nothing of wagering £30 or £40 a head on their man' and added that the Australians also bet heavily. But the Port Moresby boxing scene inevitably fell away in early 1944 with the decline of Port Moresby as a major Allied operational base.

Subsequently, Morotai Island, a large Allied airbase and staging area for Australian I Corps in the Halmahera Islands in

Corporal Bill Bertram wins the cricket ball throwing event at a Bougainville sports carnival, June 1945. AWM 092775.

the Dutch East Indies, briefly became a hub of Allied boxing. In October 1944, the RAAF's 14th Airfield Construction Squadron built a boxing stadium for weekly boxing tournaments that drew thousands of Allied troops. By the end of April 1945, the crowds had grown so large that RAAF engineers could not spare the manpower needed to clean up after tournaments and the unit closed the stadium – but not before Warrant Officer Len Waters had the chance to write himself into Australian sporting history.

Waters was a trailblazer who, through the outbreak of World War II, broke barriers to pursue a dream to fly. As he later recalled: 'I grew up in the era when the skies were being explored. There was Amy Johnson, Kingsford Smith, Bert Hinkler, Lindbergh ...' At a time when Australians feared a Japanese invasion, he enlisted in the RAAF and worked through a series of rigorous tests to ultimately join its fighter-pilot elite. In an age of racial discrimination, this was no mean feat. Waters was a Kamilaroi man, who spent his early years at Toomelah Aboriginal reserve in northern New South Wales.

The first step was graduating as a flight mechanic. This was the easy part. Re-mustering for pilot training meant getting through stringent testing. Having left school at thirteen, night school was imperative. After initial flight training and more examinations, Waters faced the Categorisation Board, whose task it was to select the category of aircrew in which he would continue training. 'I knew that I was holding my own with the majority of fellas who had transferred to aircrew and that when I went before the Board, I was keen to prove myself ... And of course everyone wanted to be a pilot.'

The night before he was to appear at the Categorisation Board, Waters was scheduled to fight in a boxing tournament. His opponent was a flight sergeant drill instructor. A mate, Wally McKenzie, warned Waters to be careful, and with good reason. Waters had thought the fight to be an exhibition bout. McKenzie put him straight: the flight sergeant's mates had money on him. Knowing this, and that Waters' skill as a boxer was likely underestimated, McKenzie put 'fifteen quid' on Waters. After the boxing match, Waters noted wryly, 'We went out and this fellow tried to put me away in the first two or three punches and as it so happened he finished up on the sick parade the next morning.'

At the Categorisation Board the next morning, an elated Waters was selected for pilot training, ultimately gaining his wings as a fighter pilot in July 1944. Promoted sergeant, twenty-year-old Waters was posted to No. 78 Squadron RAAF, which had first seen operations off New Guinea in November 1943. When Waters arrived, the Allies had been in control of the island Noemfoor, West Papua, since August that year, having taken it after two months of fighting. However, Japanese forces were stubbornly refusing to accept the all-but-certain prospect of defeat, and the squadron was to carry out patrols, sweeps and

Above: **A friendly training session for Len Waters (right front).** Courtesy Gordon Clarke.

Left: **Warrant Officer Len Waters in his Kittyhawk, Black Magic.** AWM P01659.001.

strikes to provide cover for Allied troops attacking Japanese posts and airstrips. Waters inherited a P-40N Kittyhawk that serendipitously carried the name *Black Magic*. Fate had spoken.

Waters flew forty-one strike and attack operations and a further fifty-four operational flights in the ten months he was in the islands. He remembered one such mission with more than some clarity. In January 1945, nineteen Kittyhawks set out on a mission targeting Japanese bases in the Celebes Islands. Manado had been an important Japanese coastal base, and neutralising it was a high priority. Waters was leading the flight at the time. He described how, having dropped his bombs at 3000 feet, he began to pull out of the dive in order to come back around to strafe. '[But] I felt this clunk underneath me and thought, "I've got a hit there somewhere".' He was worried, very worried.

It was a long flight back. When coming in to land at Morotai, Waters alerted the other pilots in the flight to land and clear the strip. 'I came in on my own and I just taxied to the end of the strip.' The armourers ripped open the area under the cockpit, finding a live high explosive 37-millimetre shell – a Japanese type of 'pom-pom'. Waters' luck had held. He later described it as 'the smoothest landing I've ever made! I guarantee I could land it on egg[shells] because I didn't want to jar out what was there.'

Recreational options in the islands were limited. However, there was always swimming and, of course, cricket. A makeshift coral pitch was prepared by taxiing an aircraft into position and using the draught from the engine, gunned to test revolutions, to blast the pitch clear. However, it was Waters' boxing skill that caught the attention of his squadron. As he swayed and jabbed at the punching bag, it was clear that he was more than just a competent boxer. There was something rhythmic and purposeful in his movement. He began sparring with his mates, in the process showing them the finer points of boxing and passing on the lessons he had learned from an old tent boxer at Nindigully, in southern Queensland. With a boxing tournament in prospect on Morotai, his fellow aircrew realised that they might just make a few quid in a boxing scene that had flourished throughout the war.

The stadium stood in a coral pit about a half a kilometre from the beach, fringed by coconut palms and jungle. Here up to 10,000 Australian and American servicemen would flock on Friday nights to drink beer, gamble and, for a moment or two, forget the war. Nearby, at Barney's Casino, 'two-up' was under-way as the arena quickly filled. Over the loudspeaker, the week's sporting results, which had come in over shortwave radio from Australia, were announced.

The ring was brilliantly lit and by 7 p.m., every seat was filled. Men sat on kerosene tins, stools, bomb crates, canvas chairs and a few hundred planks perched on top of old drums. The program comprised ten bouts, which because of the enervating heat, were kept to three three-minute rounds. At the end of each bout, thousands of Dutch guilders changed hands among the troops. All boxers were paid from a shower taken up midway through the night. Usually, they received about 20 guilders each (worth about $300 in 2025).

A lean 75 kilos and lanky 179 centimetres tall, Waters was a middleweight nicknamed 'Bones'. He had that toughness that comes not from the gym but from a hard, physical life. He stepped into the ring on the evening of 12 January 1945 for his first elimination bout in the Morotai Inter-Services Boxing Championship. He won this three-round event and was back flying patrols the next day. After the euphoria of the previous night, he rated the job 'very boring'. Over the next few weeks, he gradually worked his way through elimination bouts, his opponents including some of the best fighters the American marines and navy could produce. He beat them all on his way to the final. There were some 'fit fighters amongst them, too', Waters recalled.

When he entered the ring that night for the title of the inter-services middleweight champion, Waters knew he faced his toughest opponent yet. An imposing African American was in the opposite corner, a soldier with the 93rd Infantry Division. Waters' mates in 78 Squadron had backed him throughout the fights and won thousands of guilders on his victories. They were not going to stop now.

This would be his fifteenth fight, and he was determined to keep his unbeaten record. The American fought out of the corner draped with the Stars and Stripes; Waters out of the corner sporting the Australian flag. They slugged it out, with the American's punches hurting Waters. His squadron mates began to fear the worst. Flight Lieutenant Bob Crawford was among those who backed Waters in the ring that night but could see his money going to the bookies. 'The squadron had all the money on him, and at one stage in the second round it didn't look as though we were going to win, but Len came through and was the victor and we all won money.'

Waters proudly recalled: 'I won the middleweight title at Morotai. I held it for 1944 and 1945. I had fifteen fights and I didn't lose one.' No official record of the fight was kept, as it was considered an amateur sporting event, but Waters was presented with a handsome trophy in the shape of a wooden shield with two aluminium plaques proclaiming him as the middleweight champion of the region.

Many years later, Waters was asked about the fight in conversation with friends in Sydney and explained that his opponent persistently hit him with low punches. Despite two warnings from the referee, he continued to hit illegally. Just as Crawford's recollection confirmed, Waters admitted that he was in trouble, but after a further low blow from the American the referee rightly stopped the fight. Waters had won and in doing so, just like Digger Evans in the Great War, wrote himself into AIF boxing history.

Being feted as a fighter pilot and boxing hero, however, was not enough. Post-war was a different story for Waters. He returned to the town of St George in outback Queensland, married and had high hopes of setting up a regional aerial taxi service. A local businessman agreed to finance the business; all Waters needed was his civilian pilot's licence, the permit for which was under the jurisdiction of the federal Department of Civil Aviation. He would later write: 'I had to secure a permit from Canberra. I applied for it and I didn't even get a reply to my request, so it fell through.'

Bureaucracy stood in the way of a conversion of his RAAF flying accomplishments to a civilian flying licence. Waters went back to shearing, telling his wife, Gladys, 'I guess I'll have to go back to being a blackfella.' He had played his part with distinction in the Anzac legend, only to find that with the war over, the old discrimination returned.

26

CONJURING VICTORY

With fourteen months as a POW at Changi behind him, in April 1943 Captain Ben Barnett was among 3662 Australians sent by the Japanese to Thailand as part of F Force to work on the Burma–Thailand railway. Their slave labour coincided with the infamous 'speedo' period when pressure intensified to complete the line. Barnett's role was adjutant to Lieutenant Colonel Samuel 'SAF' Pond, 2/29th Battalion, a fellow Melbourne Cricket Club member.

Captain Roy Mills, 2/10th Field Ambulance, believed the former Test cricketer to be ideal for the position. Barnett was 'a gentle person' whose 'steady unflinching gaze masked a steel resolve'. A man who 'possessed a brain capable of quick analyses', Barnett was trusted and admired by all ranks. In the months ahead, his qualities would be tested to the limit.

In his diary, Mills described the galling task he and Barnett had daily in assessing which of the men were fit to work. Once informed of the number available, Barnett would barter with the Japanese, sometimes successfully but mostly not. 'If the demands were absolutely unreasonable Ben Barnett would stand up for the men and as likely as not, sustain a beating,' Mills wrote. Before their work was done, 29 per cent of F Force would be dead.

Mills remembered urging Barnett to tell cricket stories to the men, in particular his pre-war trips to England with the Australian team and of 'the superb batting of [Don] Bradman and the outstanding bowling of [Bill] O'Reilly'. A well-known cricket story of the day related to Barnett's 1938 Test teammate Merv Waite, a playboy by reputation and a corporal in the RAAF. He had been on the eight-month tour and was credited with quipping, 'Bradman got the runs, I got the roots.' In support of Waite's application to enlist in the RAAF, Bradman wrote wryly: 'Merv. has always been a very popular member of any party. He has a genial personality which enables him quickly to make friends.' (Waite played two Tests, scoring 11 runs and taking one wicket for 190 runs.)

En route to the hell that was the Burma–Thailand railway, Barnett and his fellow officers left behind their trunks filled with all the gear they could not carry at Ban Pong. Two years later, after the rail link was finished, and in transit to Singapore, Barnett stopped at Ban Pong to collect his trunk, only to find his possessions ransacked. Barnett later told the Australian War Crimes Board of Inquiry that all that remained was a lonely pair of cricket boots.

Barnett was not one to take such theft quietly. Some retribution was called for. An opportunity presented itself in the form of the POW working parties sent daily to the Singapore docks. As Captain Norm Morrison, 2/29th Battalion, recounted, Barnett was in charge of a work party in January 1945, during which his men pocketed whatever they could.

> On return the Nip in charge always searched their haversacks before dismissing them. Ben carried the loot, mainly cigars, in his bag slung over his shoulder. As the Nip turned to inspect the last rank, the end man of the

centre rank who had been ok'd and Ben would swap bags and thus Ben was able to produce an innocent haversack for inspection. All goods thus brought in were divided equally amongst the party. One occasion only did something go wrong and then the Nip confiscated all the cigars and money of the party.

Morrison's attention, however, was focused on gaining approval for a rare swimming carnival at a Singapore beach, on 10 February 1945. In the existing sports vacuum, the carnival created great interest. Anyone with any pretentions of being a swimmer began training in a bid to win selection. Morrison noted that because a limited time was allowed at the beach, it was decided to hold relay races between the various units. This would enable more men to take part. The twenty teams comprised four men each and raced over a 30-yard course – a distance that the Changi doctors said was far enough for the physical condition of the POWs. With no starting platform at the beach, the men had to improvise. As Morrison described it:

> The races were swum parallel to the beach and start was obtained, or supposed to be, by pushing off the bottom. This meant that the team nearest the shore had a bit of an advantage over those out in the deeper water. It was found to be much easier to start by pushing off from the chest of the man behind you. As there were no lanes to guide one each team had a distinctive coloured towel waving like mad to show one where to head.

After a team from the 2/4th Machine Gun Battalion won the carnival, Royal Netherlands Force POWs challenged the Australian swimmers. In a relay race of eight a side, the Dutch proved too good by about 10 yards.

Captain Adrian Curlewis, Headquarters 8th Division, witnessed the carnival, noting the Dutch victory. A few months earlier, Curlewis had organised a learn-to-swim campaign for all officers, and during his time at Changi had given lectures on surf lifesaving and board riding. As a founding member, club captain and president of the Palm Beach Surf Life Saving Club in Sydney, he was the keenest of swimmers. Curlewis had just been allowed back into the water after a long break due to malaria. 'They cut me out of swimming – one of the bad things about doctors,' he would later quip.

Curlewis was also a mate of Ben Barnett, who he thought was 'a gem and amusing'. Curlewis described an incident in which Barnett's skills as a wicketkeeper – acknowledged for his lightning-quick hands behind the stumps – came to the fore:

> He was a great conjurer, and he used to get the cookhouse Japanese to come round and watch him do conjuring tricks. They couldn't speak any English at all. But while they were out of their cookhouse some of the other boys, our boys, were robbing the cookhouse of things. Ben would be saying, 'Look, I'm running out of tricks, you chaps, shake it up. Make them get going. I can't do any more tricks.'

Bashings by guards were a matter of course for any infraction, real or imagined, and Barnett got his share, including one a couple of months later witnessed by Sergeant Jack Croft. Barnett was philosophical about the bashings, shrugging them off with the view that he just happened to be in the wrong place at the wrong time, and in more ways than one, he was.

The war was in its final year, and within two months the Allies would be victorious in Europe, with Germany surrendering on 8 May 1945. Not so in the Pacific, where the war persisted until August that year. Had he been either serving in the forces or a POW in Europe, allowing for health, Barnett would have been a certainty for the Australian Services team playing in the Victory Tests that immediately followed the end of the war. Instead, he was cooling his heels at Changi as the cricketers in Britain he knew so well began a series that would thrill crowds desperate for a return to old certainties.

War could neither blunt a competitive spirit nor stop the urge deep within Australians to challenge the English on a cricket field, wherever that may be. On New Year's Day 1945, British POW and future cricket writer E.W. Swanton remembered an England versus Australia game, with players avoiding washing hanging off bamboo lines and hitting the ball behind the wicket where spectators gathered under the trees. Swanton called it 'jungle cricket' and said that it took prisoners' minds off dysentery and cholera. Swanton himself contracted polio and convalesced at the hospital camp, Nakom Patom, where more cricket was allowed. Thousands of miles from home and in terrible conditions, the English and Australians still had their national game.

And such was the case in India. There, two cricket 'Tests', England versus Australia, were played by teams representing the RAF and RAAF in 1944 and 1945, England winning the first. The RAAF wanted revenge. To strengthen the team, Flight Lieutenant Vic Richardson, who joined the Volunteer Air Observers Corps in 1941 and served in Australia, Burma and India, was seconded from Australia. Nicknamed 'The Guardsman', the combative yet droll Richardson had represented Australia in nineteen Test matches between 1924 and 1936, including five as captain in the 1935–36 tour of South Africa, a series Australia won 4–1.

He came with a notable reputation, relishing the opportunity to ruffle English feathers – as he had done when he was Australian vice-captain during the infamous Bodyline series of 1932–33, which saw the England captain Douglas Jardine reviled for his brutal legside tactics. Richardson was one of several Australian batsmen who were hit by viciously rising balls. In the Test at the Adelaide Oval, Bert Oldfield suffered a fractured skull and the Australian captain, Bill Woodfull, was left staggering after being struck just above the heart by the lightning-fast spearhead of the England attack, Harold Larwood. Jardine called out to Larwood: 'Well bowled, Harold.' Police had to be deployed on the boundary.

After the day's play ended, Plum Warner, the English manager, knocked on the Australian dressing room door. Richardson happened to be nearest the door and asked Warner what he wanted. 'I want to speak to Mr Woodfull,' Warner said. Richardson replied, 'You can't because Bill is having treatment. What did you want?' Warner said, 'I want an apology from the Australian player who called Larwood a bastard.' Richardson turned to the Australian room and said, 'Which one of you blokes mistook Larwood for that bastard Jardine?'

Flight Lieutenant Vic Richardson (centre front) leads the RAAF cricket team, New Delhi, February 1945. AWM SEA0130.

When the two-day match began in New Delhi on 10 February 1945, Australia batted first, making 192. England replied with just 92. Following on, they could only manage 122. With Group Captain Hughie Edwards a spectator, Richardson opened Australia's second innings, scoring a quickfire 16 on his way to leading the Australians to victory. Richardson is remembered with the Victor Richardson Gates at Adelaide Oval.

With the war in its final months, one of those not there to don the whites and stride onto a cricket field again was RAAF Flying Officer Charlie Walker, a mate of Richardson's from the Adelaide cricket scene. Walker, who had been Ben Barnett's understudy on the 1938 Ashes tour of England, was the mid-upper-gunner on a Lancaster shot down over Saltau, Germany, in December 1942. He and his six crew mates had no known grave, but he is remembered every cricket season when the South Australian Cricket association presents the Charlie Walker Trophy to the best wicketkeeper in Adelaide grade cricket.

27

THE VICTORY TESTS

Unlike Ben Barnett, his good friend Lindsay Hassett was in the right place at the right time. Having enlisted in the AIF in September 1940, Hassett was a warrant officer who had served in New Guinea before being posted to Britain in July 1944. With signs that the Allies were gaining the upper hand, the Australian Command resolved that a POW Reception Group be sent to Britain to prepare for the repatriation of Australian POWs from Europe.

Bert Oldfield, a major with the Army Amenities Service, was instructed to seek out some top-line cricketers who were in the AIF to be part of the reception unit, which was to be established at Eastbourne. The proviso was that only those who had previously served in the Middle East and New Guinea were to be considered.

Besides Hassett, other first-class cricketers transferred to Eastbourne were Captain Dick Whitington, Sergeant Cec Pepper and Sergeant Alf Cheetham. Cheetham and Pepper had both represented New South Wales, and Whitington South Australia. Sergeant Charlie Price, who joined them, had played first-grade cricket in the Sydney competition.

Another first-grade cricketer in London with the RAAF was Flight Lieutenant Bruce Andrew, a fearsome fast bowler who played for Collingwood in the Melbourne District competition. Andrew was a fine all-round sportsman who had won two Aussie Rules Grand Finals with Collingwood. In 1943, he accidentally became known as 'the rugby sensation of the year' when he filled in for a RAAF rugby team that was one short and, despite never having played the game before, emerged a star. He was an automatic selection in services rugby union from then on. At the same time, he was also playing his first love, Australian Rules, as captain of an RAAF team. True to form for an all-round sportsman, he was chosen to play cricket alongside his mate Keith Miller, representing the RAAF against the RAF at Lord's.

Captained by New South Wales batsman Pilot Officer Keith Carmody, a talented RAAF side included a nucleus of capable cricketers. The team had already tested its mettle against the best England teams during 1943 and 1944. Squadron Leader Stan Sismey recalled the 1943 match at Lord's when Keith Miller prepared to bowl to the English champion batsman, Denis Compton.

> It was the first time we'd met Denis and it was the first time Denis had seen Keith, so he turned round and asked: 'What does this chap bowl?' and I said: 'He's not really a bowler at all, he just rolls his arm over, though you might find him a bit quick.' Keith nearly took his head off.

However, Carmody's opportunity to play cricket in England was interrupted when the Beaufighter he was piloting was shot down off the Dutch coast in June 1944. Taken prisoner, he was held at Stalag Luft III until the war ended, captaining the Australian cricket team in the camp. With an AIF team built around Hassett, Whitington, Cheetham and Pepper, a strong combined

Australian side was in prospect, albeit one that the RAAF would dominate.

Although programs had already been developed for both an RAAF side and an AIF XI, agreement was reached to combine the two teams to form an Australian Services XI for a series of five three-day matches against England. Although the Ashes were not at stake, these matches were to become known as the Victory Tests.

A key figure in the move to combine the Australian sides into one team was Stan Sismey, who had recently been transferred from flying duties to RAAF Headquarters in London. Pre-war, he was the New South Wales state wicketkeeper and a useful lower-middle-order batsman. After enlisting in 1941 and training in the Empire Air Training Scheme, he was promoted speedily through the ranks. In 1944, he was piloting a Catalina flying boat off the Algerian coast when he was shot down. He spent the next eight hours in the Mediterranean before being rescued, unconscious, by the Royal Navy. Recovered, he was sent to Scotland as a test pilot.

Squadron Leader Stan Sismey. AWM UK2976.

No international sport resumed more quickly than cricket. Symbolically, the game represented the triumph of old and trusted values after the horror of six years of war. Importantly, that reaffirmation could not have occurred without Australia's 'forgotten heroes', fourteen cricketers who proudly represented their country against far more prestigious opposition. The carefree cricket they played to entertain the crowds who flocked to see them was psychologically important in drawing a line through the past and, despite stringent food rationing in Britain, boosting morale for the post-war future. The British wanted change, and the Australians were there to play their part in lifting the wartime gloom, just as their predecessors had done in 1919.

As an Australian Test batsman pre-war, Hassett was the natural choice to captain the combined Australian team, while Sismey, the on-field wicketkeeper, was the official commanding officer of the Services XI. Playing alongside them in the first Test at Lord's were Keith Miller, who was vice-captain, Flight Sergeant Jim Workman, Dick Whitington, Dambusters hero Flying Officer Ross Stanford, Cec Pepper, Alf Cheetham, Flying Officer Reg Ellis, Warrant Officer Graham Williams and Sergeant Charlie Price, with Flying Officer Bob Cristofani as twelfth man. The England team was not restricted to Service personnel and was selected from the best available players, including Wally Hammond, who was captain, Len Hutton, Flight Sergeant Cyril Washbrook, Squadron Leader Les Ames, Squadron Leader Bill Edrich, Squadron Leader Walter Robins and Alf Gover.

On Saturday, 19 May, just eleven days after VE Day, play in the first Test began at Lord's in front of a packed ground of 23,000 cricket-starved fans. By the time it was finished 70,000 people had poured through the gates over the three days of play – all unaware that, according to Whitington, the Australians were filled with trepidation. 'In their hearts was a deep and haunting misgiving – almost extinguishing hope – a misgiving that they might all make fools of themselves.'

England won the toss and batted, with Hutton and Washbrook opening the innings. After Cheetham finished the first over, Hassett threw the ball to Williams, a tall fast-medium bowler and useful lower-order batsman for South Australia before the war. Williams had been liberated from Stalag IX-B in Hesse just five weeks earlier. He had graduated as an air observer (navigator) in December 1940, joining No. 39 Squadron RAF in April 1941. At the time, the North African campaign was going poorly for the Allies and the Germans were advancing on Tobruk. On 16 June 1941, he was on only his twelfth mission, a reconnaissance flight over northern Libya in a Martin Maryland bomber, when a Messerschmitt Bf 109 fighter attacked, forcing the pilot to crash-land. Captured by a German patrol, Williams and the rest of the crew served the remainder of the war as POWs. While a POW, he became a prisoner support officer, regularly communicating with the Red Cross on POWs and their needs, and even learned Braille so he could teach it to blind prisoners.

Although he was gaunt, at 31 kilos below his pre-war playing weight, nothing was going to stop Williams from tearing in against Hutton, who in his last innings against Australia in 1938 had scored a world record 364 runs. Hutton had scored a single when Williams bowled an outswinger with his third delivery. Hutton prodded and caught the edge, sending a low catch through to Sismey. As the running sheets to the official scorecard noted, the dismissal caused 'glee among the many Australians in the crowd'.

Between overs, Williams drank glasses of glucose and water to keep his energy up, but at one stage he was unable to continue bowling and Keith Miller took over. England was all out for 267, with Williams capturing the prize wickets of not just Hutton but also Hammond for 29 to finish with 2–56 off nineteen overs. Cheetham took 3–49, Reg Ellis 2–59, Charlie Price 2–24 and Miller 1–11.

With Cheetham out for a duck at 7–358, Williams put down the glucose he had been gulping and marched out to join Miller on 98. A great ovation filled the ground, Miller later describing it as 'the most touching moment I have ever seen or heard, almost orchestral in its sound and feeling'. He compared the ovation:

> with anything ever given Bradman, Lillee or Richards. But it was not the sort of clapping and cheering that greets a hundred. This is different. Everyone stood up. They all knew about Graham's captivity. He was a big fella, but he was gaunt from his experience, and he just walked round for a while as if in a trance.

To Sismey, as 'the whole crowd stood as one' and gave Williams a 'prolonged reception', it was 'one of the most emotional and moving experiences to occur on a cricket field'. Williams went on to score 53 off fifty-seven balls, Miller top-scoring with 105, Hassett making 77, Stanford 49, Pepper 40, Sismey 37, Whitington 36 and Price 35 in a total of 455.

England fought back with a second-innings score of 294, with Pepper the main wicket taker with 4–80, leaving Australia with a chase of 107 runs in seventy minutes. At 4–76, after Hassett had made 37, they needed 31 in thirteen minutes and then 5 in four minutes. With two balls left in the match as the ground clock struck 7 p.m., Pepper swept to square leg for the winning runs before 16,000 hushed spectators. Even though England were thoroughly outplayed, Hammond declined to use delaying tactics, such as changing his bowlers and slowing the over rate, to secure a draw.

In the second Test, in Sheffield at the bomb-scarred Brammall Lane ground, England scored 286 in their first innings, with Hammond scoring 100 and Washbrook 63, leading their side to a 41-run victory to square the series. The third Test began at Lord's on 14 July, with England making 254 in their first innings, and

Australia replying with 194. In their second innings, England managed 164, Needing 225 to win, Miller led the way to victory with 71 not out, to give Australia victory by four wickets. The win owed much to Vic Cristofani's match figures of 9–92.

The fourth Test was also played at Lord's, starting on 6 August, the match attended by Britain's new Labour Prime Minister, Clement Attlee, who had just won a landslide victory over Winston Churchill's Conservative wartime government. Miller again starred for Australia, scoring 118. England responded with 7–468 declared. While the game ended in a draw, Sismey had reason to remember the match. Having reached 58, he suffered a blow to his thumb and was forced to retire hurt. Team masseur Sergeant Larry Maddison, a Tobruk 'Rat', wondered how to get him back on the field and came up with a novel idea: he used three bottle tops to give added protection to Sismey's batting glove, placing two along the front of the thumb of the glove and another on the top, binding them on with adhesive plaster. Sismey returned to score one more run before being caught.

The fifth Test, at Old Trafford, began on a high note on 14 August, VJ Day, Japan having surrendered unconditionally in the Pacific. Batting first, Australia was all out for 173, Miller unbeaten on 77. England replied with 243, Cristofani snaring 5–55. In Australia's second innings, Cristofani made 110 not out in the total of 210. Batting last, England easily chased down the required runs, winning by six wickets. The series was over, tied at two wins each and one match drawn. Miller established himself as Australia's emerging star, scoring 443 runs at an average of 63.28 and taking ten wickets at 27.7. In Thailand, E.W. Swanton was on his first walk as a free man for four years when he came across a café in a Thai village on the edge of the jungle. 'Our hosts kindly turned on the English [radio] program. We were at Old Trafford and a gentleman called Cristofani was getting a hundred.'

The series had provided cricket as people wanted to see it played. By the time it was over, 370,000 men, women and

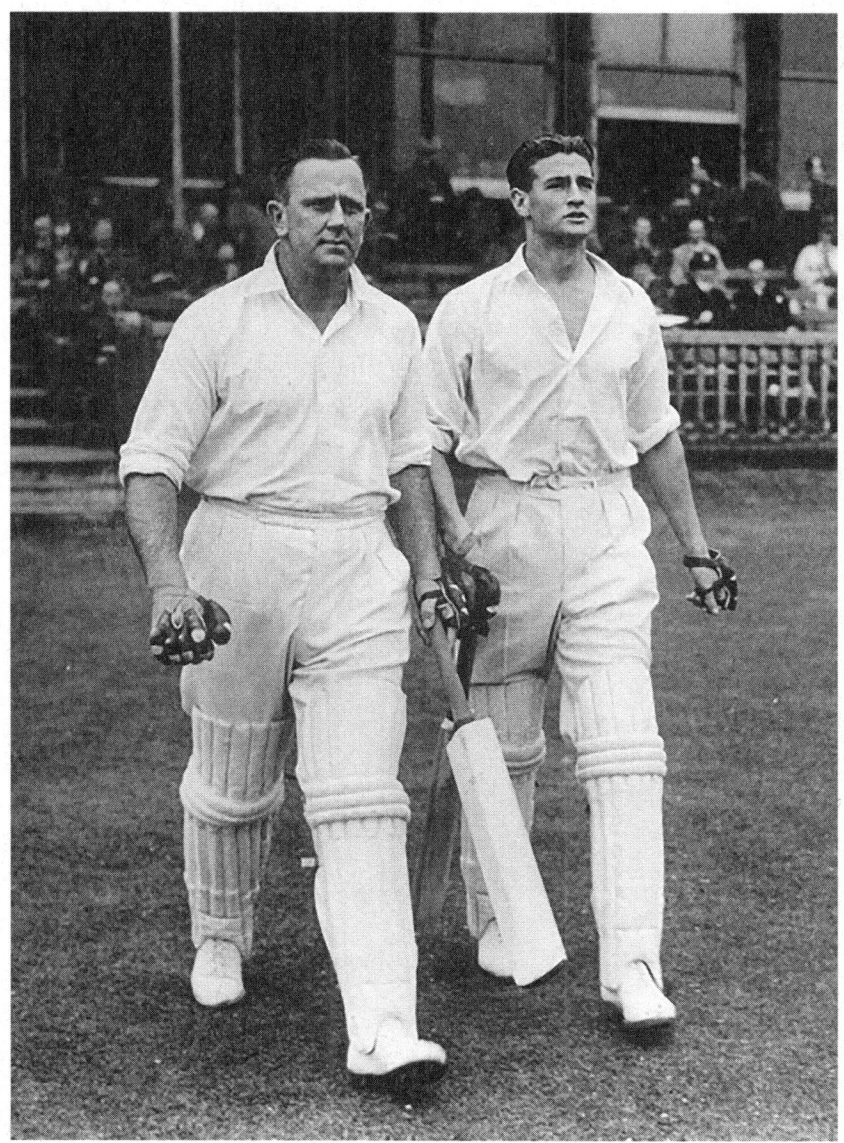

Cec Pepper (left) and Keith Miller at Lord's. AWM SUK14649.

children had watched the matches over a period of fifteen days. Stan Sismey thought it significant that on VE Day and VJ Day the Australians were playing cricket at Lord's and Blackpool; playing on the grounds that so many had given so much to protect. 'I remember the bomb-holes on Old Trafford, Lord's and Bramall Lane, and the groundsmen proudly pointing to how the turf had once more grown nicely over it,' he wrote later.

Ironically, although called the Victory Tests, the matches were not given Test match status by the participating Boards of Control. The Australian Board of Control feared their side was not strong enough to compete with a near Test-strength England. Accordingly, Graham Williams was never recognised as an Australian Test cricketer. And, after returning to Australia later in 1945, he would never play first-class cricket again.

28

WHEN SUCCESS TURNS SOUR

Shunned by the Australian Board of Control, the Services XI had succeeded in capturing the public imagination. They had played the best cricketers in England and emerged with reputations enhanced through a drawn series. So successful were they that the Australian government stepped in to capitalise on their new-found status, delaying the team's demobilisation and directing them to return home via India and Ceylon.

The brainchild of the Minister for External Affairs, Dr H.V. Evatt, the idea was agreed to by General Thomas Blamey, commander-in-chief of Australian Military Forces. By the end of September 1945, the tour of the subcontinent was approved – without the players being consulted. Nor were they consulted when, oblivious to the tour plans, the Board of Control approached Blamey asking that the team be kept together to play one match in each state on their return home.

When India formally invited the team to tour on 28 September, it left Hassett and his players only six days before they sailed from Liverpool, Miller nearly missing the ship. Still on their services pay of 12 shillings a day, the Australians found on arrival that any profit arising from the tour would be handed over to the Australian High Commissioner for distribution among Indian charities.

Lindsay Hassett kept the captaincy, with Miller his vice-captain, to lead the team for nine matches, eight of which were first-class. The touring party included most of the players who had taken part in the Victory Tests. Graham Williams and Alf Cheetham, having returned home, were replaced by Flying Officer Eddie Williams and Flight Lieutenant Mick Roper. Flight Lieutenant Colin Bremner was added to the party as reserve wicketkeeper. Instead of finally heading home to Australia to be reunited with their families, the players faced a draining schedule, travelling long distances by train in a country where steamy conditions and different food affected their health.

After a drawn opening match against the Prince's XI at New Delhi, in which Hassett scored 187 and Eddie Williams 100 not out, the team played another drawn game, against West Zone, in Bombay (Mumbai), in which Miller scored 106. In the first unofficial Test against India, at Bombay, the Services team totalled 531, with Keith Carmody 113, Pilot Officer Jack Pettiford 124 and Cec Pepper 95. India replied with 339, the match ultimately ending in a draw as the Australians ran out of time to score 103 runs in thirty minutes to win, finishing at 1–31 due somewhat to India's strategy of bowling wide of the stumps.

Sismey commented that the 'game was played under most humid and oppressive weather conditions, and the Australians were deprived of a much-merited victory by "stalling" tactics employed by the opposition'. After another drawn match, against Combined Universities, the tour was beginning to take its toll, with players succumbing to food poisoning and dysentery. The prospect of a gruelling 2000-kilometre train trip from Bombay to Calcutta (Kolkata) sparked discontent. With airmen dominating the team, they demanded to travel by air and not by train for the long journey across the continent. When this was initially refused, threats were made to abandon the tour or replace Hassett with either Miller or Carmody. Miller refused to plot against Hassett and the dispute ended when Sismey arranged for an RAAF plane already in India to transport the team.

Unsettled, the Australians at Calcutta faced East Zone, a team bolstered by a guest appearance from Denis Compton. With a century in the second innings, he led the Zone to a two-wicket victory over the Australians, who, with good reason, were distracted – and not just by health issues. As they played, war trials had begun in New Delhi for Indians who had collaborated with the Japanese during the war, fanning unrest and violence.

Twice the match against East Zone was interrupted and stopped by thousands of banner-waving demonstrators who invaded the ground and ordered all players to leave. One of the rioters who had invaded the pitch ran up to Compton, who was on 94, and said: 'Mr Compton, you very good player, but the match must stop now.' This was a phrase which Miller gleefully recalled whenever Compton went out to bat against the Australians. The demonstrators stated in no uncertain terms that 'no more cricket would be permitted' and any attempt to resume playing would result in the ground being dug up and grandstands set on fire. Hassett was said to have defused the crisis by approaching the riot's leaders and asking, 'Have you a cigarette?'

In a bid to restore order as the players were told to stay in their hotel, the governor of Bengal, former Australian Minister for External Affairs Dick Casey, called out the Indian army. 'However,' Sismey noted with some understatement, 'being escorted to and from the cricket ground under the watchful and protective eye of the army was not exactly conducive to a pleasant and enjoyable atmosphere.'

Against this background, the Australians played their second Test against India at Calcutta, the game resulting in another draw after Whitington scored 155, Pettiford 101 and Miller a quickfire 82. Pepper bowled seventy-one overs for match figures of 7–214 and Ellis seventy-one overs for 2–173. Flying to Madras to play South Zone, the Australians enjoyed a six-wicket victory. Three days later, the third unofficial Test match began, with Hassett top-scoring with 143, and Pepper notching 87 in a total of 339. Thanks to a double century from R.S. Modi, India went on to win the match by six wickets.

With the tour finished, Sismey commented that the Australians were 'subjected to much criticism' due to the 'White Australia' policy, which limited non-European immigration to Australia. However, by the tour's end 'these Service cricketers had created an enormous amount of goodwill and had proved very popular indeed'. The Indian tour analysis saw Hassett accumulate 921 runs at 83.7, Carmody 592 at 45.5, Pepper 379 at 37.9 and Miller 470 at 36.1, while in the bowling Pepper took thirty-two wickets at 35.9, Ellis thirty at 29.8 and Miller thirteen at 25.6.

By now it was mid-December 1945, and the Australians had been playing cricket for seven months – and it still wasn't over. A three-day match against All Ceylon in Colombo saw the Australians go on a run spree, with Miller scoring 132. With the spin bowling of Pepper and Ellis proving too much for their opponents, the Australians won by an innings and 44 runs.

The team arrived back in Australia on 19 December 1945 and for some, it was their first glimpse of their homeland in five years. Cricket was not high among their priorities, yet they were astonished to be presented with a program of seven four-day matches against the states, all to be played over forty days. The players were angered. Finally, the program was cut back to six three-day matches. Sismey summed up the players' disgruntlement: 'Most of the players, having spent such long periods away from homes and families, were disappointed and upset at such further extension of absences from families plus the intense concentrated demands being required.'

Sismey was unimpressed that the team's request for the program to be reconsidered drew 'scathing and unfavourable comments' from Australian cricket officials, who asserted that the criticism was not warranted and that due consideration had been given the players. He rejected this, later writing in his unpublished history of the Australian Services cricket team:

> Team members, although having been absent from Australia for some years and during that time having been closely and actively involved in total war in the truest sense, were aghast with the criticism that 'other members of the Services not in the happy position of being cricketers, are still in uniform overseas with no idea of when they will return to Australia', and 'cricketers generally will hope for more concentration on the game rather than a succession of complaints'.

The first match, against Western Australia at Perth, straddled Christmas, which the players had hoped to spend with their families. A draw resulted. Two days later, they played South Australia at Adelaide, in a match that saw Graham Williams and Alf Cheetham rejoin the team with modest contributions. While Don Bradman captained South Australia, scoring 112, he was involved in a controversy with Cec Pepper, who, after having an appeal against Bradman turned down, colourfully voiced his disapproval. The match ended in a draw.

Sismey described what happened as a 'sour note' when one of the umpires filed a written complaint against Pepper to the Board of Control. 'Having participated in continuous cricket for about 8 months under many strange and trying conditions, without any unpleasant incidents, the team was upset and dejected that back in its own country such a drastic step was taken.' At the conclusion of the tour, Pepper returned to Britain and played no further cricket in Australia. According to the champion West Indies all-rounder Sir Garfield Sobers, who later played with South Australia, 'Bradman once remarked that had Cec's mouth and his attitude been different, he would have been one of the greatest all-rounders the world has ever seen.'

Unsaid in Sismey's comments was unresolved questioning about the way Bradman had spent the war convalescing from illness. In June 1940, Bradman had enlisted with the RAAF, before transferring to the army four months later. He became a student at the School of Physical and Recreational Training at Frankston, Victoria, the plan being for him to go to the Near East as a divisional supervisor of physical training.

Bradman said he genuinely wanted to serve, but his health suddenly declined after he played four fundraising cricket matches in 1940–41. He suffered fibrositis, a frozen shoulder and eye problems that meant he had trouble seeing the ball. He was hospitalised on three occasions before being transferred to the Repatriation General Hospital in Keswick, Adelaide. On 2 April 1941, Bradman was taken off the army's roster and shortly after was given indefinite sick leave. In June 1941, he was formally discharged from the armed services and focused on building his stockbroking career in the South Australian capital.

Sismey never forgot the match at Adelaide Oval, and Bradman's century. 'I remember it clearly. Don made 112 against our Australian Services XI, and he was a sick man in all the war years, but he walked out there and batted just like Bradman always batted, getting runs, hundreds of them.' After the clash in Adelaide, Pepper was rested for the match against Victoria, which the Services XI lost by an innings and 156 runs. Dispirited, another heavy defeat followed in Sydney against New South Wales, the Services XI losing by an innings and 8 runs. The next match, against Queensland in Brisbane, was drawn, as was the match against Tasmania.

That game ended a remarkable tour of nine months of continuous cricket, yet the players were left not just jaded by its arduous demands but disillusioned by the attitude of the Board of Control and, indeed, by their reception in Australia. Sismey summed it up, concluding that it was 'amazing how the team originated, how such a tour became a reality' and how sixty-four matches with twenty-six wins and thirteen losses had been played in the UK, India, Ceylon and Australia 'without any respite'. Enormous funds had been raised for the Red Cross and other charities in all the countries visited, causing Sismey to add: 'Yet not one cent ever went to the members of the team. The players only received their normal Service pay.' And that was meagre.

As the Services XI limped to the end of their tour, Ben Barnett returned home. At thirty-six, he realised that the war had taken his best years of cricket. While he played district cricket in Melbourne, he told the press that after five years away, his first concern was to get to know his son. He could have been selected for the Australian tour of New Zealand in March 1946, but advised selectors that he would not travel without his family. He did not make the team, ending his Test career.

Like Barnett, the careers of many other cricketers had been prematurely ended by the war. As well, the Services XI, who had begun their extraordinary campaign so many months before, now found their achievements clouded by controversy not of their making; they were left jaded as their success turned sour. Nonetheless, they left a legacy: they had revitalised the spirit of cricket at a time when it was needed not just on the field but among cricket fans across a world wearied by war.

Keith Miller took this new spirit into every post-war game he played, along the way raising tensions with Bradman, with whom he had a famously tetchy relationship. At the crux of this were their contrasting experiences in the war. Miller and several Australian and British cricketers had emerged from the war believing that cricket should be played in a new, lightened spirit. However, Bradman's attitude was to continue the combative atmosphere of cricket from the 1930s. When asked many years later by TV host Michael Parkinson about pressure in cricket,

Miller responded: 'Pressure is a Messerschmitt up your arse, playing cricket is not.' Even so, Miller had only three operational flights, all in the final days of the war.

Miller, who would go on to play fifty-five Tests for Australia, at one point during the 1948 'Invincibles' tour refused to bowl when Bradman threw him the ball. Bradman reputedly grumbled in the dressing room, saying, 'I'm 40 and I can do my full day's work in the field,' to which Miller allegedly replied, 'So would I – if I had fibrositis during the war!'

Just as Jack Gregory had emerged from the World War I Victory Tests to become Australia's great Test all-rounder during the 1920s, so too Miller went on to become Australian cricket's greatest swashbuckling all-rounder. Years later, Miller nominated Keith Carmody – who never played a Test – as captain of his 'dream team' picked from his international contemporaries.

29

MATE AGAINST MATE

Abruptly, in mid-August 1945 Australia's military forces in the Pacific had gone from a war footing to having no enemy in front of them, other than those unaware that hostilities had ended and were still hiding in the jungle. Flying was reduced to two days a week and involved dropping leaflets to inform the Japanese troops of the surrender.

The Australian military was faced with the massive logistical task of bringing its forces back home. There were 224,000 troops serving across the Pacific: from Borneo and Morotai in the Dutch East Indies, New Guinea and New Britain, through to Bougainville in the north Solomons, as well as POWs in Japan and in other parts of South-East Asia. Bougainville at that time was part of the Australian Mandated Territory of New Guinea.

Men had gone from front-line action with the accompanying fear and random hits of adrenaline to wondering how to fill in time. As the Allies gained the upper hand through 1945 and Japanese forces retreated, there was now time for sport. In Solomon Islands the 58/59th Infantry Battalion staged swimming and athletic carnivals featuring underwater, freestyle and diving events in the swimming, and track and field events in the athletics. Just to show tradition had not been forgotten, there were also grenade and cricket ball throwing competitions. At subsequent 'tabloid' meets, which included events such as running backwards, winners received a case of beer. These were destined not to last long.

In the navy, sailors kept fit by playing volleyball in ship lift wells and, where possible, athletics on deck. And there was always deck hockey. The rules may have stated 'no kicking, striking or pushing an opponent', but rules are for breaking. Petty Officer George Glansford recalled playing deck hockey while serving on HMAS *Hobart*, the 12-centimetre puck made of rope.

> You had to belt this through into the goals. It was a pretty rough game I can tell you. There were sore shins everywhere. The officers had a team and the men, usually each part of ship, had a team. The torpedo men would have a team; the stokers would have a team, and they used to play one another. It was all much rivalry because the officers would get a pretty big doing over but they were good at it too and they gave as much as they got.

Ashore, sporting events were hurriedly organised. Volleyball and badminton were popular on Morotai, in the North Maluccas, and on Tarakan, a small island off the north-eastern coast of Borneo. On the island of Bougainville, in the Solomons, there were an estimated 30,000 Australians who wanted to get home, but transport was at a premium and they faced lengthy delays. The officers were intent on keeping the men occupied. Cricket, Australian Rules and rugby league were played on the site of a former US medical company hospital and evacuation centre, renamed Medco Ground. Everything was done by the book. A Bougainville Rugby League Association was formed, with Brigadier General Leslie Binns as patron. Lieutenant Tom Pedrazzini, a pre-war Brisbane rugby league official, was president, and Warrant Officer Ron Connor secretary.

In 1939, rugby league was the odd game out. Rugby union, Australian Rules and cricket were the official sports. A couple of heavy hitters from Queensland lobbied for a change. James Larkham, a state MP and former president of the Queensland Rugby League, as well as Queensland federal MP Arthur Fadden, who was briefly prime minister in 1941 and inaugural president of the North Queensland Rugby League, changed this. Rugby league was adopted by the military.

The go-ahead was given and selectors from each state met to choose their teams. With all due reverence, a trophy was commissioned by no less a person than the commander of the 3rd Infantry Division, Major General William Bridgeford. The army workshop crafted the trophy from a 120-millimetre Japanese naval shell casing, with handles either side, engraved with the words: Interstate Rugby League Series, Bougainville.

The honour of playing and watching the first 'Origin' match went to those who were based on Bougainville after the Japanese surrender. At Torokina on 16 September 1945, the Queensland

The 61st and 30th infantry battalions AIF compete in a rugby league match, South Alexishafen, New Guinea, September 1944. AWM 075814.

side, wearing maroon jerseys, ran onto Medco Ground and lined up against New South Wales, wearing blue.

It is thought to be the first time interstate teams were selected according to birthplace rather than where they were living at the time or where they enlisted. It was a unique concept that would not be replicated until the rugby league State of Origin contests began in 1980, when the selection criterion was changed to allow players to be chosen to represent their state, depending on where they played their first senior rugby league game. Up until that time, players were selected for interstate matches based on where they were playing their club football at the time of selection. The new system greatly increased the pool of talent available to Queensland.

Queensland captain Jack Barnes was an electrical linesman, who not only played first-grade footy in Rockhampton but was also a talented cricketer who represented Queensland in a Sheffield Shield match in 1941 before enlisting. Private Frank Ballard, 2/2nd Machine Gun Battalion, who had been a referee in Brisbane, controlled the game, which was broadcast to the Bougainville troops by Tom Pedrazzini.

At 2 p.m., Bobby Williamson kicked off for the Queenslanders. From the word go, the Maroon forwards were on the ball and stayed on it until the final whistle. After just a minute's play, Queensland received a penalty on New South Wales' 25-yard line and Jim Christopher slotted the kick, giving Queensland the lead 2–0. Play resumed with Queensland dominating the attack. Halfway through the first half Queensland received another free kick at the same spot and Christopher was again successful with the penalty, giving Queensland the lead 4–0.

Just before the half-time bell, with Queensland on the attack again, a scrum went down 5 yards from the New South Wales goal line. Kelly Brennan hooked the ball and Bobby Williamson worked the blind to send Jim Christopher over in the corner. Christopher failed to convert the try, leaving the half-time score Queensland 7, New South Wales 0.

The second half opened with Queensland continuing to dominate. It seemed that New South Wales would be beaten easily. However, the Blues received a free kick on Queensland's 25, and fullback Norm Parkinson's kick brought the score back to Queensland 7, New South Wales 2. Parkinson went on to convert another penalty, followed by a field goal from about 40 yards from the goal line. The kick was all the more remarkable in that the ball had hit the crossbar, bounced into the air and fortuitously fell over the bar. Queensland's lead had been reduced to 7–6. Then came the most brilliant try of the match when the New South Wales backline moved into action, all men handling from the halfback to the winger and then back to Doug McRitchie, who came around on the outside to gather the ball and score in the corner. Norm Parkinson failed to convert, but New South Wales had grabbed the lead, 9–7.

With only five minutes left on the clock before full-time, Queensland was staring at defeat. But they mounted an attack and received a free kick on the Blues' 25, about 10 yards in from the sideline; Jim Christopher failed to put the kick over. With only two minutes to go, the Queensland forwards carried the play to 10 yards from the New South Wales goal line and fierce tackling resulted. Macca Thomson, the dummy-half, gathered the ball and passed to Hec Bradshaw, who smashed his way through the New South Wales defence. Fullback Barnes launched into a desperate tackle, but Bradshaw dragged him over the line to score. Thirty seconds later the full-time bell rang. The Maroon forwards had won the game for Queensland 10–9 in a nail-biting finish. Spectators swarmed over the field and Bradshaw was carried shoulder-high to the dressing shed.

In a report of the match published shortly after in the Rockhampton *Morning Bulletin*, Ron Connor praised the standard of play. 'I witnessed one of the most spectacular and exciting games of Rugby League I have seen. Personnel who have just returned from leave on the mainland, said that the standard of football on Bougainville was equal, if not better, than A grade football played on the mainland.' A second match followed, with Queensland again victorious, 20–13.

In the following 1946 season in Brisbane, the army handed over the trophy to the Queensland Rugby League during a club match. Bearing the names of both teams, the trophy remains at Brisbane's Victoria Barracks military museum. Significantly, the series it commemorates is now regarded by rugby league historians to be the first ever State of Origin contest.

On the other hand, with the war over, the navy set their sights on building a strong rugby union team. As with World War I, the code was again reeling, having lost nine Wallabies and many state representatives during this war.

Prominent among the navy's footballers was Sub-Lieutenant Ian Wrigley who had been the Physical and Recreational Training Officer on the RAN's flagship HMAS Australia during the war. Now, in peacetime, he was at the forefront of the navy's efforts to re-build rugby union. 'The RAN, despite being numerically the smallest service, was determined for the first time to go all out and win the Rugby Services Premiership,' Wrigley, a lock forward, recalled. 'We were a happy band of post war "Rah Rahs" where rank or rating meant nothing in our determination to win the premiership because those of us who were "hostilities only" had been told that we would not be demobbed until we had done so.'

Faced with that challenge, navy played and beat the army 23–14 at Victoria Barracks in Sydney on 9 July 1946, having beaten the RAAF at North Sydney Oval a week earlier, 8–6 in a tough, hard-fought game. 'The navy was fairly chuffed that we had in fact for the first time ever, won the Australian Services Rugby Premiership.' In the post-war euphoria of the time, the navy side went on a country tour before they were finally demobbed. Civvy street beckoned – but not for all.

Post–World War II

30

RUNNING HARD

A frozen wasteland of destruction confronted the Australians in the British Commonwealth Occupation Force (BCOF) when they arrived in the Japanese city of Hiroshima in February 1946. There were no shops, dancehalls or sports fields in a city where the first atomic bomb had been dropped just a few months earlier in August 1945 to help end the war in the Pacific. More than 70,000 of the city's buildings had been damaged or destroyed and an estimated 140,000 people killed.

The BCOF troops were dismayed at what was in prospect as they prepared to oversee Japan's demilitarisation and demobilisation, and the establishment of democratic government. Based at Kure, a city in Hiroshima prefecture, the Australian component of the BCOF was responsible for more than twenty million Japanese citizens and 57,000 square kilometres of country as Japan began to rebuild from the ruins of its World War II defeat.

The lack of facilities did little to improve the negative attitude the Australians already held towards the Japanese, given the bitter wartime experience of the treatment of POWs, the attacks on the Australian mainland and battles in the Pacific. The Australians were part of an occupying force of 45,000 Commonwealth troops from Britain, India and New Zealand, as well as more than 150,000 American troops. The Australians also had another role to play: to establish their nation's credentials as a post-war Pacific leader. In quest of this, the Australian government insisted that Lieutenant General John Northcott be appointed commander-in-chief of the BCOF, a post he held until mid-1946.

Against this uneasy background, organised sport was considered imperative for the occupying force – remedying the lack of playing fields and sports equipment being an immediate priority. Northcott was quick to act. A year later, Queenslander Private Kevin Rosenstengel voiced his satisfaction with the 'three tennis courts, two basketball courts, football, hockey, baseball and cricket fields' that had been established. The new Anzac Park enabled a cricket competition to begin. Sapper Norm Sacree, from Melbourne, was now more than happy with the lifestyle and amenities. 'We have a good swimming pool and good outside swimming. The water is warm and there are no sharks. Every sport is catered for, more so than ever before in the Army.' This included bicycle racing, which was a major sporting activity of Australians posted to the main military training ground at Haramura, a valley in the Hiroshima prefecture. Races organised by the 34th Infantry Brigade Cycling Club were held over a section of road from Kure to Hiroshima. At Haramura, Warrant Officer 'Jack' Harwood sat on the edge of the track using a loudspeaker to commentate on the progress of races.

As had become the norm, the presence of New Zealand troops meant rugby union – with results that would become depressingly familiar for Australian rugby fans over the years ahead. This was apparent in a match between the 2nd New Zealand Expeditionary Force and the 34th Australian Infantry Brigade in a semi-final of the newly established rugby competition in May 1948. The services newspaper, *Bcon*, concluded that the New Zealand side, which won 48–0, was 'probably the best team ever to play the game in BCOF'. It went on: 'The superbly conditioned Kiwis, playing Rugby that would have been a match for most top teams in New Zealand or Australia, overwhelmed the Australians, mainly drawn from Rules and League teams.'

A month later, the Australians made a closer contest of a match against an understrength New Zealand side at Osaka, going down 18–8 in a contest for the Duntroon Cup. Back to full strength for a game at Tokyo a week later, the Kiwis downed Australia 37–8 in a rugged game played before more than 15,000 spectators. *Bcon* reported: 'The Australians hung on desperately in the hard, rugged second half, but although the Kiwis did not get their combinations working so often, the Australians could not stop them from increasing their lead.' The Osaka and Tokyo games showed a level of interest among local Japanese, with 6000 people watching the match at Osaka and 15,000 at Tokyo. The new BCOF commander, Lieutenant General Sir Horace Robertson, was reputed to have observed, 'It would be very beneficial to spread rugby in Japan.'

The BCOF began to wind down its operations, and from the end of 1948 the Australians were all that remained, and they too were being withdrawn gradually. But their immediate future and hopes for peacetime life were abruptly shaken when North Korea invaded South Korea on 25 June 1950. In a historic first, the United Nations intervened by sending armed forces mandated by the Security Council Resolution 82. Stationed in Japan, No. 77 Squadron RAAF was promised immediately, as were HMAS *Shoalhaven* and her relief in Japanese waters, HMAS *Bataan*. By early July, Australia was part of a UN multinational force comprising units from sixteen nations. As the crisis deepened, the Australian government promised an infantry battalion, to be incorporated into a British-led Commonwealth brigade. By October 1950, troops from 3rd Battalion, Royal Australian Regiment (3 RAR), were an important part of the effort to drive the North Korean communist forces out of South Korea. A year later, Australia sent the aircraft carrier HMAS *Sydney*, from which aircraft flew ground attack sorties.

Jim Parsons, an aircraft armaments fitter, Fleet Air Arm, sailed on the *Sydney*, and was pleased that sport was organised in port. 'We always had Aussie Rules and rugby teams, and soccer teams, and play competitions with teams from other ships and shore depots.' Ordinary Seaman Stephen Joyce recalled tennis, cricket and rugby inter-service games against Royal Australian Navy (RAN) and Australian army teams in Korea. 'Actually, that's where I learnt to hit a tennis ball, up there.'

One of the Australians serving in Korea with 3 RAR was platoon commander and signals officer Captain Claude Smeal, a long-distance runner. A New Guinea campaign veteran who had joined the army in February 1939 as a twenty-year-old, he regularly participated in marathon events in Australia, his preparation often involving running about 160 kilometres a week. When Smeal joined 3 RAR in Korea in late October 1951, his battalion had just completed Operation Commando in the Battle of Maryang San, a tactically important steep hill overlooking the Imjin River. Their task now was to patrol the no-man's land between the two opposing trench lines that ran along the 38th Parallel.

Despite landmines scattered across the countryside and the threat from ever-present snipers, Smeal continued training, jogging near sections of the front line, and was warned by his commanding officer, Lieutenant Colonel Floyd Walsh, to 'keep his head down'. Every morning, he set out in his St George Athletics Club singlet, tracing a path through the surrounding rice paddies.

In mid-1952, the Australian press picked up his story when he applied to the New South Wales Athletics Association for inclusion in the Australian Olympics team for the approaching Olympic Games in Helsinki, Finland. With the support of his battalion commander, Smeal undertook a trial marathon, crossing the finish line just twenty minutes outside the world record. With two war correspondents from Australia acting as timekeepers, the time was good enough for selection for the Olympics. The story immediately aroused interest back home. Sir Frank Packer, proprietor of the *Daily Telegraph*, threw his support behind the campaign to have Smeal included in the Australian team. The Minister for the Army, Joe Francis, granted special leave from the army for Smeal, who was added to the team. On 26 June 1952, the 3 RAR war diary noted his selection and on 2 July recorded that 'Captain C V Smeal marched out en route for Helsinki'.

Heading off to London to join the Australian team, Smeal was provided with a pair of specially fitted light canvas running shoes with ribbed crepe soles; they were handmade by a Japanese shoe craftsman. A gratified Smeal commented, 'These are the best shoes I have ever had.' Stepping off the plane in London, still wearing his army uniform and carrying a basic kitbag, Smeal was hastily kitted out with his Olympic uniform.

On 27 July, Smeal lined up with sixty-five other runners for the start of the marathon. With him on the starting line was the incomparable Czech Emil Zátopek, who, having already won the 5000 metres and 10,000 metres, was attempting his first marathon with the aim of completing an unprecedented winning treble of the major Olympic distance races.

Zátopek, dubbed the 'human locomotive', set a killing pace, burning off his challengers to win in a time of 2 hours 23 minutes 3 seconds. His feat of winning all three distance gold medals has never been equalled. Smeal finished forty-fifth, with a time of 2 hours 52 minutes 23 seconds in a race that saw thirteen runners drop out through exhaustion. Back in military uniform and suffering from badly blistered feet, he was soon on a plane back to Korea. Smeal reflected that he had not had nearly enough training on roads. 'However, I am happy I completed the course.'

Army Minister Francis commented, 'Any runner going straight from actively fighting an enemy in a bitter campaign to compete with the world's best must be expected to appear under a handicap.' Posted to a non-combat role in Japan, Smeal made light of any handicap. He continued training, with the goal of leading a signals unit marathon relay team in an annual 29-kilometre race between Kure and Hiroshima. On 19 November 1952, he led his team to victory in record time.

While Claude Smeal made his mark in athletics, no campaign could go unmarked by 'Test' cricket between Australia and England, and such was the case in Korea when the 'Korean Ashes' were staged annually between 1953 and 1955. While the war had ended with the signing of an armistice on 27 July 1953, three years and one month after the war began, a peacekeeping force continued, with the Australians remaining until 1957.

Lieutenant Gus Breen played in the Australian services cricket team in Korea and recalled that the 'Korean Ashes' matches were 'very serious stuff'. After England won the first series in 1953, the Australians were determined to take the 1954 series, to be played on a desolate field, designated 'The Oval', only a few kilometres behind the Demilitarized Zone. News of the contest in October caught the attention of Test cricket star Keith Miller, who sent the Australians a note of support, urging them to 'twist the lion's tail'. Miller threatened to dump the Australian team into the Imjin River if they lost the Korean Ashes, and offered to let the diggers tip the Aussie Test team into the Yarra if they failed in Australia.

No doubt spurred on, the Australians won with three wickets in hand, prompting the Australian captain, Lieutenant Joe Taggart, to reply to Miller, 'We have given the Lion's Tall a preliminary twist, the rest is up to you.' Three weeks later, the Australian Test side defeated England in Brisbane by an innings and 154 runs. However, England went on to take the series 3–1, thus retaining the Ashes. The final contest for the Korean Ashes –

Australian and English troops eye the announcement of the 'Korean Ashes'.
AWM HOBJ5413.

a brass urn made from shell cases – was played in October 1955 at 'Lord's', a sun-baked dirt oval near the truce line, with the English defeating Australia by 43 runs. The year had not been a good one for Australian cricket – neither on civvy street nor the defence force. Whether the diggers ever got to tip the Australian cricket team into the Yarra, having lost the Ashes, was never reported.

Among the Australians who served in Korea was Captain Reg Saunders, who commanded his company through the fiercest, coldest fighting Australian troops endured in Korea. Saunders, a Gunditjmara man who was nineteen when World War II broke out in 1939, was a war hero who had fought in Libya and Greece and survived on the German-occupied island of Crete, living among the locals for eleven months, before making it back to Australia. Reassigned to fight the Japanese in New Guinea, he volunteered again when the Korean War broke out. In April

1951, now a captain, he led his C Company troops at the Battle of Kapyong, in which the Australian 3rd Battalion was awarded the United States Presidential Citation for 'extraordinary heroism'.

A sportsman of note, he had the satisfaction of knowing that he had played football of three different codes – rugby league, rugby union and Australian Rules – in five different countries, including Japan and Korea. Saunders had a reputation for playing as hard as he fought. An officer from the 3rd Battalion described to biographer Harry Gordon how he and Saunders were once politely asked to leave an American officers' club in Japan – 'not because of Reg's colour, simply because he had a strong urge to keep demonstrating rugby tackles'. On another occasion, at Hiroshima, the two had returned home at 4 a.m. after a heavy night out. 'Three hours later he was hammering on my door, dressed immaculately in white shorts and shirt, demanding that I play tennis with him.'

Back in Australia and out of the army, and living in Melbourne, there was a move for Saunders to be given the honour of carrying the Olympic torch on its final lap around the Melbourne Cricket Ground and light the flame that would burn for the duration of the Olympic Games. With his background in sport and notable wartime service to Australia, he seemed a natural choice. The Olympic Organising Committee vetoed the idea. The first Indigenous Australian to become an officer in the Australian army was denied that honour.

31

VUNG TAU

From the arrival of the first members of the Australian Army Training Team Vietnam in South Vietnam during July and August 1962, more than 60,000 Australians, including infantry, air force and navy personnel, would serve there. Along with the Americans, their goal was to stop North Vietnam's push to unify the country under a single communist regime modelled after those of the Soviet Union and China. The war led to the deaths of 523 Australian troops, with almost 2400 wounded. Among the dead, in November 1965, was Warrant Officer Kevin Wheatley, VC, a tough, knockabout digger who had spent most of his adult years soldiering, but whose nickname, 'Dasher', stemmed from his storming exploits on rugby union fields. In Vietnam, opportunities for sport were limited, especially in the early days of the campaign.

The war was the cause of the greatest social and political dissent in Australia since the conscription referendums of World War I. A key part of Australia's involvement in South Vietnam was the introduction of conscription, which saw most twenty-year-old men having to register for National Service between 1965 and 1972. Names of potential conscripts were selected by a birthday ballot, where numbered wooden marbles were drawn by lottery from a barrel, the numbers on the marbles matching a secretly maintained list of birthdays. The ballot saw more than 63,000 men conscripted into the Australian army during the conflict, with nearly 16,000 serving in the war. Of these, more than 200 'Nashos' died and at least 1200 were wounded on active duty.

The Vietnam commitment came on top of Australia's presence elsewhere in the region, with two RAAF fighter squadrons and a bomber squadron stationed at Butterworth, Malaysia, throughout the 1950s and '60s as part of direct Commonwealth military support for Malaysia during *Konfrontasi* – a dispute between Malaysia and Indonesia. Australian troops were also stationed at the Terendak Garrison in Malaysia during that time as part of the 28th Commonwealth Infantry Brigade Group. As in campaigns past, wherever Australian troops were gathered, sport followed. At Butterworth, competitions between Australia, New Zealand and Britain were played in various sports, including cricket, rugby union, soccer, tennis, water polo, volleyball and softball.

But it was Vietnam that saw by far the largest Australian presence. In March 1966, Prime Minister Harold Holt announced a significant increase in the number of troops to be deployed in Vietnam, from the initial 1500 of April 1965 to a 4350-man task force that, for the first time, would include conscripts. With New Zealand troops deployed to Vietnam from June 1966 and integrated within the 1st Australian Task Force at Nui Dat in Phuoc Tuy province, Anzac rugby union matches were inevitable.

Helping troops to stay fit on the voyage either to or from Vietnam on HMAS *Sydney* – dubbed the Vung Tau Ferry after the Australians' destination port in Vietnam – were some notable physical training instructors (PTIs), among them the World Cup rugby league star Bobby Fulton, a conscript drafted in 1968. Along with another Nasho, nuggetty Balmain halfback Keith Outten, 'Bozo' Fulton travelled with the 1st and 5th Battalions RAR, keeping them fit on the way up and conditioning them as best he could on the return voyage. Fulton also represented the army in the inter-services annual rugby union competition, leading the team to big wins over the RAAF, 17–0, and the RAN, 17–6, in August 1968. As a PTI, Fulton was attached to an artillery unit and played rugby union against army teams, including the 101st Infantry Workshop, Ingleburn.

Years later, one of the Workshop's players, Eric Cupitt, remembered Fulton's team thrashing them 101–2. 'I did tackle Bobby Fulton on the try line. I stopped that try and he then picked me up said, "Are you alright mate?", and carried me off the field.' Fulton, who was honoured as an original Rugby League Immortal, won premiership titles and Ashes series as a player, captain and coach. As coach, he used to take his teams up to the North Head artillery barracks for training to expose them to the army parade ground environment. In retirement, he spoke to journalist Roy Masters about his time in the army:

> Think of the toughest footballer you have ever seen. Any soldier who goes to war is tougher than him. They went up there as fresh-faced, bright-eyed 20-year-olds and, a year later, returned as mature, hardened men. I was fortunate enough to get involved in something I loved, which was physical training in the army and playing football for Combined Services and Manly. These guys were getting involved in something which could kill them.

If sport can be seen as 'guts and glory', Fulton understood that in war this is taken to another level altogether. His role as a PTI was to ensure the troops he had charge of were physically fit and ready to fight when they landed. Doug Collins, then an able seaman who would rise to lieutenant commander in the RAN, made two voyages on the *Sydney* to Vietnam. He recalled that there was a limited amount of gym equipment on the former aircraft carrier. 'She was a very large ship with lots of space, three aircraft hangars and a flight deck. There was always fitness training; lots of running, and just as you would get in a normal gym, freestanding weights, and some rudimentary stationary bicycles.'

There was also rifle practice. 'The army used to float balloons off the ship, they'd be on the aft end of the flight deck and shoot at the balloons as they drifted away.' The ship's physical training staff would organise other recreational activities such as 'mini-Olympics', which would include a variety of events including tug-of-war (always keenly contested). Volleyball, played on the forward aircraft lift, was a popular activity. 'On my first trip to Vietnam,' Collins recalled,

> the shipwrights erected a 'home-made' swimming/ plunge pool on the flight deck for the crew to enjoy when not on watch, as we transited through the tropics. Sport and fitness training were welcome interruptions to the ship's daily routine and while there was a core of regular participants, the organised departmental competitions provided an opportunity for the development of teamwork, team building and a sense of camaraderie within the ship's crew.

Ashore in Vietnam, Gunner Steve Lewis, 12th Field Regiment, remembered the main leisure activity at Vung Tau being volleyball – played every afternoon he and his unit were in camp. Volleyball courts could be quickly prepared, with jungle cleared and a net strung between trees. The game was a mainstay for quick and easily accessible sport, usually followed by a few convivial beers. Lewis was a keen surfer, but without much in the way of surf at Vung Tau, he was restricted to a 'paddle around in the South China Sea'.

Rugby was soon being played. On 2 October 1966, a team fielded by 6 RAR played members of New Zealand's 161st Artillery Battery at Ba Ria, the capital of Phuoc Tuy province.

The match was played in searing heat with 80 per cent humidity, and replacements were allowed throughout to avoid heat exhaustion. Hundreds of Vietnamese, including scores of young boys, together with more than a hundred Australian and New Zealand soldiers, watched the match on an oval marked with white mine tape. The New Zealand side won the match 14–5; an Australian doctor commented that he was amazed there were no casualties in the oppressive conditions. This he attributed to the fitness of the task force soldiers.

There was no getting away from the enervating heat; it just had to be accepted and playing arrangements tailored to keeping men on the field if they were to remain fit for war. This was uppermost in the minds of 5 RAR's Lieutenant Roger Wainwright and Major Paul Greenhalgh when they organised what they believed to be the first Australian Rules football match in Vietnam. Before 5 RAR deployed from Vung Tau to the task

From left, nursing sisters Lieutenants Ann Hall, Ruth Page and Diane Lawrence at Vung Tau beach, Vietnam. AWM BEL/69/0831/VN.

force's main base, Nui Dat, about 25 kilometres from the port, in May 1966, Wainwright recalled various sporting activities on Vung Tau's Back Beach. 'We did kick a ball around but there were no formal matches up to this point. Hence my belief that the first game was the one at Nui Dat.'

Played between C and D Companies 5 RAR in late July 1966, the game took place at the airstrip at Nui Dat. It had not long been secured, and perimeter defences, including weapon pits and wire, were still being constructed when Wainwright and Greenhalgh decided their troops deserved a break with a game of footy before heading out on field operations in a few days.

They looked to the airport field to stage the game. The runway had not yet been bitumenised and the dirt surface was quite smooth, having been recently levelled by bulldozers. There was enough space to mark out a regulation Aussie Rules field, but goalposts were another question. In the end, the teams made do with 44-gallon drums, double-stacked for the goal area and singles either side for the behinds. GP military boots were the preferred footwear. Wainwright captained the C Company team and remembered the conditions as hot and humid, with frequent water stops in the ten-minute quarters. C Company won convincingly by ten goals. A matter of days later, 5 RAR deployed on Operation Holsworthy, the cordon and search of the village of Binh Ba.

It was not long before an Australian Rules competition was organised at Vung Tau, where the 1st Australian Logistic Support Group Base was established. Known as the Vietnam Football League, afficionados took wry delight in the abbreviation, VFL. They took further delight from the knowledge that the genesis of the VFL came when a Service Corps Nasho, in trouble with his commanding officer, was given two options: either organise a game of Aussie Rules or face detention.

Eight units competed, with two Ordnance teams, and teams representing the Engineers, Field Hospital, the RAAF,

Service Corps, Field Workshops and Signals. The first game was played in late 1966, with a full competition beginning in 1967, divided into two premiership seasons. Because most matches were held on a rectangular soccer ground, games were played with fourteen a side instead of the usual eighteen. The RAAF won the first premiership in 1967, with 5th Company Service Corps winning the second title that year. In 1968 the 2nd Advanced Ordnance Depot (2AOD) won both trophies, only to lose their crown in the first of the 1969 competitions – due, it has been conjectured, to a failure to stay off the grog the night before the big game; a farewell party naturally took precedence.

In the second season of 1969, 2AOD returned to the winners' list but not without a brutal struggle against the 17th Construction Squadron. A member of the team, Private Stan Middleton, recalled that 2AOD's captain was Wayne Closter, a former Geelong star. In the other team was a brilliant and tough Aboriginal footballer, Glenn James, who later became a VFL umpire. Middleton recalled:

> As there was no trial by video in those days, Glenn was given the job of taking out Wayne Closter at the opening bounce. He did this to perfection and Wayne was useless for the first three quarters. At three-quarter time the scores were level. Wayne finally came good and kicked five goals in the last quarter, to bring 2AOD home.

Wayne Closter remembered the match:

> We met the Nui Dat engineers in the grand final. I'd kicked 12 in the semi, so the word was out: 'Get Closter'. Early on, my eye ran into Glenn James' elbow. Years later, Glenn, then a top VFL umpire and a good mate, said he was sorry – sorry that I'd got up! I kicked 11 and we won.

The games played at Vung Tau caught the attention of Lance Corporal Ian Granland, 104th Signals Squadron. When he arrived at Nui Dat in 1969, organised sport was almost non-existent – 'apart from the occasional dart tournament at the boozer'. Granland, a Nasho, had been an Australian Rules player in Sydney and was keen to promote the game in his new role. He set about organising a match against 106th Field Workshops at Nui Dat.

Granland located a ground within the wider task force area that could be made suitable with some work. His unit possessed an old Massey Ferguson tractor, with which they were able to slash the 1.2-metre-high grass to prepare the field the day before the game – rifles at the ready. Granland umpired, recalling:

> The players turned up in their Land Rovers and trucks, even an armoured personnel carrier. But there were ample players of all ages, size and shape, all primed for a game, and there were some bloody good footballers among them too. It was my first go at blowing the whistle and I loved sticking up the sergeants and junior NCOs on the field, penalising them 10 yards when they got a bit cheeky.
> I copped a bit of abuse from the opposition and maybe a bit from my side as well. It was in the days of the one central umpire. The out of bounds on the full rule had only recently been introduced and of course I applied it.

The match finished with 104th Signals Squadron winning. 'There was no function, after the match,' Granland remembered, 'no speeches or best player awards; there was three cheers from either side for the opposition then just back to the units. But it was a good relief, something a bit different because obviously, most who played loved the game.'

Australian Rules players were not alone in their love of their game. Unit rugby union teams also played competition games, including at the provincial capital of Ba Ria. One Australian reporter wrote that the standard was remarkably high, 'considering such problems as 100-degree heat, tropical rain, the lack of goalposts and the tendency of local youngsters to steal the ball'.

Among the Australians were some accomplished players, including Major Malcolm van Gelder, an engineer and a Wallaby breakaway. He had a long rugby representative career behind him, not the least of it in the army, beginning with his years at Duntroon in the 1950s, when he was selected in the college's First XV, and winning the Australian Capital Territory rugby premiership in 1955.

Selected for representative matches in Canberra, van Gelder played alongside Major Ian Mackay, who also went on to serve in Vietnam. Another teammate was Kevin Newman, who rose to the rank of colonel and also served in Vietnam before entering federal politics. Like van Gelder, Mackay had been in the frame for inclusion in the Wallaby team for the long world tour of 1957–58. Despite the disappointment of missing out, Mackay had no doubt about the importance of sport to the military. With no military operations to head off to after he graduated from Duntroon in 1955, he later opined: 'No problems in motivation, whatsoever. Once you get heavily involved with sport …'

Van Gelder was posted to Vung Tau in 1968–69, where he commanded the 17th Construction Squadron and played inter-unit rugby regularly on local soccer fields. 'We had no shortage of rugby players, and we played almost continuously throughout the year against other army units. I considered it good for the troops as a morale boosting and good exercise diversion from the sappers' normal work.'

Whatever the code, playing football in Vietnam often came with hazards. When RAAF Vung Tau Rugby Union Club played No. 2 Squadron RAAF at Phan Rang at a soccer field in a village near the airbase, concern for security was such that engineers swept the pitch with mine detectors to ensure that the Viet Cong had not planted booby traps. Moreover, throughout the match RAAF airfield defence guards armed with automatic weapons patrolled the perimeter to protect the teams from possible attack.

Similarly, Leading Aircraftman Geoff Irvin, who had just turned twenty when he went to Vietnam, recalled a rugby union match with an RAAF team playing an army side on a field just outside the Vung Tau base. Minutes before the game began, all the players were told to line up and link arms.

> And then we had to walk the length of the field with our toes, bare feet, toes, sifting in through the soil to see if we could find anything that was dangerous, whether the enemy had put some bloody mines there or whether it was sharp or glass objects. We had to sift our way up the field and then down the field several times to make sure that we were free of anything.

With the air force leading, an army player lashed out at one of the RAAF players, knocking him out cold.

> The referee, who was an army captain, he blew the whistle, and he called the guy over and he said, 'You are off.' Sent him off. And the bloke argued with him and he said, 'You're off.' And the bloke turned around and smacked him right in the mouth, one of those one punch jobs and flattened him. And then we were all in onto this one bloke and we carted him off in pieces. I think the army were just as upset as we were, but they were one man short and we went on to win the game.

After that moment of madness, body collisions and hard tackles seemed like an anticlimax to Irvin.

If a bit of 'biffo' brought the familiarity of home to a football field in Vietnam, there was also the chance to bet on horse races in Australia through the inevitable presence of SP bookies at Nui Dat. Ian Granland witnessed the operations of the SPs, one a staff sergeant and the other a lance corporal. He recalled that troops were able to hear the Saturday races live from Sydney via Radio Australia and rebroadcast through Australian Forces Radio. The unit's bookies had a crony in a signals unit in Watsonia, Victoria, who sent through a telex message on Thursdays with a complete list of acceptances for the following Saturday for the Sydney, Melbourne and Brisbane races. A clerk in the orderly room then typed out and printed hundreds of copies listing the horses in each race, along with their form. The guide was then circulated around the base, which at times was home to 5000 troops.

Granland remembered that both bookies had jobs where they could 'disappear' on Saturday afternoons to their tents, where both had phones connected so they could take bets.

> Soldiers from other units, both in the field and inside Nui Dat, would ring their bets through which were listed by the bookies. The dispatch riders would take the winnings to the various units the following Monday and/or collect the bets from those who lost. It was a lucrative but dangerous business.

However, many betters absconded back to Australia when their time was up, sometimes owing thousands to the bookies. And, of course, everyone had to be paid: 'the bloke at Watsonia, the receiver of the telex in the Coms Centre building, the clerk who typed out the sheets and of course the dispatch riders. But the bookies certainly made a quid.'

Just like at any corner pub back home on a Saturday afternoon.

32

THE PARADOX

The pilot's voice crackled through the intercom as the passenger jet began a steep descent into Saigon airport. Apologetically, he explained that he had chosen to come in high and drop into the airfield, because Viet Cong were known to hide in the surrounding paddy fields from where they could take pot shots at incoming aircraft. As eighteen young Australian soccer players looked out the jet's window, they saw huge bomb craters alongside the runway and the airfield buzzing with military aircraft. Such was the unsettling scene that greeted the Australian national soccer squad in November 1967. 'We didn't think we were going into a war zone until we landed in Saigon. We thought it was just a tour of Asia,' Australian midfielder Ray Richards said later.

Football and the Australian military took various forms in Vietnam, but perhaps the most unexpected was the role the army played when the original Socceroos flew in for the South Vietnam Quoc Khan Cup, or Friendly Nations Tournament, in Saigon. There to greet the team as they collected their bags was Private Doug Brian, a signaller. Importantly, he was a childhood mate of the Australian goalkeeper, Ron Corry. When Brian read that Corry was coming to Vietnam he arranged to be at the airport, figuring it would ease the team's entry into a city in the grip of war.

The arrival of the young Australian team, with an average of age of twenty-two, stemmed from a visit to Australia in January 1967 by South Vietnam's Prime Minister, Air Vice Marshal Ky. He extended a surprise invitation to Australia along with New Zealand, to participate in the tournament. Besides Australia, New Zealand and Vietnam, another five countries – Singapore, Indonesia, Thailand, South Korea and Malaysia – were invited and agreed to take part.

Even at the time it reeked of propaganda, a South Vietnamese effort to stop already lukewarm international support for the war from collapsing further. The Australian government, despite its military involvement, was wary about the prospect of civilians going into a war zone. It was several months before the Department of External Affairs extended cautious support for the tour going ahead – 'subject to the security situation'.

To Corry, arriving in Saigon was a big adventure. 'We were going to somewhere where we probably shouldn't have been going, but we were assured that everything would be okay, that it was safe and that the war hadn't really hit Saigon. But it wasn't very far away.'

The reality of Saigon was very different from anything the young Australians had imagined. They were immediately confronted by the trappings of war – the might of the American military presence on show, the rumbling of helicopters and the sound of mortars in the distance. To add to their sense of unease, the bus transporting the players to the hotel housing them and the other seven teams was first checked for mines. Vietnamese security police – known as the 'white mice' – accompanied their transport the entire visit. 'We were worried,' Corry recalled.

For the Socceroos, the presence of Australian soldiers was crucial to dealing with events as they unfolded. The hotel was filthy and run-down, the food rancid and the water undrinkable. Striker Ray Baartz recalled that, initially, a few of the army boys organised to supply the team with some steak and milk – 'which was honestly a life saver'. Through Doug Brian, the team was invited to the mess at the Australian headquarters in Saigon. Corry said: 'Dougie looked after us. He would take us down there every second or third night and we could have a couple of beers and a hamburger and watch a movie and things like that. Everyone was hanging out to go to the mess.' While the mess was regarded as safe zone, a visit there was nonetheless accompanied by a cautionary warning, according to Corry. 'If you hear a gunshot, don't worry about it. If you'll hear two gunshots, it's still okay, but if you'll hear three hit the floor because there could be trouble.'

Outside the team hotel, the Australians became aware that the nearby Presidential Palace was being incessantly shelled and cars being blown up within earshot. Getting some sleep amid the sounds of gunfire and explosions that filled the Saigon night was not easy. 'At night we used to be able to sit up on the roof and watch the tracer bullet flares go up and fly across the sky and you would hear the big guns,' Corry recalled.

Friendships were forged and the Australian soldiers became regular and enthusiastic spectators at each of the team's games. Fullback Stan Ackerley recalled:

> These were hardened young soldiers – and I mean young soldiers – they had seen more than we could ever dream of in a lifetime. But they made us very welcome. They took care of us. They said they didn't know much about it [soccer] in them days – they were mainly rugby league supporters – but we invited them to come to the games, and they did.

Training for the tournament was different. Mornings, the players would head off under police escort to train while the soldiers marched off to duty. The team's captain, soccer legend Johnny Warren, caught the paradox. 'While they went out to fight, we went out to play football. It was a surreal experience.' The training ground the Australians were allocated was mostly a quagmire. More unsettling was the order that when a ball was inadvertently kicked over the 2-metre-high fence, there would be no retrieval due to the hidden presence of landmines in the surrounding fields. At one point, the players even trained on the concrete roof of the team hotel.

When the tournament began, Baartz recalled that outside the stadium there were 'soldiers going around with mine detectors under cars and the bus making sure there weren't any nasties hanging around'. Machine-gun-carrying South Vietnamese soldiers also patrolled the perimeter. The tournament began well for the Australians with a 5–3 win against New Zealand.

However, it was in the third match against the hosts, South Vietnam, that Baartz remembered that 'all hell broke loose' in the packed stadium when riot police were called and tear gas used to quell a melee that broke out among the partisan 30,000 Vietnamese spectators. In the first half, Johnny Warren kicked a goal. At half-time Air Vice Marshall Ky went to the home side's dressing room, offering the players six months' wages to turn the game around. Australia hung on, winning 1–0. 'After the game we were in our dressing room and they started throwing rocks,' Baartz said.

Despite the tension of constant danger, Australia did well, winning all their preliminary games and reaching the final on 14 November to face the heavily favoured South Korean team. 'Everyone was very excited because this was the first time Australia had made a final anywhere – especially overseas in the situation we were in,' Corry said.

Against the backdrop of flares in the night sky and the sound of mortars in the near distance, Australian soldiers turned up to the stadium to support their team. But the stadium was sold out, leaving no seats for the diggers. On hearing this, the Australian team management issued an ultimatum: they would refuse to play unless their military mates were allowed in. Facing a crisis, the organisers quickly found extra seats, giving the soldiers a bird's eye view of the match. Their cheers rang out to support the Australians as they ran out in the heat and humidity onto a pitch heavy with mud and a night laden with tension from a war that was going badly.

What caught the Australians by surprise was the support of the South Vietnamese spectators, who because of old enmities, were hostile to the South Koreans. The crowd – variously estimated at anywhere from 35,000 to 65,000 – loudly barracked for the Australians. The dislike ran so deep that before the final, a bomb had been found on the South Koreans' floor of the hotel.

From the whistle, the energy-sapping conditions were a challenge. As Baartz explained, 'When you're playing in that heat and humidity, and the ground's such heavy going, and you haven't had a great diet, it obviously takes its toll on you. It was a good game, a hard game.' In goal, Corry could see that the South Koreans were 'very, very sharp and very, very quick. But once again, we had some great players in our side, and we'd been playing well and gelling well.' The Australians dug deep, calling up their team spirit to win the championship final 3–2, making it the first international trophy for Australian soccer. Overjoyed, the Australians sang, laughed and joked as they shared the moment with their military mates at the stadium, and later at the mess. 'I can remember at the end it was really a terrific celebration. Everybody was ecstatic about winning the tournament,' Corry said.

The series over, the team flew to Vung Tau to play a post-celebration match against Australian troops. Flying in an RAAF Caribou, the Australians were told to ignore bullet holes in the aircraft. 'The Caribous had open doors at the back, and we flew across the sea about six to eight feet above the water,' Corry remembered. 'We had a game against the Australian troops, and the worst part of it was that we got a penalty, and I went up and took it. They still haven't found the ball to this day, and no one was going to go in and get it,' he explained about deliberately missing the chance to score a winning goal. The friendly over, the Australians – Socceroos and diggers – relaxed over a few drinks. 'It was an unbelievable day, they had a barbecue for us. It lifted their spirits.'

A few weeks after the Australians' Saigon victory, a soccer competition was organised at Vung Tau, with seven teams competing in a knockout series. No doubt inspired by the Socceroos' win, an RAAF team defeated teams from No. 2 Composite Ordnance Depot, No. 110 Signals Squadron, and in the final beat No. 5 Company Services Corps 2–1. The Australians also played against Vietnamese teams, one such match occurring on 17 June 1971 when a combined 1st Australian Logistic Support Group side played a local provincial side, the game ending in a 1-all draw.

The '67 Socceroos never forgot the contribution of Signaller Doug Brian, making him an honorary squad member, and including him in a future fiftieth anniversary reunion. As Corry explained: 'I was the only one that Dougie knew before we all got over there. And when he met us at the airport, he got to know everyone. Doug was very important because he organised so much for us. I didn't ask him to organise. He was the one that did it all.'

While winning an international trophy went largely uncelebrated in the broader Australian community, the experience of victory in adversity forged a new sense of camaraderie among the team members. Eight of the players, captained by Johnny Warren, became the nucleus of the Socceroos who in 1974 qualified for the World Cup for the first time. Corry and his teammates had no doubt that the 1967 tournament in Saigon was the crucible which forged the spirit of the Socceroos. 'The birth of the Socceroos name happened in '67.'

To Warren, who died in 2004, the tour stood apart as a footballing triumph and national milestone. He thought it unfair that the team — unlike entertainers who performed there — were denied the Vietnam Logistic and Support Medal for representing Australia in Vietnam. He believed the team should march in Anzac Day parades because of the role they played in the war.

> Even the entertainers that toured Vietnam were in a controlled situation at the Australian bases, while we were right in the middle of the action. Here we were, a bunch of young kids, who were expected to play soccer while a major war raged around us. I don't think the team has ever received the recognition it deserved for its war efforts.

The government would later argue that only individuals who were under government or military jurisdiction during their time in Vietnam were eligible for official recognition. At least the players got to keep their tracksuits.

33

THEY DON'T UNTEACH YOU

At 195 centimetres, Tony Dell was a shade taller than Jack Massie and, like Big Jack, was a lethal left-arm fast bowler. His in-swinging thunderbolts made him an awkward proposition for opponents among Brisbane first-grade cricketers. In the 1960s, cricket stars Peter Burge, Wally Grout, Ken Mackay and Tom Veivers knew he was a future leader of the Test attack with the potential to be Australia's next Alan Davidson. But just as the path to state selection was opening up, Dell had to put his burgeoning cricket career on hold. War called.

Born on 6 August 1945 – the day the Americans dropped the first atomic bomb on Hiroshima – Dell had just turned twenty when the second ballot for National Service was held in September 1965. Of the numbered marbles placed in a barrel, one bearing his birth date was among those drawn. He accepted the quirk of fate with alacrity and went off to basic army training at the Singleton army base. After six months recruit and corps training, he was posted back to Brisbane and 2 RAR. The training hardened his physical fitness. 'I loved it,' he recalled. The move to Brisbane was fortuitous, allowing him to resume weekend first-grade cricket.

Tony Dell. Courtesy Tony Dell.

Doug Walters, just a few months younger than Dell, and already a Test star, was also conscripted, in 1966–67. Stationed at Holsworthy army base, outside Sydney, Walters was briefly batman to a future deputy prime minister, Second Lieutenant Tim Fischer, also a conscript. It was Walters' job being to bring the junior officer an early-morning cup of tea at six o'clock. Fischer cancelled the arrangement after three days. 'As a simple farmer I could not agree to a Test cricketer bringing me my tea each day.' Soon after he was conscripted, Walters was exempted from Vietnam service in order to pursue his professional career in cricket, to which he returned in 1968. His nickname among his teammates was 'Hanoi' – 'He got bombed every night,' says Dell with a laugh.

Dell's path was different. His posting to 2 RAR at Enoggera, Brisbane, enabled him to play weekend club cricket. In preparation for Vietnam, jungle training followed at Canungra, but while on exercise Dell fell from a cliff edge, sustaining a leg fracture. The injury meant that he did not complete the course and, with 2 RAR about to be posted to Vietnam, as a national serviceman he had the option of not going with them. Psychologically, he had prepared himself for the army: the first year to train to be a soldier, and the next year to go to Vietnam. There was no hesitation in his decision.

> What was I going to do? Sit back in Australia and just do parades and possibly bloody peel spuds. I mean, you'd done all that training, why would you waste it? You were 21, you were bloody physically fit. You were with a whole raft of mates, because I mean, the camaraderie within the military is second to none. I was young, I was full of testosterone, and this was boys' own stuff, every boy's dream, but you know, you're going off to be a soldier and fighting the war.

So, in 1967, Dell went with his unit to Vietnam where he spent the best part of a year. Initially, as he 'gradually got into the groove and became very much part of the whole battalion and task force strategy', he enjoyed the experience, arduous though it was at times: 'Spending lots of time in the jungle, in the paddy fields and water and foliage and checking your body and your nuts every night to make sure that there weren't too many leeches attached and burning them off with the lighted end of cigarettes. It was just surreal when I think back.'

There were crises on search and destroy operations where Dell and his mates faced imminent death, where terror engulfed them and they fought for self-control to ward off panic. Another time, on operations, his patrol became lost as dusk approached and he quickly realised that 'boys' own stuff' could turn deadly serious. His patrol was thrust into a life-or-death near confrontation with more than 100 Viet Cong troops. Trapped overnight with bullets whizzing overhead, the whispers went out to shut up and keep down.

> I had the radio, and I turned it off so that the squelch wasn't audible, and we just sat there and really crapped ourselves. We didn't know where to fire, and we would've been cannon fodder. And then come daylight, we called in the gunships and artillery and just cleared the whole perimeter, and we were able to get out.

A memory from that encounter was vividly imprinted on Dell's mind: the sight of VC bodies with heads blown off. 'But you've got a job to do. You just compartmentalise the crap and move on because you can't shirk or nick off or go and have a rest or sit down. That one incident resonated with me.'

It was like a bizarre dream that Tony Dell found himself in. Tim Fischer recalled similar challenges as he tried to deal with 'the cacophony of experience' that was Vietnam, and which so often left him chilled to the core. Just like Dell, he tried to store such memories away 'in a box in his head'. In their downtime away from operations, there was often limited time for sport, a chance to regain the composure and ordinariness of life.

Lieutenant Adrian d'Hagé, who served in Vietnam as a platoon commander in 6th Battalion, recalled that organised sport was not a major feature for infantry battalions. 'This was principally because we spent most of the time out on patrols and operations. On average, we would return to Nui Dat for two days every month, which was spent on short R&R in Vung Tau before launching back into the jungle.'

When South Australian Aussie Rules legend Private Graham Cornes served in Vietnam with 7 RAR as a Nasho in 1970, he took with him a football that the Glenelg club had given him as a farewell gift, but he had little chance to use it.

> I was in an infantry battalion; we were out in the scrub and just didn't have time to play footy. We were either on operation or back in camp or had a couple of days leave, but we just never got a chance to. Our lines were in the rubber plantation, so we could kick between the rubber trees, just a bit of the end-to-end stuff.

At fire support bases he grabbed opportunities to rig up a net and play volleyball. 'But then when I got transferred out to an infantry platoon, there was nothing. You couldn't possibly, it's full-on operational.' Cornes admits to being rankled when he heard there was a footy competition in Nui Dat.

Fischer sought relaxation with games of volleyball, but Dell has little memory of sport in Vietnam. The battalion's official history reveals improvised games of cricket took place between the lines of tents at Nui Dat. Years later, looking at an action photo of a group of his mates, stripped to the waist, with a plank for a bat and boxes for the stumps, Dell was perplexed.

Vietnamese villagers watch as Private Frank Baker, 5th Battalion AIF, hits out.
AWM COL/67/0151/VN.

It seems we did play cricket. I run into blokes now and then saying, you bowled me a bouncer in the lines at Nui Dat. It was probably a tennis ball, but what it seems to have done is to stay in their memories, lifted their morale. Something like that takes you away to another world for maybe an hour.

Dell returned home from Vietnam physically fitter than he had ever been. 'But unknown to me not quite right mentally. I saw things in Vietnam that the human brain is not meant to experience.' In the space of a few weeks, he went from a 'botched-up night ambush' outside Nui Dat to being demobbed at Enoggera Barracks in Brisbane and then back to his civilian job. 'They teach you to kill, but they don't unteach you.' A profound statement that typified the experience of Dell and others suffering from the effects of war. Post-traumatic stress disorder (PTSD) can emerge without warning.

He settled back into a life in Brisbane revolving around cricket, rugby and his job with an advertising agency, describing himself as a workaholic. He would later understand that this was 'the brain's way of masking the garbage that's in there'. In the summer of 1968–69, intent on success in cricket, he was soon among the leading wicket takers in the Brisbane competition. So committed to cricket was he that he would later say that if it hadn't been for the game, he might well have stayed in the army and gone on to officer training. 'I loved the army, I loved just getting fit and completing the tasks that we had to complete. But cricket was top of my mind, and that's all I wanted to get back to again.'

Dell loved the camaraderie of team sport, preferring the environment that surrounded it to individual sport. The dressing-room banter was infectious, and success soon followed when he was picked in the Queensland Sheffield Shield side in 1970.

Elevation to Shield cricket suited him. 'It was the big stage with the added adrenaline, and the harder wickets with more bounce made up for the better batsmen. And a six-foot-five left-hander with a late inswinger will stuff up anyone.' He was soon bowling to elite batsmen, among them Ian and Greg Chappell, Barry Richards, Ian Redpath, Keith Stackpole and Doug Walters. He had a fearsome bouncer that troubled anyone who faced him. Bowling at a similar pace to current Australian left-arm opening bowler Mitchell Starc, Dell was a handful for the world's best.

Test selectors took note, and with Australia struggling in the 1970–71 Ashes series against England, Dell was selected for the final Test at the Sydney Cricket Ground, playing under new captain Ian Chappell. In a match that Australia lost by 62 runs, Dell was the most successful fast bowler on either side, bagging five wickets to Dennis Lillee's three, Bob Willis's and Peter Lever's four, and John Snow's two. Ian Chappell told him afterwards that he had out-bowled Lillee in the match. Years later, when he reflected on his time in the army, he reckoned that 'twelve months in Vietnam was very good training to be in Ian Chappell's dressing room'. Chappell, of course, had the same larrikin streak as his grandfather, Vic Richardson, with a similar attitude to English cricketers.

Despite his impressive performance in the Test against England, it would be two years before Dell was selected to represent Australia again, this time against New Zealand on a flat MCG wicket that gave fast bowlers no help. Although Australia won by an innings and 25 runs, he took just one wicket and was made twelfth man for the next Test at the SCG. Dell was hit hard. 'I caught a cab to the airport with Australian selector Sam Loxton, and we chatted all the way and I told him that I didn't want to play anymore. I had no idea why I said it but he accepted it.'

Loxton wished him good luck. When Dell told Greg Chappell, who by then was his Queensland captain, Chappell told him: '"Bullshit. I've just convinced Jeff Thomson to play for us and you have to open the bowling with him next season." That was an offer I couldn't refuse so I played one more season and then gave it away.' While Queensland finished second in the Sheffield Shield that season, the competition was a triumph for Dell (twenty-nine wickets) and Thomson (twenty-seven wickets), with left-arm seamer and future international Geoff Dymock leading the way with thirty-eight wickets. Despite the foundations for future Sheffield Shield success having been laid, Dell walked away from first-class cricket.

The 1980s marked the beginning of a downward spiral for Dell. First, he was fired from the job he had given up cricket for, then lost his own advertising business in the 1990 recession, which was followed by the break-up of his marriage. 'I lost everything and eventually lost my family too. I'm not sure how I survived.' He had become isolated and alone, ignoring annual

Anzac Day parades and refusing invitations to reunions. Many veterans had returned to Vietnam in the hope that by revisiting old haunts they could heal the wounds that lingered.

Like Dell, Graham Cornes was shocked by the sudden transition from Vietnam back to Australia.

> We were in Nui Dat on Thursday morning, flew to Saigon, caught a charter flight from Saigon to Sydney. Got in late, went to Kings Cross, missed my first flight out on the Friday morning, got back into Adelaide and I played for Glenelg the next day, Saturday, in the reserves. We just had no preparation for coming back.

Cornes believes the discipline and infrastructure around the club at the time 'probably saved my life'.

He initially believed that when he returned from Vietnam, he did so without the trauma that so many others had endured. But the impact of the 'tough, dirty, tiring work' on patrol lingered. There were flashbacks of horrific moments, and violent dreams. 'Those hands, that head, the jammed M60 machine-gun. They say war is heroic and romantic. It's not. It's ninety-five per cent boredom and routine with five per cent terror, exhilaration and grief thrown in.'

He masked the demons enough for a successful playing career to follow, before a career as a media personality. One Anzac Day in Adelaide, one of his old 7th Battalion mates saw him in the crowd and dragged him into the march. 'At the end of the march, my mate came up again and said: "I listen to you on the radio, and you need to see someone because you're suffering." He was as blunt and as bold as that.' The comment hit home. Cornes had never been able to admit that he needed to seek psychological help. When he did, twenty or more years after his time in Vietnam, he was diagnosed with PTSD.

Lieutenant John Stevenson instructs Hue, a young Vietnamese orphan boy, in batting. AWM THU/67/1167/VN.

Aussie men, particularly, see it as sign of weakness. In fact, it's the opposite. It takes a certain strength to admit there is a problem and to seek help for it. We can see the physical wounds but it's so easy to disguise the psychological ones for fear of being stigmatised. However, there should be no stigma attached to mental illness, be it depression, post-trauma stress or anxiety.

Cornes regards himself as 'one of the lucky ones'. Belatedly, Tony Dell's luck began to change too. In 2007, a retired colonel, aware that he was the only Test cricketer to have served in combat in Vietnam, approached him to be guest of honour at the inaugural International Defence Cricket Challenge to be held in Canberra in November that year. Teams from the Australian army, navy and air force were to compete against defence force teams from New Zealand and Britain, and Dell was given a standing ovation.

Dell's involvement in the series led him to reluctantly visit the veterans' drop-in centre at Cotton Tree on the Sunshine Coast. He stayed longer than he expected, other veterans wanting to talk to him about cricket and Vietnam. After a while, one veteran said to Dell: 'You've got PTSD.' He was flabbergasted. 'Bullshit,' he said.

That moment was the first time that Tony Dell became aware of the existence of the condition. Although initially dismissive, he listened again to what the volunteers were saying, gradually accepting that if they had been through the war themselves and been diagnosed with PTSD then they spoke from experience. Importantly, he came to understand that they had learned to live with it. The reason for the years of darkness began to make sense: he had suffered for all that time from PTSD.

A psychiatrist confirmed the Cotton Tree veteran's opinion, entitling Dell to free medical treatment and care. Dell says: 'I had lost the will. I had always been a fighter, but I had lost the fight.' The fog began to lift, and he turned his focus to helping fellow Vietnam veterans suffering from depression and mental health problems. Out of this new understanding he established a charity, Stand Tall 4 PTS, to aid awareness and raise funds to assist sufferers. Despite a brief interlude of cricket at the highest level early on, for Tony Dell it was the effects of Vietnam that became a life-long journey.

For his friend Doug Walters, time in the army had different consequences. In 1969, while touring India with the Australian side, he was targeted by the Communist Party of India after rumours spread that he had served in the Australian army during the Vietnam War and had killed women and children. Years later, while speaking to the *Hindustan Times*, Walters recalled, 'There were about 20,000 Communist protesters outside the team hotel. They had been wrongly informed that I had served in Vietnam. I didn't take it too seriously. They were just protesters. Some windows of the hotel were smashed by a few angry ones.'

Walters does not believe his time in the army affected his cricketing career. 'Not really, as I had my best ever series soon after I came back, against the West Indies in 1968.' In that 1968/69 series, Walters plundered 699 runs from four Tests, becoming the first player in history to score a century and a double-century in one Test.

In 2015, he and Dell were part of a panel at the Queensland Cricketers Club for a Gabba Legends lunch to raise money to fight depression. With Test greats Ian Chappell, Jeff Thomson and Len Pascoe also present, Dell was lauded as the only Vietnam veteran to play Test cricket – indeed, the only living Australian to have fought in a war and played Test cricket since the death of former Australian opening batsmen Arthur Morris a few weeks earlier.

Thirty-five years after he quit Test cricket at the end of 1973, Dell was in a PTSD research program and asked a psychologist why he quit cricket when he did.

> She explained that right from the start of recruit training, the army drills into you that the section or platoon is only as strong as its weakest member. She then said that in your PTSD-befuddled mind, you thought that you were the weakest member at work because you were always off playing cricket.

Tony Dell finally got his answer.

34

EVEN A WARPED BAT WILL DO

In 2001, former Test captain Steve Waugh recognised the link between cricket and military history when he led the Australian cricket team to Gallipoli on the way to England to do battle for the Ashes. In his autobiography, Waugh reflected on the importance of Gallipoli:

> True bonding experiences stand the test of time and become part of you and, most certainly, visiting Gallipoli together on our way to England for the 2001 Ashes tour had a profound effect on most of the squad. In the limited-overs tournament, we put to good use the increased unity we had gained from Gallipoli, and dominated our matches. We elevated the aggressiveness in our play and tried to consume our opposition as quickly and ruthlessly as possible.

Waugh's book was released in 2005, coinciding with that year's Ashes series and a tour by an Australian Combined Services team to mark the sixtieth anniversary of the 1945 Australian Services side that played the five Victory Tests against an England XI. A surviving member of that side, Stan Sismey, farewelled the eighteen-man squad, with the deeds of Keith Miller and Lindsay Hassett and the courage of Graham Williams a guiding light for the young team.

And in the Middle East that same year, the cricketing flame of old was reignited in the form of the 'Desert Ashes', reviving memories of Tibby Cotter in World War I, and the 'Test' at Tobruk in World War II, as well as the 'Test' played at Batufa in northern Iraq in June 1991 between Australia and England. The teams were drawn from members of a multinational operation to provide humanitarian aid to Kurdish refugees fleeing Iraqi forces in the wake of the Gulf War, with Australia winning. Twelve years later, in March 2003, Australia had joined a US-led 'coalition of the willing' to locate and destroy suspected weapons of mass destruction in Iraq, with all three branches of the Australian Defence Force (ADF) serving during a deployment that generated massive protests across the nation.

The first game of the five one-day matches was held at Camp Smitty in southern Iraq in July 2005. Although some Australian commandos at the base were known to be uneasy about the focus on the series, contending that it interfered with planning for military operations, the series was no scratch affair: Cricket Australia and the England and Wales Cricket Board flew in equipment, and a matting-covered concrete wicket was laid inside the protective walls of the compound at Al Muthanna.

The Australian side for the match was drawn from members of the Al Muthanna Task Group, which formed Australia's main ground force contribution to the multinational force during the Iraq War. Prime Minister John Howard – a self-confessed 'cricket tragic' – sent a letter of support to the team before the Australians strode onto the dusty, grassless field wearing green and gold uniforms identical to those worn by the Australian cricket team for international one-day matches. The toss of the coin was synchronised with the toss at Lord's in London for the first Test between Ricky Ponting's Australians and Michael Vaughan's England side.

Under the leadership of Captain David Carew, the Australians won the toss and chose to bat in the 50-degree-plus heat. 'This will be the hottest game of cricket in the world,' he commented with some understatement. The Australians immediately took to the British bowling, with 12 runs coming from the first over. Revelling in the conditions, Major Steve Mott hammered the British bowling and top-scored with 103 runs in the Australian total of 221. In reply, the British were all out for just 102 runs, with Australia's Captain Nathan Schurmann taking 4–17.

At Lord's, the Australians also won, defeating England by 239 runs. But while the Australian army went on to win the Iraq series and the replica Ashes urn 4–1, the Australians in England lost the Ashes 2–1. Army's crushing victory in the desert restored some measure of national pride. And as Ponting's men struggled,

Sergeant William Ross and Trooper Robert Lavendar, raise the 'Desert Ashes' in 2005. Courtesy Australian Department of Defence.

the Australian Combined Services team added further to the army's success, playing ten games, winning six, losing three and drawing two.

A few months later, intelligence officer Major Sarah Watson was deployed to Iraq, underscoring the increasingly important role of women in the ADF. Stationed at Ali Air Base in southern Iraq for seven months, she recalled that the battle group organised army cricket games or touch footy games with the Iraqi military. 'We were there to mentor and train as well.'

Watson soon found herself questioning Australia's involvement in the war, given the failure to find the alleged weapons of mass destruction that was the Howard government's justification for the original deployment of Australian troops. 'It became clear we were there for political reasons – alliance with the US – as opposed to any real interest in Australia's national security. It was also clear that the local population did not want the troops there,' she would later submit to an inquiry.

Nevertheless, Watson threw herself into her job of providing top-secret intelligence feeds to the battle group in 2006–07. The aim was to provide the best early warning and help the teams avoid ambush. Working sixteen-hour days, seven days a week, began to take its toll. She kept her growing anxiety to herself. 'That was the way we were raised in the military, to crack on, don't show weakness, don't be the weak link in the team.' Sport and physical fitness provided an outlet for Watson, who had been awarded the fitness excellence prize at Duntroon.

> If there was a scratch match, I played touch footy. Doing sport and fitness in Iraq was critical for me to keep myself on an even keel given the high stakes and the stress that I was experiencing over there. I would always try and get involved as that just helps so much in bringing down the stress levels and bringing up the endorphins, which is critical in good mental health.

A unique opportunity emerged: the Iraq edition of the Boston Marathon. Although having never run a marathon, Watson decided to compete in a race that coincided with the running of the famous American race. The 42.2-kilometre route took the runners past the Ziggurat of Ur, a 4000-year-old monument within the base's 30 square kilometres. 'We started at four in the morning and did four laps of the course that went out around the Ziggurat of Ur, which was surreal, running around the house of Abraham.' Watson finished second among the women runners, completing the course in 3 hours 54 minutes. Pleased though she was, there had been an unforeseen challenge. 'A dust storm hit at about 30 kilometres in. I was already struggling to breathe but having to suck down dust and grit in your eyes and barely able to see ten metres in front was quite character building.'

Australians were also based in one of Saddam Hussein's lesser palaces within the huge and heavily fortified American base at Baghdad, Camp Victory, where they had to be inventive with sport and physical fitness requirements. (Recruits to the armed services must reach a fitness standard to enlist and are subject to compulsory retesting every six months.) With security at a premium, the Australians resorted en masse to the relative safety of the gym. They also made use of the protective high stone walls, running and walking inside the perimeter – often as rocket-propelled grenades (RPGs) flew overhead. At the end of the week there would be informal, well-attended races. Commander Jill Buckfield, who was attached to the Australian headquarters, recalled:

> We carried weapons all the time; it just became normal. Even with sport, we had F88 Steyrs slung to our backs with a magazine strapped to the weapon. The security threat was so great that playing sport wasn't something you did lightly. From a safety point of view, we had to go in pairs if we were running and walking. So, team

building sport was not a thing we could do. Outside was dangerous, and even within the base.

There was one novel approach to sport in the compound, which featured a large lake with a tiny island in the middle – a tempting 150-metre drive with a fairway wood. The challenge for the ADF's golfers was to drive a ball over the water onto the island. More balls landed in the lake than on the target, much to the bemusement of onlookers.

While the Australian presence in Iraq was more recent, the ADF's post-World War II presence in the region began 1982, when peacekeepers first joined the Multinational Force & Observers, overseen by the United States, to supervise the 1979 Israel–Egypt peace treaty. Withdrawn in 1986 before being recommitted in 1993, the Australia's peacekeeping presence has seen joint detachments from the RAN, Australian army and RAAF. Continuing to the present day, around 1300 Australians have served as peacekeepers in Egypt, their primary role having been to support the Fijian and Colombian battalions on the Sinai Peninsula. One army veteran, who did not want to be named, recalled playing rugby with the Fijians.

> While our Australian contingent tended to attend structured physical training courtesy of a PTI, the huge Fijian lads, who were all built like props, could be found each morning at sunrise and sunset playing rugby – sometimes touch, often full tackle – in a totally unregulated fashion. There was no marked field, there were no lines, no forward passes, no free kicks – the gist of the enterprise appeared to be to see how creative one could be with passing the ball, goose-stepping and keeping the pill alive – movement was life. One's best efforts at creativity were rewarded with whooping and clapping and laughing, which could be heard the length of the base.

I can remember running in the total dark, and above my breath hearing the strains of a full-throated 60-strong Fijian choral effort during their worship, made even more poignant by the fellow standing atop the guard tower looking out over the Red Sea singing along by himself, rolling a rugby ball back and forth beneath his feet.

The serenity of such a scene contrasted with the Australian presence in Afghanistan, where Australia deployed special forces units, including the Special Air Service (SAS) Regiment, to participate in counterterrorism operations following Al-Qaeda's 2001 terrorist attacks in the United States. They would remain there until 2021. The commitment, which was part of the International Security Assistance Force, included combat and combat support operations, as well as reconstruction and training. Amid patrols, there was time for cricket, and scratch games not only helped troops relax by defusing tension but also helped build alliances with locals. Often, spontaneous hits with bat and ball in a military base, village lane or rock-strewn field would bring curious locals into the game to field, bowl or bat.

At Asadabad, capital of the north-eastern Afghan province of Kunar and near the border with Pakistan's Federally Administered Tribal Areas, an Australian SAS unit spent a few days at Camp Wright. As the Taliban routinely targeted the compound with RPGs, the SAS returned fire into the surrounding cornfields. They also wove cricket into their response – but they needed a bat. They asked their interpreter, 'John' – a universal moniker for locals – if there was any chance he could get them one. John said he could, and the Australians scraped together US$100.

One SAS veteran who was present at the time recalled that John was gone for three days after crossing into the dangerous Pakistani tribal areas. 'We thought he would just duck up the street to get it. After thinking we had done our money, he returned with a carpet rolled up on the back of his bike.' Inside was a well-used cricket bat bearing the image of Pakistani cricket star Shahid Afridi, wearing his ubiquitous aviator sunglasses.

The bat was warped and 'curved like an oar', but they now had a bat, and that meant they could have a hit.

> We were having a game when one of the locally employed kitchen hands was on the sideline looking very interested. We called out for him to have a bowl. I was batting and he bowled to me off a 20-metre run, which somewhat amused me. He came in off this long run-up and to my amazement, he bounced me. He was very quick, and I had to sway out of the way. He smiled at me; I could only smile back.

In that very human moment, it was an exchange that needed no words. John got to keep the change and the carpet. As for the cricket, the game was stopped when RPGs fired by the Taliban flew overhead, too close for comfort.

In late 2005, at a town centre near the SAS base at Tarin Kowt, a suicide bomber ran into a gathering of around 200 men and boys gambling on dog fights. He detonated the bomb and blew himself up, killing and injuring scores of locals in the chaos that followed. All through the afternoon an ADF doctor worked feverishly to save the injured while SAS troops moved the dead and dying. That evening, needing to unwind, predictably, they played a game of cricket, the horror of the day temporarily forgotten in the old certainties of a sport firmly embedded in the nation's psyche.

35

FIGHTING BACK

Over the past century, in the two world wars, Korea and Vietnam, the nature of danger on the battlefield changed, but the end results were no different. Iraq and Afghanistan have only served to underline this. In Afghanistan, ADF combat engineer Curtis McGrath had his own life-changing moment – one that would lead him to sporting glory.

Sapper McGrath's duties ranged from building structures and converting seawater into drinking water for both the army and the local inhabitants, to destroying bridges and clearing mines and booby traps – all in between a spot of rock throwing. As McGrath saw it, 'rock throwing is a sport in the army, something we always do. Whenever there's a lull, rocks will be found, and rocks will be thrown'. But for McGrath, his life came crashing down in a remote part of the Afghan province of Urōzgān in August 2012. About halfway through a six-month deployment, he and his team were given the task of clearing a checkpoint that had been used by insurgents. He had an odd feeling – 'like we were underprepared' – about the five-day patrol. But that couldn't stop what happened next.

> I stepped right on top of a small IED [improvised explosive device] that detonated beneath me and immediately took both my legs off, severely injured my left hand and perforated my right eardrum – the injuries were significant. I knew my legs were gone as soon as it happened.

Seriously injured but still conscious and aware he'd bleed to death within minutes, McGrath, as the unit's chief first-aid officer, directed his comrades to apply tourniquets and administer an IV and morphine. As he was stretchered to a helicopter, he feared he would never see his family again. Once on board, it was likely the morphine that allowed him to joke that he planned to become a Paralympian.

Just months later, McGrath was up and walking on prosthetic legs, motivated by the opportunity to march with his unit in their welcome-home ceremony. Deciding to live up to his words, he took up kayaking. With the Paralympics in mind, he and his father, Paul, paddled 900 kilometres from Sydney to Brisbane to raise funds for Mates4Mates, a charity that supports current and former ADF members. Instantly hooked on the sensation of gliding across water, he began training six days a week. 'I loved the sense of purpose it gave me. The promise I'd made while I was waiting to die had changed my life.'

In 2014, McGrath captained the Australian team at the inaugural Invictus Games in London. Founded by Prince Harry for wounded, injured or ill veterans, the games aim to provide a sports-focused pathway to recovery, both physical and psychological, for veterans injured while serving their countries.

A clear way ahead opened for McGrath, with the Australian army giving him 'elite sportsperson status', something he hadn't known existed. 'It meant my place of work was officially on the water. My service to the army would be by way of sport.' Within four years of his injury, McGrath won gold in the

Kayak Single 200m KL2 at the Rio 2016 Paralympic Games, winning gold again in the same event at the 2021 Tokyo and 2024 Paris Paralympics. With a gold also in the VL3, McGrath won four Paralympic gold medals overall to add to twelve world paracanoe titles. As a World and Paralympic champion, McGrath acknowledges the impact of sport as an 'an amazing tool', with its use in rehabilitation allowing people to 'reconnect'.

Sarah Watson also embraced the Invictus Games. As a result of her service in Iraq, she was diagnosed with PTSD, and subsequently medically discharged from the army in 2015. Through the national charity Soldier On, she took up competitive cycling and represented Australia at the 2017 Invictus Games held in Toronto, Canada. Competing in the Cycling Time Trial and Criterium, she won silver and gold respectively.

Watson's and McGrath's experiences in the Middle East throw more light on the importance of sport in the defence forces. From the perspective of his service in Vietnam, Tony Dell remains strong in his belief that sport and the military go hand in hand.

> The teamwork, the mateship and the reliance on others is like, say, the combination between a halfback and the five-eighth, just what happens there in the understanding they develop. In the army, it's the gunner and the gunner's mate. You've got a forward scout and he's the first one that knows that there's enemy ahead or the bloke behind him is conscious that someone's watching them. The rapport between the five-eighth and the halfback wins games but the rapport between the soldiers saves lives. There's a saying that's rammed into you in the army that the section or the platoon is only as strong as the weakest member. It's something that you learn very early on, and it's carried through. Even fifty years later, I'm still connected by that sort of brotherhood with blokes I served with.

Major Sarah Watson celebrates gold in the 1500 metres during the 2017 Invictus Games in Toronto, Canada. Photo by Claus Andersen/Getty Images for the Invictus Games Foundation

Already a champion paracanoeist and swimming medallist, Australian Army Sapper Curtis McGrath (right) demonstrates his all-round sporting versatility as he chases a loose ball against Tyron Lincoln of Team Canada in a wheelchair rugby match during the 2017 Invictus Games. Photo by Claus Andersen/Getty Images for the Invictus Games Foundation

In World War II, American general Douglas MacArthur believed that team sports helped develop attributes in athletes that made them better leaders in combat. In the contemporary ADF, leadership is regarded as a side benefit of sport, with egalitarianism playing a key role. As RAN retired lieutenant commander Doug Collins sees it, a junior seaman can be captain of a sports team that might include a superior officer. 'That's where it comes into play, where there is no rank in the team on the playing field. It allows people to develop their leadership skills in managing the team on the paddock.'

In World War I, rugby union star and Gallipoli veteran Tom Richards reluctantly accepted that war was no longer – if it ever had been – marked by old-fashioned sporting values of 'honest open hand-to-hand or man-to-man conflicts', where brave and strong men fought gallantly for the honour of their country. However, hand to hand fighting is far from a thing of the past, as experience showed.

The nature of modern warfare highlighted a soldier's need for close quarter combat skills. American forces, for example, conducted surveys of returning soldiers from the two wars and recorded more than 900 cases of individuals engaging in hand-to-hand combat.

The ADF's experience of this was small by comparison, but on one night raid in Afghanistan in 2007, Sergeant Paul Cale, a veteran of the elite 2nd Commando Regiment and a black belt in eight different styles of martial arts, was forced into a deadly, bare hands fight with a Taliban commander. His personal hand-to-hand combat experience, and those of his fellow commandos, guided the development of a new program, the Kinetic Fighting system, involving mental and physical training designed to instil a survival mindset.

In 2017, this became the foundation of the ADF's Army Combatives Program. With every soldier required to have a minimum level of fitness to survive a physical encounter and retain their weapon, the program utilises combat sports such as Brazilian jiu-jitsu, mixed martial arts, boxing, wrestling, karate, judo, taekwondo and Muay Thai. While they can never replicate real-world fighting scenarios, the ADF believes combat sports are crucial preparation for deployment.

The one thing that would have baffled Tom Richards is the decline of boxing in the services. Throughout its history the ADF has had many notable boxing champions. More recently, Private Billy McAllister, 6RAR, represented Australia at the 2022 Birmingham Commonwealth Games.

A century earlier there were Tiny Ryan and Digger Evans in World War I, Len Waters in World War II and then Joey Donovan, an RAN quartermaster gunner in the Vietnam years. Donovan's career of 159 fights for 150 wins is one of the greatest records in Australian boxing history. The Indigenous champion – nicknamed the Prince of Stuart Point as well as the Smithtown Whirlwind – won a gold medal at the 1967 Asian Games. A year later he represented Australia at the Mexico Olympic Games and went on to represent Australia at the 1974 Commonwealth Games. He was Australian amateur champion six times in three different weight divisions. In recent decades, amid the intense pace of ADF operations and overseas deployments, boxing has been discouraged, reflecting a view at senior ADF levels that it carries an unnecessary risk of head injury. Now boxing is just one of several combat sport options within the services.

36

JUST A GAME OF FOOTBALL

In her book *The Season*, Helen Garner relates a conversation in which a friend describes football as 'a mirror of war, a mirror we can look into safely', with the knowledge 'that war is as close as we ever get to being in the midst of life and death simultaneously.' In wars over the past century, sport has provided a means for diggers, however briefly, to put mortal fear to one side and lose themselves in a game among mates, perhaps for just an hour away from the combat. Conversely, war itself was never 'a good, rugged scrap', as Lieutenant Les Seaborn portrayed it in his efforts to build a Sportsmen's Battalion in World War I. It quickly became evident that bombs and bullets don't discriminate, killing and maiming at will. Haunted by the fate of the unit he had so enthusiastically formed, Seaborn took to alcohol on his return to Sydney. Perhaps he looked into the mirror and saw the truth about a 'scrap' that was never good.

In the two world wars, more than 830,000 Australian troops were deployed overseas – for some, for as long as five years. Two-thirds became casualties. About 16,000 Australians served with the BCOF in Japan in the wake of World War II, with another 18,000 serving in the Korean War. Service in the Vietnam War for more than 50,000 diggers was restricted to twelve months, while deployments to Afghanistan for nearly 40,000 troops and 2000 more in Iraq, together with nearly 7000 peacekeepers in Timor-Leste and the Sinai, were very much shorter, but more frequent. The changed nature of deployment now sees women serve overseas with the ADF in war zones.

Unlike the two world wars, troops in recent years have often been encamped in hostile environments with an amorphous front line, frequently leaving room only for spontaneous games.

Former army psychologist Captain Melissa Harries witnessed the impact of the emerging changes during deployments to Timor-Leste, Iraq and Afghanistan. As the battlefield psychologist for 3 RAR, she saw communication specialists being flown into Afghanistan and taken out to small patrol bases. While conditions were basic and often without running water, amazingly there was Wi-Fi, 'and they could Skype the missus' along with catching up with the latest footy scores. This highlights the seismic shift in communications over the past century – from Gallipoli's handwritten letters, through World War II's telephone exchanges and telex machines, to today's Wi-Fi and smartphones bringing all-important and instantaneous access to home.

In Iraq and Afghanistan where the conditions of deployment often dictated how, or even if, organised sport was possible, it became clear to Harries that troops still needed 'a healthy way to let off a bit of steam', to interact with each other in ways that were not work-focused, to have a laugh about stuff that's not serious and to just exist in a different headspace.

> If you're only going to do one thing for your mental health, then sport's probably a big-ticket item because it just covers so many bases. You're usually outside, you're doing something active, you've got a shared goal with others, and it lifts your mood. What we get from sport is to be a bit of a kid again, we get to play and have fun. It

is a huge shift to your mindset. The research is clear about how important each of those factors individually is, and you get it all with sport.

In Iraq and Timor-Leste there was soccer and touch football, often played on concrete carparks, with typically little difference in the sports men and women played. Volleyball would spring up if someone discovered a patch of sand where a net could be erected. Running was ubiquitous, and the most common way of keeping fit. For daily exercise, Camp Phoenix in Timor-Leste had a 300-metre running track. Harries recalled that with hundreds of people living in accommodation there, 'we ran a lot in circles'. Spontaneous games were created in the gym by the PTIs, often involving complicated rules. It might be throwing a ball that would have to bounce off several designated surfaces before landing in a bucket. Over-exuberance often led to the game being stopped. Of one thing she is certain: 'I don't think I've ever seen Australians go into any kind of sporting match, whether at home or overseas, and not be absolutely determined to win. We are naturally very competitive people.'

The presence of women meant netball; when mixed, this created a different kind of sport. 'It's not the same as women's netball. It is very quick, quite aggressive, more physical than when you're playing with women. But loads of fun, humbling for the men, I think, to be outplayed by women,' Harries added wryly. The importance of sport to the troops was clear. 'I saw how people looked after a game of volleyball, or soccer; there was a visible sense of peace, they would just flop, and the tension would just drain away.' It was the spontaneity of games that had a huge impact on troops. 'When it is mandated it's so much less fun. Part of the value of sport, in a world in which you have so little choice, is the choice to participate.'

Pat Cummins, as captain of the Australian men's cricket team, trod in Steve Waugh's footsteps when he and the Australian

Cricket World Cup squad went to Gallipoli in 2019. During a four-day stopover in Türkiye, the Australians laid a wreath, recited the 'Ode of Remembrance' and had a minute's silence. Reflecting on the stories of Australians who fought at Gallipoli, he commented that many of the men were not necessarily best mates. 'But you know they've got each other's back when the going gets tough. Just sticking it out, punching above their weight, doing all those things – no doubt there's going to be times during the World Cup when we're going to be up against it.' Cummins had no doubt about the importance of the visit. 'Just spending time together in a place like this, you can't help but learn something about yourself, about your teammates. Just learning about the ANZAC spirit – the fight, the mateship, just the incredible values they held here in 1915.'

For the Australian veterans of Afghanistan, the power of connection has spawned annual T20 cricket matches between the ADF and the Afghan interpreters and translators who resettled in Australia after the country's fall to the Taliban in 2021. It was natural that retired Afghan veteran SAS Captain Harry Moffitt, a cricket tragic, should lead the RSL XI in a match in Adelaide in December 2022. The Afghans were too strong, scoring 117 runs to the RSL XI's 98 in reply.

Such matches are emblematic of the link between sport and the military. Troops on overseas deployment will always find a bat or a ball for a hit or a kick around. For POWs, especially in World War II, sport fulfilled needs and met imperatives by allowing troubles to be temporarily forgotten.

However, the risk is that sport is too easily merged into the Anzac myth, with matches projected as having the same pivotal consequences as war, and team values seen in parallel. For instance, former Australian cricket captain Michael Clarke has spoken of how vital camaraderie, friendship and mateship are, concluding that 'the Anzacs represent that more than any other team that we've ever had in this country. As a sporting team you look up to the soldiers because of that spirit and because of that mateship and you try and build that camaraderie amongst your team.'

Hallowed though the Anzac myth is, sport is intrinsically not war. However, sport and combat do share some traits. In 2017, writer Rachel Hibbert put the issue to Afghanistan veteran Lieutenant Robert Andrew, who returned from his deployment initially contemptuous of such suggestions. However, after meeting the Queensland State of Origin rugby league team and the Queensland Firebirds netball team, he changed his mind. 'My perception of professional athletes altered. I never once got the impression that they were using an affiliation with Anzac. On the contrary, they seemed more humbled to meet us [soldiers] than we were to meet them. I believe sport and combat do share a lot of traits and for that reason I think associating sport with the Anzacs is the best way to bring the recognition of servicemen and women to the fore in society whilst keeping it relevant to almost every red-blooded Australian sports fan.'

In recent years, recognition of the role of sport has become an important part of the commemoration of Anzac Day. In Brisbane, the ADF cricket team plays the Brisbane Lord Mayor's XI in an annual Anzac Day match that honours the Shell Green game. More widely, football codes have their own direct links to the Anzac story, with players who have enlisted and served in the military over the past century.

In Australian Rules, a unique link was forged through the Barassi family and the father–son rule, which allowed a player to be recruited to the club his father had played for. The rule circumvented the zoning system in the VFL, the forerunner of the AFL. Introduced in 1949, the rule stemmed from the lobbying of the Melbourne club to have the young Ron Barassi follow in the footsteps of his father, Ron Barassi senior, who had been killed at Tobruk. When the time came, Barassi junior signed with Melbourne and began a stellar career. In the years to come, on Anzac Day Barassi often marched with the 7th Division, and his father's mates, on a hallowed day when, for him, football and the army became as one.

Not without coincidence, the various football codes have embraced the Anzac legend as part of their usual competition rounds to mark the connection with the nation's military history. Matches on 25 April are now a significant part of Anzac Day. To arrive at that point in Victoria, it took an act of the state Parliament in October 1958 to lift a ban on Anzac Day sport. However, sporadic scheduling of matches on Anzac Day in the years ahead brought varying degrees of success.

It was Essendon coach Kevin Sheedy – himself a national serviceman in the army from 1969 to 1971 – who pushed for greater recognition of the day. Sheedy envisioned honouring Australia's servicemen and women with an Essendon–Collingwood clash at the MCG on Anzac Day. He organised a meeting between officials from both clubs and the RSL and the concept was born. 'In the end we can never match the courage of people who went to war. But we can actually thank them with the way we play this game, with its spirit. We're very, very lucky people in this country,' he explained.

When the clubs met at the MCG on 25 April 1995, a crowd of 94,825 witnessed an epic draw. The Anzac Day match between the Magpies and the Bombers is now firmly written into the traditions of the day. A trophy is awarded to the winning team each year, with the names etched on it of footballers who died during war, and the Anzac Medal is presented to the best player on the ground.

To former Collingwood captain and coach Tony Shaw, it would be wrong to compare a football game with war, but it is okay to emphasise the lessons that players can learn from soldiers – discipline, hard work and camaraderie. Of the annual match, he believes the build-up is like no other game, but 'you can't make the game something it's not – it's not a war. Sure,

"The Last Post" is emotional, and for that minute's silence we reflect, but when the siren blows it's just a game of football.'

For former Essendon captain James Hird, there's nowhere else he would rather be than the MCG on Anzac Day. In his 2006 autobiography, *Reading the Play*, he declared Anzac Day 'the greatest day to play football apart from the last one in September. There's nowhere else I'd rather be. It's an awesome experience, genuinely moving, almost spiritual in its weight of sadness and respect you feel for those who didn't return from war, and the families they left behind.'

In rugby league, the NSWRL premiership first staged games on Anzac Day in 1927, and since 2002 in the NRL, St George Illawarra and the Sydney Roosters have played for the Anzac Day Cup, the match arguably the biggest on the code's calendar outside finals and State of Origin. In Super Rugby, an Anzac Weekend Round is held, and there has been talk of an Anzac Day Bledisloe Cup Test match between Australia and New Zealand.

Importantly, the names of two men who played for both the British and Irish Lions and the Wallabies are commemorated in international rugby. Since 2001, the British and Irish Lions have competed with the Wallabies for the Tom Richards Cup. A further military link was announced on Anzac Day 2025 when Rugby Australia and the British and Irish Lions unveiled the Blair Swannell Medal for Player of the Match ahead of a combined Australia–New Zealand Invitational team that would play the Lions at Adelaide Oval during the tour.

Although not played on Anzac Day, soccer internationals between Australia and New Zealand began in Brisbane in June 1923 when the long-forgotten 'Anzac Soccer Ashes' were created – a match in which Judy Masters represented Australia. An elaborate wooden casket made from New Zealand honeysuckle and Australian maple was crafted to hold ashes of cigars smoked by the captains of the two teams at a 'cigar night' after that match. The ashes were housed and sealed in a silver-plated razor case that was carried at the Gallipoli landing. The trophy served as the prize for the two nations' clashes. Lost from 1954, it was rediscovered in 2023 and is now awarded to the winner of trans-Tasman contests.

Be it be soccer, AFL, NRL or rugby union, the various football codes have now embraced the Anzac tradition in perpetuity.

Epilogue

General Sir Peter Cosgrove, whose appointments as Chief of the Defence Force and then Governor-General capped his distinguished military career, was a life-long sports enthusiast. At Duntroon in the 1960s, he remembered that physical training was relentless and unceasing. 'Sport was king', and for Cosgrove, that was rugby and cricket. After commanding an infantry platoon in Vietnam, he saw how jungle warfare restricted opportunities for sport. With Vietnam over, there was a change, and he recalled that physical fitness and sport came back strongly on the agenda.

In the contemporary ADF of 2025, more than 7000 men and women of the 55,000-strong force are involved with competitive sport in the services, with thirty-one associations and annual inter-service competition in AFL, cricket, rugby union, rugby league and hockey. A key development in the post-Afghanistan era has seen the emergence of an ADF Adaptive Sports Program. The concept materialised in the United States with the warrior games for men and women who had suffered physical or psychological injuries resulting from their service. Britain then followed with the Invictus Games.

In 2016, the Chief of the Defence Force, Air Chief Marshal Mark Binskin, directed Brigadier Phil Winter, head of the ADF Sports Cell, to develop the program. He subsequently assumed the role of Chef de Mission for ongoing Invictus and Warrior Games from 2016 to 2025. A high point for the ADF was the hosting of the Invictus Games in 2018 in Sydney, where 500 competitors from more than twenty nations competed in a variety of sports.

The Sports Cell has also been instrumental in the development of the Pacific Sports Program since 2018, aimed at growing sports capabilities in Papua New Guinea, Tonga, Samoa, the Solomons, Nauru and Vanuatu. An important goal is to create pathways for players, referees, coaches, sports medicine practitioners and family programs. A regional highlight is the annual soccer contest between Timor Leste and Australia for the Cosgrove-Gusmão Cup, named after two of the men who played significant roles in the tiny nation's transition to independence: General Sir Peter Cosgrove and Xanana Gusmão. Cosgrove was Commander of the International Force for East Timor (INTERFET) from 1999 to 2000, while Gusmão was the new nation's first president.

It's a long way from kicking a footy on New Britain in World War I and the 'State of Origin' rugby league match on Bougainville at the end of World War II, but through sport the ADF is maintaining a crucial link to the region. Of necessity, sport has had to adapt to ever-changing strategic demands, its role now is perhaps more important than ever.

In other ways, too, the connection has been strengthened. In 2024, the enduring link between cricket and the Australian military reached a significant milestone when Flight Lieutenant Vic Richardson's great-grandson, Air Marshal Stephen Chappell, was appointed Chief of Air Force. A promising cricketer in his youth, he was inspired by the movie *Top Gun* at age nine and never wavered from his dream of becoming a fighter pilot. Awarded his wings in 1997, Chappell deployed to the Middle East for operations in 2003 and 2014.

His father, legendary former Australian Test captain Greg Chappell, was in no doubt about the significance of the appointment from a family that also saw his elder brother Ian captain Australia, and younger brother Trevor play for Australia. After his son was handed the sword of the forefather of the RAAF, Sir Richard Williams, Greg Chappell said: 'His achievement is greater than anything that I've ever achieved.' Stephen Chappell is now the captain of a different team – and the game is not over.

Acknowledgements

War holds a fascination for me and has thus been the inspiration of six previous books, but looking at sport in the context of war has been very different experience – both surprising and immensely enjoyable. I owe a debt of thanks to a range of people for their contributions.

The book stemmed from an idea from Brigadier Phil Winter, the inaugural Director General of the ADF Sports Branch, who made the suggestion over coffee one morning in 2022. Along the way, Phil has been generous in his time, assistance and encouragement.

Thanks go to Lieutenant Commander Dave Devlin and Lieutenant Colonel Craig Johnson for their help with sourcing material.

Spanning so many different sports over 110 years of wars and conflicts involving the Australian military has required input from many people contributing their thoughts and experiences.

I would like to thank Kylie Best of the State Library of Victoria for her help with the papers of Padre Bennett, and also to Robyn Van-Dyk at the Australian War Memorial for her help with the untold story of the 'Test' cricket match at Gallipoli. Thanks go to Sandra Smith and Michael Bell for their help with the story of Tiny Ryan. Ian Hodges kindly shared his research on post-WWI returned soldiers. Further thanks go to historian

Tony Cunneen for kindly sharing his research paper on Leslie Seaborn and the Sportsmen's Unit in World War I.

I am grateful to Kristen Alexander for her help with World War II Bomber Command POWs; and to Ian Chappell for his grandfather Vic Richardson's story.

Thanks go to Rod Duncan for sharing the story of his father, Vic Duncan, in the sinking of HMAS *Perth*; to Liam Kane for sharing his thesis on sport in Papua New Guinea in WWII, and Yasushi Washo, who generously provided research from Tokyo on sport in the post-WWII occupation force in Japan.

These acknowledgements would not be complete without reference to Kevin Blackburn and the remarkable amount of research he has undertaken regarding the story of the Australian POWs at Changi.

Julian Croft shared his father's POW experiences from Changi, while Doug Heywood again shared the heart-rending story of his father, Scott Heywood.

Col Hutchinson provided material on Australian Rules in the ADF. Additionally, thanks go to Ian Granland and Roger Wainwright for their memories of playing football in Vietnam. I owe a special debt to cricketer Tony Dell and footballer Graham Cornes for their frank accounts of the effects of their Vietnam experience.

Ron Corry deserves a special mention for his colourful description of the experience of the Socceroos in their extraordinary soccer tour to Saigon in November 1967.

Thanks also to Tim van Gelder for his generous help with the story of his father, Malcolm van Gelder. Chris Masters alerted me to the story of his grandfather, 'Judy' Masters, while his brother Roy Masters shared his story of the late Bobby Fulton. Thanks go to Lieutenant Commander Doug Collins for his help with RAN recollections.

Particular thanks go to Curtis McGrath for the telling of his remarkable story and to Jill Buckfield, Sarah Watson and Melissa

Harries for sharing their thoughts on women and sport in the ADF in recent years, while I would also like to thank Rachel Hibbert for her contribution.

A special debt is owed to Peter Rubinstein, who has been a source of ideas and research and shared interviews. His encouragement, insights and friendship are deeply appreciated. Likewise, commentary from my daughter, Gemma, was important in shaping the final narrative of this book. Most importantly, there is Sue Langford, who carries responsibility for so many roles in the life of this book. No words can do justice.

Notes

WORLD WAR I

1 Players by Nature
For the source of references to Jack Massie in this and following chapters, see the AWM 3DRL/3701(A).
The C.E.W. Bean quote is from the *Official History of Australian in the War of 1914–18*, Vol. 1, *The Story of ANZAC*, Angus & Robertson, Sydney, 1936.
For the quote from William Throsby Bridges, see *Duntroon*, C.D. Coulthard-Clark, Allen & Unwin, Sydney, 1986.
For *The Winner*, see 17 February 1915; the columnist J.W. in *The Australasian*, 10 April 1915; and *The Referee*, 25 November 1914.
For the reference to playing 'the greater game', see article by Rebecca Britt, *Wartime*, Issue 33, January 2006.
For the Tom Richards quote, 20 October 1914, see AWM 2DRL/0786.
According to the Australian War Memorial, the physical requirements for enlisting in August 1914 were 19–38 years, height of 5ft 6in and chest measurement of 34 in. In June 1915 the age range and minimum height requirements were changed to 18–45 years and 5ft 2in, with the minimum height being lowered again to 5ft in April 1917. During the first year of the war, approximately 33 per cent of all volunteers were rejected. However, with relaxation of physical standards of age and height, as well as dental and ophthalmic fitness, previously ineligible men were now eligible for enlistment.
Lieutenant Ralph Robertson died in an aircraft training accident at Aboukir, Egypt, in May 1917.

2 And the Pyramids Watched

For the account of the situation with Australian troops in Cairo in January 1915 and the later reference to venereal disease, see *The War Work of the Y.M.C.A. in Egypt*, James W. Barrett, H.K. Lewis & Co. Ltd, London, 1919.

The Matheson account was published in the *Morwell Advertiser*, 12 February 1915.

See *The Australasian*, 10 April 1915, for the account of the match involving Clyde Donaldson.

The account of intense training for the troops was sourced from an account by Harold Fawcett, 2nd Battalion Australian Infantry, published in the *Armidale Chronicle*, 27 March 1915.

Corporal Hector Hallam's letter was published in the *West Wimmera Mail and Natimuk Advertiser*, 16 April 1915.

Tom Richards' graphic account of playing football in the Nile Delta country was published in the *Sydney Mail*, 13 September 1916, several months after the evacuation from Gallipoli.

The Richards quotes were sourced from his diary entries for 21 February 1915, 5 February 1915, and 21 February 1915, AWM 2DRL/0786.

The Observer, Adelaide, published the account of the match involving the Adelaide-raised 10th Australian Infantry on 27 March 1915.

The criticism of the film *Gallipoli* was published by Neil Jillett, *The Age*, Melbourne, 13 August 1981.

3 The Red Rag

Cliff Halloran was published in *The Sun*, Sydney, 16 May 1915, and 25 May 1915.

The 'Bull' Ryrie account was published in Phoebe Vincent's, *My Darling Mick: The Life of Granville Ryrie*, National Library of Australia, 1997, pp. 71–72.

Charlie Rowe's letter was published in the *Northern Miner*, 28 May 1915.

See *Australians and Egypt 1914–1919*, Suzanne Brugger, MUP, Melbourne, 1980, for the complaint about the behaviour of cricketers at the Gezira Sporting Club.

For the Henry Gullett reference, see *Official History of Australia in the War of 1914–1918, Vol. VI, Sinai and Palestine.*

The Richards quotes were sourced from his diary, 23 February, 28 February and 24 April 1915, 2DRL/0786, AWM.

For the C.E.W. Bean quote on 'playing the game', see Peter Rees, *Bearing Witness*, Allen & Unwin, Sydney, 2015.

The Arthur Blackburn account was published in *The Register*, Adelaide, 6 August 1915.

For Tom Whyte's letter, see AWM PR04722.

For Bean's account of the landing, see Commonwealth of Australia Gazette, No. 39, 17 May 1915.

The Ryrie letter was published in the *North Western Courier*, Narrabri, 18 June 1915.

For the Bean quote about Australian country life, see *Bearing Witness*, op. cit.

The British officer quoted about the Australian race was John Graham Gillam, 29th Divisional Train, Army Service Corps. See *A Gallipoli Diary*, George Allen & Unwin, London, 1918.

The Jack Massie letters were dated 5 May, 14 May and 18 August 1915; Massie AWM file, op. cit.

For the football match quote and the Wally Hale reference, see Bill Gammage, *The Broken Years*, ANU Press, Canberra, 1974.

For the Blair Swannell story, see *The Referee*, 27 October 1915.

For Bean's references to Ted Larkin, see *Official History of Australia in the War of 1914–18*, vol. 1, op. cit.

Ted Larkin's story was told at the AWM Last Post Ceremony, 21 April 2015. Also see *The Life and Death of Sergeant Ted Larkin*, Geoff Armstrong, Stoke Hill Press, 27 April 2016, www.stokehillpress.com/blog/the-life-and-death-of-sergeant-ted-larkin.

4 Cricketing Bombs

The figure of 774 AFL-level players was supplied by the AFL's former official historian, Col Hutchinson.

Regarding enlistment of soccer players, see Ian Syson, 'Fronting Up: Australian Soccer and the First World War', *The International Journal of the History of Sport*, 28 April 2014.

For information on James 'Judy' Masters, see article by Chris Masters, *Sunday Telegraph*, 23 June 2013.

The reference to Judy Masters in the *South Coast Times* was published on 16 June 1916.

J.W.'s column in *The Australasian* was published on 10 April 1915.

Dale Blair discussed 'muscular Christianity' in 'Beyond the metaphor: Football and war, 1914–1918', *Journal of the Australian War Memorial*, issue 28, April 1996.

For reference to 'the greater game', see Murray Phillips, *The Sports Factor*, 'Lest we forget – sport and war', ABC RN, 19 April 2002. Ultimately, it has been estimated that 5000 Australian rugby players went on active war service between 1914 and 1918. This figure represents about 98 per cent of the playing numbers in the game, outside of the schools, in 1914. See: www.rugbyfootballhistory.com/rugbyatwar.html#WorldWar1.

Syd Middleton was quoted by *The Referee*, 15 December 1915.

For Michael McKernan, see his book with Richard Cashman (eds), *Sport in History: The Making of Modern Sporting History*, University of Queensland Press, St Lucia, Qld, 1979.

The quote from *The Bulletin* was published on 27 January 1916.

For the Thomas Baker quote, see: www.iwm.org.uk/history/voices-of-the-first-world-war-sport-in-war.

The Tom Richards quote was published in the *Sydney Mail*, 13 September 1916.

For Padre Tom Bennett, see Bennett papers, State Library of Victoria, MS 10138.

For the quote by Jim McKinley, 4th Divisional Signal Company, see AWM, S00287, https://s3-ap-southeast-2.amazonaws.com/awm-media/collection/S00287/document/1865630.PDF

For the Ernest Brooks quote, see AWM G00406.

Arthur Mailey's quote was published in *The Referee*, 15 December 1915.

For the Massie quote, see his AWM file, op. cit.

The reference to Frank Lugton was sourced from the Northcote Cricket Club, Facebook page: www.facebook.com/NorthcoteCricketClub.

C.E.W. Bean's musing was reported by *The Advertiser*, Adelaide, 21 July 1915.

Bean wrote about the death of Wilfred Harper in the *Official History*, op. cit., Vol. II.

Details of the extraordinary cricket 'Test' match played at Outpost No. 3 are to be found in Sergeant Leslie Sutherland's file, AWM 2DRL0988.

For Bean's reference to the Shell Green ruse, see AWM38 3DRL 606/23/1 – Diaries, Notebooks and Folders, December 1915. Also see Bean's *Gallipoli Mission*, AWM, 1948.

For Ryrie's reference to the match, see *My Darling Mick*, op. cit.

For Harold Suttor's remarks, see Andrew Shepherdson, *Journeys of a Light Horseman*, self-published.

Among men from Ryrie's 2nd Light Horse Brigade who died in action were boxing champion Teddy Reynolds, who was killed on 21 July 1915.

5 Slingshot Thunderbolts

References to Tom Richards' diary in this chapter are dated 11 June 1915, 13–14 September 1915, 14 December and 29 December 1915, 20 and 26 January 1916, and 13 May 1916. 2DRL/0786, AWM. Also see Bean, *The Story of ANZAC*, op. cit., p. 802.

For James McKenzie's diary, see 5 July 1915–21 January 1916, State Library of New South Wales: https://transcripts.sl.nsw.gov.au/page/104171/edit.

For Judy Masters' reference to soccer against the Tommies, see the *South Coast Times*, 28 June 1916.

Jimmy Clarken's quote regarding the Australian nurses was published in *The Referee*, 15 December 1915.

For the diary of Walter Bruce Rainsford, see State Library of New South Wales: https://transcripts.sl.nsw.gov.au/page/item-02-walter-bruce-rainsford-diary-1-january-1915–31-december-1915-page-364.

The Murphy quote was published in *The Referee*, 1 March 1916.

For the description of Tibby Cotter's bowling, see article by Max Bonnell, *Sydney Morning Herald*, 30 October 2017.

The Alcock remark was quoted by Daniel Lane, *Sydney Morning Herald*, 21 April 2013.

For the match between the Australians and the Yeomanry, see Peter Rees, *Desert Boys: Australians at War from Beersheba to Tobruk and El Alamein*, Allen & Unwin, Sydney, 2011.

For the story of Midnight, see Peter Haydon, Midnight Warhorse: www.haydonhorsestud.com.au/wp-content/uploads/2023/02/Midnight-Warhorse-original-.pdf.

6 The Game Changes

For Gerald Evans, see GV Evans, MM, *Recollections of the 1914–1918 War*, privately published, 1982.

Tom Richards' quotes are from his diary entries, op. cit., for 3 May, 28 May, 10 June, 6 July, 8 July, 9 July and 10 July 1916.

For James Gibb, see New South Wales State Library: https://transcripts.sl.nsw.gov.au/page/item-04-james-brunton-gibb-diary-14-june-31-december-1916-page-10.

For C.E.W. Bean's account of Fromelles, see *Official History*, Vol III.

7 Somewhere in France

For Edgar Rule's comments, see *Reveille*, 1 January 1935.

Background regarding the London exhibition match was published in the *Sporting Globe*, 27 August 1949.

For 'mobbing', see Dale Blair, op. cit.

The Winner, 20 December 1916, published an account of the match, together with details of Claude McMullen's footballs.

For Lionel Short's account of the Western Front match, see *The Argus*, 10 May 1917.

The 3rd Australian Division team was captained by Lieutenant Bruce Sloss, who had played for South Melbourne in the VFL competition. Others in the team were Lieutenant Jack Brake (University and Melbourne), Dan Minogue (Collingwood), Carl Willis (University and South Melbourne), Leo Little (University), Bill Sewart (Essendon), James Pugh (Launceston), Harry Moyes (St Kilda), Percy Jory (St Kilda), Charlie Lilley (Melbourne), Les Lee (Richmond), Cyril Hoft (Perth), L. Martin (University), Ted Alley (Williamstown, ex South Melbourne), Hugh James (Richmond), Ben Mills (Brunswick), Jim Foy (Perth) and Billy Orchard (Geelong).

Charles Perry, a chaplain from the Norwood club in Adelaide, captained the Combined Training Units team. Under his leadership were Jack Cooper (Fitzroy), Percy Trotter (East Fremantle, ex Fitzroy), Clyde Donaldson (Essendon), Harry Kerley (Collingwood), John Hoskins (Melbourne), Harold Boyd (Association), Italo Cesari (Geelong), Ossie Armstrong (Geelong), James Scullin (South Fremantle), Stan Martin (University), E. Maxfield (Fremantle), Thomas Paine (Northam), EF Beames, George Bower (South Melbourne), L. McDonald (Essendon 'A'), Lieutenant Colonel Alfred Jackson (Essendon), H. Moore (South Australia).

Those players who were killed in coming months were:

Divisional team

B.M.F. 'Bruce' Sloss (South Melbourne), team captain, 10th Machine Gun Company AIF, killed in action at Armentières, 4 January 1917.

J. 'James' Pugh (City), 40th Battalion AIF, killed in action, Houplines-Pont Ballot, 28 January 1917.

J.F. 'Jim' Foy (Perth), 44th Battalion AIF, killed in action, near Armentières, 14 March 1917.

L.E. 'Les' Lee (Richmond & Williamstown), 10th Brigade Machine Gun Company, killed in action during the Battle of Messines, 8 June 1917.

Australian Training Units team

S.C. 'Stan' Martin (University), 22nd Battalion AIF, killed in action at Bullecourt, 3 May 1917.

J.T. 'Jack' Cooper (Fitzroy), vice-captain, 8th Battalion AIF, killed in action during the Battle of Passchendaele, 20 September 1917.

D.F. 'Dan' Scullin (Mines Rovers), 51st Battalion AIF, killed Polygon Wood, 26 September 1917.

Further to these deaths, in the Divisional team, Carl Willis (South Melbourne), Australian Army Medical Corps Dental Detail, died of pleurisy and pneumonia, accentuated by the effects of gas in World War I at the age of thirty-seven.

In the Training Units team, O.R. 'Ossie' Armstrong (Geelong), 14th Battalion AIF, was captured by the Germans on 11 April 1917, and was a prisoner of war.

John Hoskins (Melbourne), 6th Battalion AIF, was wounded twice in action: gassed, July 1918; gunshot wounds to thigh – fractured femur, etc., August 1918.

T. 'Thomas' Paine (Union Football Club, Northam, Tasmania), 16th Battalion AIF, wounded twice in action: gunshot wounds to hand, June 1917; gunshot wounds to head, September 1917.

8 Bowling Against the Wind

For Harry Chauvel's letters, see *Desert Boys*, op. cit.

For the water sports meeting at Ismailia, see *A Regatta and Water Sports*, 22 June 1917, AWM25 897/2.

For the Rafa race meeting, see Elyne Mitchell, *Light Horse: The Story of Australia's Mounted Troops*, Sun Books, Melbourne, 1978.

The Trooper Lewis letter was published in *The Referee*, 4 July 1917.

The Eustelle Overy interview was recorded by UNSW Australians at War Film Archive, 10 June 2000: https://australiansatwarfilmarchive.unsw.edu.au/archive/2544.

The Advertiser, Geelong, 22 May 1917, reported the death of Joe Slater.

For the River Douve story, see F.C. Green, *A Record of the 40th Battalion AIF*, 40th Battalion Association, Hobart, 1922.

For background to the Robert Grieve VC, story, see Greg Growden's book, *Cricketers at War*, ABC Books, Sydney, 2019, and Wesley College, Melbourne: www.wesleycollege.edu.au/news-events-and-publications/lion-magazine/lion-september-2023/the-robert-grieve-vc-ow1904-commemorative-memorial.

For the 7th Brigade Sports Day, see Reg Telfer: https://digitize-vwma.s3.amazonaws.com/I/documents/6642/file/DAD_S_WAR_MASTER__Reg_Telfer__30_Aug_2013.pdf.

The Argus, 16 July 1917, reported the Barbour letter.

The Referee, 5 September 1917, reported Barbour's assessment of Lord's and the Oval.

9 Surely the Moment for a Test Match

For details of Bert Oldfield's war experience, see Kersi Meher-Homji, *The Roar*, 31 May 2010.

Tiny Ryan's career was reported by the *Dubbo Liberal and Macquarie Advocate*, 28 August 1914, with further Indigenous background provided by researcher Sandra Smith.

Tiny Ryan's letter was published by *The Sun*, Sydney, 15 August 1915.

For coverage of Tiny Ryan's defence of Les Darcy and his death at Polygon Wood, see *The Referee*, 7 and 14 November 1917; see also Indigenous Histories: https://indigenous-histories.com/2017/04/25/alfred-tiny-ryan-the-boxing-soldier/.

For details of the 12th Brigade's sports meeting, see unit war diary, April 1917.

For Walter Belford's observations, see *'Legs Eleven': Being the Story of the 11th Battalion AIF in the Great War*, Chapter XXXI.

For Arthur Moore's diary, see entry for 11 November 1916–11 January 1918, p. 98, State Library of New South Wales.

The Referee, 19 September 1917, reported the mixed-rules football match.

Cyril Dennys's recollections were recorded by the Imperial War Museum, www.iwm.org.uk/history/voices-of-the-first-world-war-sport-in-war.

Scotty Bolton's account of the death of Tibby Cotter was published in *Desert Boys*, op. cit., p. 213.

Ern Mitchell's account of the night in Beersheba was reported in *The Referee*, 20 February 1918.

For Gordon Campbell's comments on Jack Massie, see *The Arrow*, 14 July 1917; also Blackwood Soldiers Project: http://blackwoodsoldiersproject.blogspot.com.

The *Sydney Morning Herald*, 25 April 1917, reported the push for the Sportsmen's Battalion. Other details were drawn from research and a paper by historian Tony Cunneen, 'Be a sport and enlist: Leslie Seaborn and the Sportsmen's Unit in the First World War': https://supremecourt.nsw.gov.au/documents/Publications/The-War-Memorial-Project/Cunneen_20170327_Seaborn.pdf.

Billy Hughes's comments were reported in the *Sydney Morning Herald*, 27 July 1917.

See Douglas Booth and Colin Tatz, *One-Eyed: A View of Australian Sport*, Allen & Unwin, Sydney, 2000, for details of the enlistment by sportsmen.

Regarding injuries on the playing field resembling injuries on the battlefield, an example was former Sydney Australian Rules player Joseph Ashton, twenty-two. In December 1917, he broke his collarbone while playing in a 3rd Battalion inter-company game at Boulogne where the unit was resting and training. Admitted to hospital, the examining medical officer assessed the injury as a severe fracture of the left clavicle. Ashton had a history of the same injury from his football days and the bone did not mend easily, requiring the wound to be reopened and the bone wired. His fighting days were over. (NAA, Ashton J.F., B2455; also, see Paul Macpherson and Ian Granland, *A Game to be Played: The Great War and Football in Sydney*, The NSW Australian Football History Society, 2015).

Regarding earlier sportsmen's battalion recruitment efforts, in one instance the League of Wheelmen appealed for Sydney bike riders to enlist.

10 Put Our Scores on the Board!

Cec Healy's article was published by the *Sunday Times*, Sydney, 2 February 1913.

For Walter Belford's observations, see Belford, op. cit.

Monash's remarks were published in *War Letters of General Monash*, edited by F.M. Cutlack, p. 268, Angus & Robertson, Sydney, 1934.

Monash's comments were published in George Cuttriss's *Over the Top with the 3rd Australian Division*, London, Charles H. Kelly, 1918.

The vote in favour was 1,015,159 and the vote against 1,181,747. The AIF vote overseas was 103,789 for and 93,910 against, with 1978 informal.

Les Seaborn was attached to Sports Control Board in February 1919.

Monash's protest to senior British civilian and military figures regarding the British downplaying the feats of his men went to the nub of official British government policy to stop distinguishing between Dominion and British troops by calling them all 'British'. Australian resentment at being denied credit would only grow.

11 All Dressed Up and Nowhere to Go

For background on Australian POWs of the Turks, see Kate Ariotti and Martin Crotty, 'The Role of Sport for Australian POWs of the Turks during the First World War', *The International Journal of the History of Sport*, 2014, vol. 31, no. 18, pp. 2362–2374.

For Monash's comments about 'fighting morale', see Bean, op. cit., *The A.I.F. in France 1918*, Vol. VI.

For Gerald Evans' comments, see his book, op. cit., *Recollections of the 1914–1918 War*.

See the 3rd Battalion's War Book, p. 142, regarding sport and the weather.

The Jimmy Clarken story is drawn from *Classic Wallabies*: https://classicwallabies.com.au/players/james-clarken/388.

For George Goddard's comments on football codes, see George Goddard, *Soldiers and Sportsmen*, AIF Sports Control Board, London, 1919.

12 A Golden Decade Begins

The Inter-Allied Games, Paris, provided a detailed account of the Games.

Historian Thierry Terret's comments were drawn from Thierry Terret, 'The Military "Olympics" of 1919', *International Society of Olympic Historians*, vol. 14, no. 2, 2006.

For Syd Middleton's involvement with the Games, see 'Correspondence regarding Inter-Allied Games in Paris 1919', www.awm.gov.au/collection/C2740041.

Also see George Goddard, *Soldiers and Sportsmen*, op. cit., for material in this chapter.

See *The Fortian*, November 1919, for the comment on the 800-metre relay team.

At the Covered Courts Championship meeting at Queen's Club, London, the AIF entered a seven-man team, consisting of well-performed representative players: Lieutenant Stan Doust, Major Rodney Heath, Captain Gerald Patterson, Sergeant Ron Thomas, Captain Pat O'Hara-Wood, Gunner A.B. Jones and Gunner Randolph Lycett.

13 The Noble Art

See 'Correspondence regarding Inter-Allied Games in Paris 1919', for Middleton's views on the boxers: https://s3-ap-southeast-2.amazonaws.com/awm-media/collection/AWM2020.8.1251/bundled/AWM2020.8.1251.pdf.

For Digger Evans, see comments to biographer J.M. Rohan, *The Old Tin Shed*: http://sydneystadium.blogspot.com/2010/11/digger-evans.html.

The W.F. Corbett article on Gordon Coghill was published in *The Referee*, 9 July 1919.

For the account of the wrestling, see George Goddard, *Soldiers and Sportsmen*, op. cit.

14 The Awesome Oarsmen

The Referee, 1 October 1919, reported on the Bisley King's of 1919.

Further accounts of the shooting were published in the Launceston *Daily Telegraph*, 6 October 1919.

See Scott Patterson's *The Oarsmen: The Remarkable Story of the Men Who Rowed from the Great War to Peace*, for a fuller account of the King's Cup victory.

After much debate, King George V finally decreed two years later that the King's Cup be used as the permanent trophy for the interstate eight-oared race of Australia, and it is still awarded at the Australian Rowing Championships.

Crews for Henley:

No. 1 Crew. – Sgt. A.R. Robb, 11st. 10lbs. (bow); Lieut. F.A. I House, 11st. 12lb. (2); Lieut. T. McGill, 12st. 10lbs. (3); Gunner A.V. Scott, 13 st. (4); Lieut. H. Hauenstein, M.M. 13st, 9lbs. (5); Major S.A. Middleton D.S.O., 13st. 6lbs. (6); Gunner G.W. Mettam, 11st. 12lbs. (7); Capt. H.C. Disher, 11st. 1lb. (stroke); Sgt. A.E. Smedley, 8st. 1lb. (cox).

No. 2 Crew. – Lieut. J. Howieson, 10st. 11lbs. (bow); Sgt. G.M. Penny, 11st. 9lbs. (2); Sgt. E.J. Harrison, 12st. 2lbs. (3); Lieut. H.A. White, 12st. 5lbs. (4); Major W.A. Audsley, D.S.O. 13st. 3lb. (5); Corpl. J.K. Cogle, 12t. 3lbs. (6); Gunner J.A. Begg, 13st. 1Ib. (7); Lieut. H.R. Newall, 11st. 6lbs. (stroke); and Lieut. O.J. Wood, 10st. (cox).

Crew for Paris:
Sgt. A.R. Robb (bow), Lieut. H.R. Newall (2), Lieut. L.S. Davis (3), Gunner A.V. Scott (4), Lieut. T. McGill (5), Lieut. F.A. House (6), Gunner G.A. Mettam (7), Capt. H.C. Disher (stroke) and Sgt. A.E. Smedley (cox).

15 A Fighting Force

The report of Massie's performance was published by *The Referee*, 12 September 1917.

For Massie's letter of 19 August 1917, see the Massie file, op. cit., AWM 3DRL/3701.

For Collins' account of the cricket, see *The Sun*, 9 March 1941.

The Referee published an assessment of the tour's success on 8 October 1919 and 3 December 1919.

For Claude Tozer's story, see Greg Growden's *Cricketers at War*, and the Ku-Ring-Gai Historical Society Inc. newsletter, vol. 38 no. 11 December 1920.

For details of the Tuggeranong Twisters, see *Bearing Witness*, op. cit.

Historian Ian Hodges' account of local sport in Wagga Wagga was sourced from his book, *'He Belonged to Wagga': The Great War, the AIF and Returned Soldiers in an Australian Country Town*, Australian Scholarly Publishing, Melbourne, 2022.

For background, see Iain Payten, 'Anzac Day: The champion team of war-weary soldiers that "saved" Australian rugby in 1919', *Sydney Morning Herald*, 25 April 2019, www.rugby.com.au/news/2019/04/25/anzac-aif-team-1919.

The AIF team comprised seventeen players: Gunner Eric Bull, Lance Corporal Herbie Collins, Major Cyril Docker, Lieutenant Jack Gregory, Chaplain Harry Heath, Lieutenant Charlie Kelleway (captain), Sergeant Allie Lampard, Captain Ed Long, Sergeant Hammy Love, Gunner Jack Murray, Corporal Bert Oldfield, Captain Nip Pellew, Warrant Officer Bill Stirling, Staff Sergeant Charlie Winning, Gunner Johnny Taylor, Captain Bill Trenerry and Captain Carl Willis.

Willis topped the runs aggregate with 1652 at 41.30, followed by Collins with 1615 runs at 38.45. Pellew and Taylor also topped 1000 runs, while Trenerry with 961 and Gregory with 942 were close. Gregory was the outstanding bowler, capturing 131 wickets at 18.19. Collins took 106 at 16.55, with Lampard next best with 69 at 23.26 including the best analysis by an Australian of 9 for 42 against Lancashire. He also scored 821 runs to underline his usefulness as an all-rounder. Long and Oldfield shared wicketkeeping duties, claiming thirty-one and twenty-eight scalps respectively.

WORLD WAR II

16 The Old and the New
For Nicky Barr, see AWM interview, 1990: www.3sqnraafasn.net/subpages/AWMBarr.htm
For coverage of the match between the First and Second AIF, see the *Sydney Morning Herald*, 5 January 1940.

17 Tout Juste
The 2/1st Infantry Battalion War Diary, March–April 1940, refers to the match against the French: https://s3-ap-southeast-2.amazonaws.com/awm-media/collection/RCDIG1021830/bundled/RCDIG1021830.pdf.
For D.R. Jackson's memoir, see AWM MSS 1193.
For Bill Travers's letter, see J.R. Gorham and C.J.L. Hewett (eds), *The Torch Bearers: War Service of Shore Old Boys 1939–1999, The Torch Bearers: War Service of Shore Old Boys 1939–1999*, Sydney Church of England Grammar School, 1999.
For Phil O'Brien's account, see Phil O'Brien and Bernie Dowling, *Towards Peace: A Worker's Journey*, Social History Publishing Enterprise with LeftPress, 1992: https://workersbushtelegraph.com.au/books/ttowards-peace-a-workers-journey.
Stan Vesper refers to the surf life saving club at Gaza in his book, *Those Who Served*, Playright Publishing Pty Ltd, Sydney, 2015.
Kenneth Slessor's account of the football match was published by the *Wodonga and Towong Sentinel*, 18 October 1940.
Fred Howard's description of the cricket appeared in *Soldiering On*, AWM, Canberra, 1942.
For Chas Daintree's account see *Desert Boys*, op. cit.

For the Tobruk cricket game, see Rupert Goodman, UNSW Australians at War Film Archive: https://australiansatwarfilmarchive.unsw.edu.au/archive/923.

Also see *Australia in the War of 1939–1945*, Volume III, Tobruk and El Alamein, 1966.

The Australian team at Tobruk comprised Capt. I.F. McMaster, Lieut. B. Trebock, Capt. N.N. Fletcher, Cpl. J. Laing, L/Cpl. W. Jones, Lieut. M.D. Vincent, Pte. W.T. Collins, WO (II). S. Pearson, Pte. W.D. Pearson, Cpl. M. Ready, and Pte. Chataway.

18 An End to the Good Times

Background to the 8th Division's deployment to Malaya and Singapore was drawn from Peter Rees and Sue Langford, *A Week in September*, HarperCollins, Sydney, 2021. Also, see references to the diary of Warrant Officer Scott Heywood on which *A Week in September* is based.

Kevin Blackburn's well-researched book, *The Sportsmen of Changi*, NewSouth Publishing, Sydney, 2012, was also drawn on for valuable background material and as a reference to other primary sources.

Newspapers drawn on for this chapter are the *Malaya Tribune*, 3 March 1941; and the *Straits Times*, 22 September 1941, 2 November 1941, 9 November 1941 and 23 November 1941.

For the account of Ben Barnett, see the *Sporting Globe*, 29 September 1945.

For the account of the Australian Rules match on the palace *padang*, see Corporal Lex Arthurson, *The Story of the 13th Australian General Hospital*, AWM MSS1377.

19 The Changi Tests

For the reference to cricket balls, see Donald (Norman) Morrison VX28610, *History of B Company, 2/29 Battalion*, AWM PR05395.

Regarding rivalry with the British, see Arthurson, op. cit.

For Mike Hubert's account of the match, see AWM PR01123.

Pamela Cohen, 'Behind Barbed Wire', *Sporting Traditions*, vol. 23, no. 1, November 2006, provided background material for this chapter, as did Kevin Blackburn's *The Sportsmen of Changi*, op. cit., in particular the note from Barnett to Scott.

For the recollections of Dick Curtis, see Cyril Bix interview, 'The Changi Ashes': www.far-eastern-heroes.org.uk/Changi_Ashes/.

For Dr Charles Huxtable's assessment of Ben Barnett's skills, see his book, *From the Somme to Singapore: A Medical Officer in Two World Wars*, Kangaroo Press Kenthurst, NSW, 1987.

For Frank Day's comments, see AWM PR03884.

For Jack Croft's diary, see https://merewethercarlton.com.au/wp-content/uploads/2023/03/Jack-Croft-War-Diary.pdf.

See the *Straits Times*, 22 September 1941, for the baseball match the AIF played against the Japanese Baseball Club.

20 Not Just a Diversion – a Lifeline

Jim Makeham's comments in this chapter were published by the *Sporting Globe*, 13 October 1945.

Kevin Blackburn's *The Sportsmen of Changi*, op. cit., provided important background for this chapter, along with David Leydon's article on Wilfred 'Chicken' Smallhorn, 'Wilfred "Chicken" Smallhorn: The spirit of the ANZAC Fitzroy legend, Changi legend', 2023: www.fitzroyfc.com.au/latest-news/wilfred--chicken--smallhorn-the-spirit-of-the-anzac-fitzroy-legend-changi-legend.

Vic Duncan's recollections were drawn from the Duncan family memoir of his war service, *An Odyssey*.

Also, see:

Lex Arthurson, *The Story of the 13th Australian General Hospital*, op. cit., 2/4th Machine Gun Battalion Ex Members Association, 7 June 2024; 2nd4thmgb.com.au.

Allan Grant's article, 'The Changi Brownlow – Peter Chitty', published in *Almanac Footy History*, has further background: footyalmanac.com.au.

Regarding football injuries, see diary of Norman Morrison, op. cit., AWM PR05395.

For background on the Wallabies Changi, see classicwallabies.com.au.

For Frank Day's comments, op. cit., AWM PR03884.

Bill Flowers' comments were drawn from his manuscript, AWM MSS1575.

21 Mates

Sue Ebury's authoritative biography, *Weary: The Life of Sir Edward Dunlop*, Penguin, Ringwood, 1994, provided valuable information on Weary Dunlop's wartime experiences.

Also see Tom Uren's autobiography, *Straight Left*, Random House, Sydney, 1994, for his recollections on the Burma–Thailand railway, his friendship with Weary Dunlop, and his maiden speech to the House of Representatives, 26 July 1959.

For Ray Parkin's regard for Weary Dunlop, see his book, *Into the Smother: A Journal of the Burma-Siam Railway*, The Hogarth Press, New Zealand, 1963.

For Tom Hamilton's comments, see AWM PR00219.

The account of the 1943 Melbourne Cup, plus Weary Dunlop material, were drawn from Hank Nelson's book *Prisoners of War: Australians Under Nippon*, ABC, Sydney, 1985.

For Scott Heywood's comment about the Melbourne Cup, see *A Week in September*, op. cit.

For the story of Jim Downie, see Anzac portal: https://anzacportal.dva.gov.au/resources/comradeship-stories-friendship-and-recreation-wartime#6.

For the Kenelm 'Mac' Ramsay story on the *Montevideo Maru*, see Max Uechtritz, *The Roar*, 29 June 2017, 'Remembering Wallaby "Mac" Ramsay – WW2 Hell Ship victim': www.theroar.com.au/2017/06/30/remembering-wallaby-mac-ramsay-ww2-hell-ship-victim.

Also see Classic Wallabies for background on 'Mac' Ramsay, James 'Blow' Ide and Stan Bisset: https://classicwallabies.com.au/bios.

Stan Bisset was interviewed for the Australians at War Film Archive: http://australiansatwarfilmarchive.unsw.edu.au/archive/1223.

For Stan Bisset's war record, see Australian National Archives: VX21199.

22 The Demon

Aviation writer Stanley Brogden was quoted by Christopher Warner in *Military History*, 'War Athletes: Keith Truscott', 19 April 2021 www.military-history.org/war-athletes/war-athletes-keith-truscott.htm.

The critique of Bluey Truscott's flying skills appeared in the *Journal of the Melbourne Cricket Club*, issues 50 & 51, 2013.

For Bluey Truscott's war record, see his RAAF Pilot's Training Card, personnel file and progress report, National Archives of Australia, Series Number A9300.

The *Army News*, Darwin, articles were published on 7 December 1941 and 5 February 1942.

Truscott's embarrassment was covered in the *Sun News-Pictorial*, 18 May 1942.

The George Smeaton story was published by the *Sporting Globe*, 25 April 1953.

The story of the meeting with Bill Woodfull was published by the *Sydney Morning Herald*, 22 April 2007.

The Ian Johnson story was published in *The Yorker*, The Melbourne Cricket Club magazine, Issue 51, 2013.

Biographer Ivan Southall described the circumstances of Bluey Truscott's death in his book *Bluey Truscott*, Angus & Robertson, Sydney, 1958.

For Harold Ball material, see *The Mercury*, Hobart, 18 December 1941, and a letter held by the Australian War Memorial, AWM, PR05406.

For Roland Le Folet Hoffman's comments, see Pamela Cohen, op. cit.

23 Kriegies

Background for the operations and wartime careers of Australian airmen who flew with Bomber Command was drawn from several sources, including my 2013 book *Lancaster Men* and Kristen Alexander's self-published 2023 in-depth study of POWs, *Kriegies: The Australian Airmen of Stalag Luft III*.

A valuable source of information is the Laurie Field collection of papers related to No. 460 Squadron RAAF, including interview transcripts, notes, correspondence and replies to questionnaires, AWM MSS1489.

Also see Warwick Franks, 'Sport in prisoner-of-war camps, in the army and on the Home Front': https://crescentbeachcayman.com/defreitas/files/Cricket-in-Stalag-344---Sport-in-German-Prisoner-of-war-camps-during-World-War-II.pdf.

For the Keith Miller cricket match, see *Sydney Morning Herald*, 7 June 1943.

Material on Bob Henderson was sourced from an interview conducted by Laurie Field, op. cit., as well as from Ross Pearson's *Australians at War in the Air*, Kangaroo Press, Kenthurst, NSW, 1995, vols I and II; and the 1945–46 annual report of the Mosman Cricket Club.

Information about George Archer came from his son, David. One of George Archer's golf balls remains in the family. Another golf ball made by a POW was given to the museum of the Royal and Ancient Golf Club of St Andrew's, and two more were donated to the USGA Museum.

For Tony Burcher, see Laurie Field, op. cit., and for Arthur Schrock, see AWM65 4573.

Information about RAF fighter pilot Oliver Green was sourced from Brendan Moloney's article, 'The hardest course of all', *Golf in Victoria*, June/July 1996.

For background on Bill Sampson, see Craig Sampson's article 'Great escape' in *Forty Degrees South*, Issue 78, 2015.

For details of sport at Stalag 383 at Hohenfels, Bavaria, see Pamela Cohen, op. cit., and also for the quote from the camp magazine, *One Year*, which covered the sporting activities between 1942 and 1944.

The *Ersatz Ashes*, compiled by POWs Jim Welch and Jim Davies, is held at the AWM, 3DRL/3566.

For the cricketing exploits of Pat Ferraro, see *The Record*, Emerald Hill, 18 December 1943.

Sporting Globe published the story of Roy Bailey on 18 November 1942.

24 Playing for Australia!

Background for this chapter was drawn from Kevin Blackburn's book, op. cit., and Ian Shaw's book on the fate of Australian nurses aboard the coastal freighter *Vyner Brooke*, Ian Shaw, *On Radji Beach*, Pan Australia, Sydney, 2012.

Also see Wilma Oram's (Young) eulogy for Betty Jeffrey: https://muntokpeacemuseum.org/?page_id=987.

For Betty Jeffrey's diary, see AWM PR01780.

25 Black Magic

Background for the development of sport in wartime PNG, including horse racing at Buna and boxing in Port Moresby, is drawn from Liam Kane's thesis, which he kindly shared with me: 'Embattled coalition: Australians and Americans at war against Japan, 1941–1945', UNSW, 2020.

The Jika Travers anecdote is drawn from his book *Let's Talk Rugger*, Eyre & Spottiswoode, London, 1950.

The story of Len Waters and his boxing exploits is drawn from my book *The Missing Man*, Allen & Unwin, Sydney, 2012.

26 Conjuring Victory

For the Merv Waite anecdote, see Chris Harte and Bernard Whimpress, *The Penguin History of Australian Cricket*, Viking Penguin, Melbourne, 2003. For Bradman's letter, see NAA Series no. A9301, Control symbol 47878.

For the story of Ben Barnett's cricket boots, see AWM54 1010/4/10.

For the Singapore docks story about Ben Barnett, plus the swimming races, see diary of Norman Morrison, op. cit.

Adrian Curlewis's recollections were sourced from his letters published in the book *Of Love and War*, Philippa Poole, Century Publishing, London, 1983.

For the Curlewis references to doctors and Ben Barnett, see AWM, interview with Hank Nelson: https://s3-ap-southeast-2.amazonaws.com/awm-media/collection/S00035/document/1865596.PDF.

Regarding the bashings, see Croft diary, op. cit., 24 March 1945.

See E.W. Swanton for the cricket match on New Year's Day 1945: 'War culture: Cricket in WWII', *Military History Matters*, 20 December 2013: www.military-history.org/feature/war-culture-cricket-in-wwii.htm.

The Vic Richardson story was related by former Australian captain Ian Chappell in a personal communication with the author. According to Chappell, this is the correct version of the story, which he heard from his mother, Jeanne, Vic Richardson's eldest daughter.

27 The Victory Tests

Gideon Haigh reported the story about Denis Compton and Keith Miller in *The Australian*, 16 January 1995.

Material for this chapter drew on the unpublished book *History of the 1945 Australian Services Cricket Team*, by Stan Sismey, the manuscript for which is held by the AWM, MSS1615.

R.S. Whitington's *The Quiet Australian: The Lindsay Hassett Story*, Heinemann, Melbourne, 1969, provided background on Lindsay Hassett.

For the story of Graham Williams, see Greg Growden's book, *Cricketers at War*, ABC Books, Sydney, 2019.

The ball-by-ball record for the 'Victory' Tests was compiled by Barry Valentine, a member of the Association of Cricket Statisticians and Historians: 'The "Victory" Tests 1945': https://archive.acscricket.com/research/The_Victory_Tests_1945.pdf.

For the E.W. Swanton story of listening to Vic Cristofani's century, see 'War culture: Cricket in WWII', op. cit.

28 When Success Turns Sour

For background to the travails of the Services team, see Stan Sismey, op. cit.

For the story of Lindsay Hassett defusing the riot, see Gideon Haigh, *The Australian*, 16 January 1995.

For the Cec Pepper story, see Sismey, op. cit., and Garry Sobers, *My Autobiography*, Headline, London, 2002.

Cricket writer Phil Wilkins reported Sismey's story of the controversial Adelaide match in the *Manning River Times*, 24 June 2009.

The *Sydney Morning Herald* reported the Bradman–Miller exchange on 23 September 2012.

For Keith Miller's view of Keith Carmody, see Tony Barker, *Keith Carmody – Keith Miller's Favourite Captain*, Association of Cricket Statisticians and Historians, Cardiff, 2012.

29 Mate Against Mate

David Trist, Corporal, Australian Jungle Warfare Centre in WWII, kindly shared his records of the carnivals.

George Glansford's recollections were recorded by the AWM in January 1989. See: AWM S00516.

The teams for the State of Origin match were:

Queensland: Fullback, Jack Barnes (capt.); three-quarters, Jim Christopher, Lewis Ashmore, C. King, E. Lade; halves, N. Hoare, Bobby Williamson; lock forward, Hec Bradshaw; second row, M. Treseder, T. Kraft; front row, Macca Thomson (vice-capt.), Kelly Brennan, H. McLennan.

New South Wales: Fullback, Norm Parkinson; three-quarters, W. Peachy, Doug McRitchie, Tommy Briggs, Herbie Dhu; halves, Horrie Marjoribanks (capt.), R. Miller; lock forward, Harry Taylor; second row, M. Love, C. Smith; front row, J. Hobson (vice-capt.), Don Sinclair, H. Freeman.

The *Morning Bulletin*, Rockhampton, published a report of the rugby league match on 27 September 1945.

For the Wrigley account, see *Rugby in the RAN – the Navy's first Australian Services Rugby Premiership*, Ian Wrigley, September 2013, Naval Historical Society of Australia: navyhistory.au/rugby-in-the-ran-the-navys-first-australian-services-rugby-premiership/

POST–WORLD WAR II

30 Running Hard

The AWM holds interviews with troops explaining why they signed on for a second tour of duty in Japan under the British Commonwealth Occupation Force (BCOF): S00016, 13 February 1947.

Bcon was the official all-services newspaper for the BCOF in Japan. Relevant dates for editions of the publication in this chapter are 19 April, 17 May and 25 May 1948.

Mr Yasushi Washo, a teacher from Shizuoka Sangyo University who specialises in sports history and is a member of the Prisoner of War Research Network Japan, provided valuable help with this chapter.

For the interview with Jim Parsons, see AWM S02779.

For the interview with Stephen Joyce, see AWM S02795.

The Argus, 29 July 1952, reported Claude Smeal's comments.

For the story of Reg Saunders, see Harry Gordon's book *The Embarrassing Australian*, Lansdowne Press Pty Ltd, Melbourne, 1962.

31 Vung Tau
See *RAAF News*, 1 September 1968, for details of the matches in which Bobby Fulton played.
Eric Cupitt's recollection of Fulton was published on Facebook, 25 May 2021.
The Fulton interview with Roy Masters was published in the *Sydney Morning Herald*, 3 June 2016.
Doug Collins' recollections were given in a personal interview.
Steve Lewis's recollections were given in an interview with the UNSW, Australians at War Film Archive, 19 November 2003: https://australiansatwarfilmarchive.unsw.edu.au/archive/1154.
For the doctor's comments about fitness, see: www.awm.gov.au/collection/F03807.
Roger Wainwright's recollections were given in a personal interview.
For the Wayne Closter–Glenn James incident, see 'Stan Middleton reports on the Vietnam Football League in the 1960s', Vietnam Swans, 22 April 2011: https://hanoiswans.wordpress.com/2011/04/22/stan-middleton-reports-on-the-vietnam-football-league.
For Glenn James's later comments, see: 'Closter's memories', One In Hoops: www.geelongcats.com.au/news/329428/closters-memories.
Ian Granland's recollections were personally conveyed. Also, see: http://www.au104.org/Veteran_Stories/vetstory94.html.
For the interview with Ian Mackay interview, UNSW, see: https://australiansatwarfilmarchive.unsw.edu.au/archive/htmlTranscript/1501?asPdf=y.
Malcolm van Gelder's comments were drawn from his unpublished autobiography, held by his family.
For background on the Vung Tau Rugby Union club, see *RAAF News*, 1 August 1970.
Geoff Irvin's recollection of the match came in a personal interview.

Ian Granland's account of SP operations at Nui Dat came in personal correspondence.

Units that competed in the VFL competition included 2nd Composite Ordnance Depot (1967, changed to 2AOD in 1968), 2AOD (2nd Advance Ordnance Depot), 17th Construction Squadron (Engineers), 1st Field Hospital/8th Field Ambulance (Australian Army Hospital), RAAF, 5th Company Royal Australian Army Service Corps (RAASC), 102nd Field Workshops, and 110th Signals.

Following Malcolm van Gelder's selection, Bob Brown was the next army officer to be selected as a Wallaby. An incisive running fullback with safe hands, he entered the Royal Military College Duntroon in 1971 and graduated into the Infantry Corps in 1974. Brown played his first representative rugby for New South Wales Country and the ACT in 1973. A year later he made his New South Wales debut against Queensland. In 1975 he earned a Test debut against England in Sydney and was retained for the second Test, dubbed 'the Battle of Brisbane', at Ballymore. When Brown dislocated his shoulder later that season he chose to focus on his army career. One of Brown's Duntroon mates, Lieutenant Terry Beaton, represented Australia at the 1974 Christchurch Commonwealth Games, where he finished eighth in the men's decathalon.

32 The Paradox

For Ray Richard's recollections, see Australian National Football Team Reunion at the SCG, YouTube, 18 February 2018.

Ron Corry recalled the tour during a personal interview, and also in an article in the *Sydney Morning Herald*, 10 November 2017.

For Johnny Warren's comments, see his book with Andy Harper and Josh Whitington, *Sheilas, Wogs and Poofters*, Random House, Sydney, 2002.

Ray Baartz's view of the game appeared in an article by Richard Cooke in *The Guardian*, 6 June 2013.

For further background on the tournament and lack of recognition of the players, see John Didulica, *Football Belongs: Eight Matches that Explain Australia*, independently published, 2021.

33 They Don't Unteach You!

For Tim Fischer's comments about his Vietnam experience, see my biography *I Am Tim: Life, Politics and Beyond*, MUP, Melbourne, 2023.

Material for this chapter included personal interviews and communications with Tony Dell. I also drew on Greg Milam's biography, *And Bring the Darkness Home: The Tony Dell Story*, Pitch Publishing, UK, 2021. Further comments were drawn from an interview he gave to Thomas Kaye in a podcast published on 21 September 2021: https://podcasts.apple.com/au/podcast/116-tony-dell/id1271200777?i=1000536036737.

Adrian d'Hagé's recollections came in a personal interview, as did the recollections of Graham Cornes.

Further comments from Tony Dell appeared in articles by Daniel Lane in the *Sydney Morning Herald*, 30 June 2013, and Grantlee Kieza, *Daily Telegraph*, 25 November 2013.

Besides a personal interview on the subject, Graham Cornes discussed his PTSD in *The Advertiser*, Adelaide, 14 November 2014. Also see the article published by the South Australian Mental Health Commission about Graham Cornes: 'I could never admit that I needed help': https://ssamentalhealthcommission.com/graham-cornes-never-admit-needed-help.

The story of the panel hosted by the Queensland Cricketers Club for Gabba Legends was published by the *Brisbane Times*, 23 October 2015.

34 Even a Warped Bat Will Do

For Steve Waugh's comment, see his autobiography, *Out of My Comfort Zone*, Viking, Camberwell, 2005.

For the account of the Desert Ashes, see *Army*, 11 August 2005.

Sarah Watson's comments were given in a personal interview, and for her views on the reasons for the deployment to Iraq, see: https://independentpeacefulaustralia.com.au/wp-content/uploads/2022/10/175-Sarah-Watson.pdf.

Jill Buckfield's recollections were given in a personal interview.

The Multinational Force & Observers (MFO) veteran's recollections were given in a personal interview. He wished to remain unnamed, as did the SAS veteran who told the story of the Shahid Afridi bat.

For further background, see Harry Moffitt's autobiography, *Eleven Bats*, Allen & Unwin, Sydney, 2020.

35 Fighting Back

For the Curtis McGrath story, see his autobiography, *Blood Sweat & Steel*, HarperCollins, Sydney, 2021.

For further background on the Curtis McGrath story, see *The Big Issue*, 2 September 2021, and Oympics.com.

See *Army*, 11 and 25 August 2005, for coverage of cricket in Iraq and the Combined Services team's visit to Britain.

Sarah Watson's comments about the Invictus Games were given in a personal interview.

Tony Dell's views on sport and the military were given in a personal interview.

Unarmed Combat in the ADF: 'The Next Evolution' provides background on developments in this area of training. See Australian Army Journal, vol 9, number 3,

For boxing background in the RAN, see Occasional Paper 93, 'Boxing in the Navy', by John Smith, October 2020, Naval Historical Society of Australia: navyhistory.au/occasional-paper-93-boxing-in-the-navy.

36 Just a Game of Football

For the Helen Garner quotes, see *The Season*, Text, Melbourne, 2024.

Melissa Harries' comments were given in a personal interview.

Pat Cummins' comments were published in an article by Louis Cameron, 'Aussies inspired by Gallipoli visit', Cricket.com.au, 18 May 2019: www.cricket.com.au/news/3301742/aussies-inspired-by-gallipoli-visit.

For Michael Clarke's comments, see https://auscricket.com.au/news/cricket-and-the-anzac-spirit.

For the comments by Lieutenant Robert Andrew and Tony Shaw, see the article by Rachel Hibbert, 'I wasn't a fan of football on Anzac Day ... until I changed my mind', *Sydney Morning Herald*, 20 April 2017.

Kevin Sheedy's comments were published in an article by Ben Collins, 'How footy and Anzac Day overcame a tempestuous beginning', afl.com.au, 25 April 2015.

James Hird's comments were published in his autobiography with Peter Wilmoth, *Reading the Play*, Pan Macmillan, Sydney, 2006.

Epilogue

For Sir Peter Cosgrove's recollections, see his autobiography, *You Shouldn't Have Joined ... A Memoir*, Allen & Unwin, Sydney, 2020.

Greg Chappell's comment on Stephen Chappell was quoted in *The Australian*, 11 April 2024.

Bibliography

BOOKS AND MONOGRAPHS

Kristen Alexander, *Kriegies: The Australian Airmen of Stalag Luft III*, privately published, 2023,

Tony Barker, *Keith Carmody – Keith Miller's Favourite Captain*; Association of Cricket Statisticians and Historians, Cardiff, 2012.

James W. Barrett, *The War Work of the Y.M.C.A. in Egypt*, H.K. Lewis & Co. Ltd, London, 1919.

Walter C. Belford, *'Legs Eleven': Being the Story of the 11th Battalion AIF in the Great War*, Andrews UK Limited, 2023.

Kevin Blackburn, *The Sportsmen of Changi*, NewSouth Publishing, Sydney, 2012.

Douglas Booth and Colin Tatz, *One-Eyed: A View of Australian Sport*, Allen & Unwin, Sydney, 2000.

Russell Braddon, *The Naked Island*, Lloyd O'Neil Pty Ltd, Hawthorn, Melbourne, 1975.

Suzanne Brugger, *Australians and Egypt 1914–1919*, MUP, Melbourne, 1980.

Peter Cosgrove, *You Shouldn't Have Joined ... A Memoir*, Allen & Unwin, Sydney, 2020.

F.M. Cutlack (ed.), *War Letters of General Monash*, Angus & Robertson, Sydney, 1934.

George Cuttriss, *Over the Top with the Third Australian Division*, Charles H. Kelly, London, 1918.

John Didulica, *Football Belongs: Eight Matches that Explain Australia*, independently published, 2021.

Vic Duncan, *An Odyssey*, Duncan family.

E.E. Dunlop, *The War Diaries of Weary Dunlop*, Nelson, Melbourne, 1986.

Sue Ebury, *Weary: The Life of Sir Edward Dunlop*, Penguin, Ringwood, 1994.
Bill Gammage, *The Broken Years*, ANU Press, Canberra, 1974.
Helen Garner, *The Season*, Text, Melbourne, 2024.
John Graham Gillam, *A Gallipoli Diary*, George Allen & Unwin Ltd, London, 1918.
George Goddard, *Soldiers and Sportsmen*, AIF Sports Control Board, London, 1919.
Harry Gordon, *The Embarrassing Australian*, Lansdowne Press Pty Ltd, Melbourne, 1962.
J.R. Gorham and C.J.L. Hewett, *The Torch Bearers: War Service of Shore Old Boys, 1939–1999*, Sydney Church of England Grammar School, 1999.
F.C. Green, *A Record of the 40th Battalion AIF*, 40th Battalion Association, Hobart, 1922.
Greg Growden, *Cricketers at War*, ABC Books, Sydney, 2019.
Greg Growden, *Gold, Mud 'N' Guts*, ABC Books, Sydney, 2001.
Chris Harte and Bernard Whimpress, *The Penguin History of Australian Cricket*, Viking Penguin, Melbourne, 2003.
Roy Hay, *Football and War: Australia and Vietnam 1967–1972*, Sports and Editorial Services Australia, 2016.
James Hird with Peter Wilmoth, *Reading the Play*, Pan Macmillan Australia, Sydney, 2006.
Ian Hodges, *'He Belonged to Wagga': The Great War, the AIF and Returned Soldiers in an Australian Country Town*, Australian Scholarly Publishing, Melbourne, 2022.
Charles Huxtable, *From the Somme to Singapore: A Medical Officer in Two World Wars*, Kangaroo Press, Kenthurst, NSW, 1987.
Elyne Mitchell, *Light Horse: The Story of Australia's Mounted Troops*, Sun Books, Melbourne, 1978.
Curtis McGrath, *Blood: Sweat & Steel*, HarperCollins, Sydney, 2021.
Michael McKernan and Richard Cashman (eds), *Sport in History: The Making of Modern Sporting History*, University of Queensland Press, St Lucia, 1979.
Harry Moffitt, *Eleven Bats*, Allen & Unwin, Sydney, 2020.
Hank Nelson, *Prisoners of War: Australians Under Nippon*, ABC, Sydney 1985.

Phil O'Brien, *Towards Peace: A Worker's Journey*, Social History of Australia Publishing Enterprise, https://workersbushtelegraph.com.au/books/ttowards-peace-a-workers-journey.

Ray Parkin, *Into the Smother: A Journal of the Burma–Siam Railway*, The Hogarth Press, New Zealand, 1963.

Scott Patterson, *The Oarsmen: The Remarkable Story of the Men who Rowed from the Great War to Peace*, Hardie Grant Books, Melbourne, 2019.

Ross Pearson, *Australians at War in the Air*, Kangaroo Press, Kenthurst, NSW, vols. I and II, 1995.

Philippa Poole, *Of Love and War*, Century Publishing, London, 1983.

Peter Rees, *Desert Boys: Australians at War from Beersheba to Tobruk and El Alamein*, Allen & Unwin, Sydney, 2011.

Peter Rees, *Lancaster Men: The Aussie Heroes of Bomber Command*, Allen & Unwin, Sydney, 2013.

Peter Rees, *Bearing Witness: The Remarkable Life of Charles Bean, Australia's Greatest War Correspondent*, Allen & Unwin, Sydney, 2015.

Peter Rees, *The Missing Man: From the Outback to Tarakan, the Powerful Story of Len Waters, Australia's First Aboriginal Fighter Pilot*, Allen & Unwin, Sydney 2018.

Peter Rees, *I Am Tim: Life, Politics and Beyond*, MUP, Melbourne, 2023.

Peter Rees and Sue Langford, *A Week in September: A Story of Enduring Love from the Burma Railway*, HarperCollins, Sydney, 2021.

Ian Shaw, *On Radji Beach*, Pan Australia, Sydney, 2012.

Andrew Shepherdson, *Journeys of a Light Horseman*, self-published, 2002.

Garry Sobers, *My Autobiography*, Headline, London, 2002.

Soldiering On, AWM, Canberra 1942.

Ivan Southall, *Bluey Truscott*, Angus & Robertson, Sydney, 1958.

B.H. Travers, *Let's Talk Rugger*, Eyre & Spottiswoode, London, 1950.

Tom Uren, *Straight Left*, Random House, Sydney, 1994.

Stan Vesper, *Those Who Served*, Playright Publishing Pty Ltd, Sydney, 2015.

Johnny Warren with Andy Harper and Josh Whitington, *Sheilas, Wogs and Poofters*, Random House, Sydney, 2002.

Steve Waugh, *Out of My Comfort Zone*, Viking, Camberwell, 2005.

MAGAZINES, PODCASTS AND DIGITAL

Kate Ariotti and Martin Crotty, 'The role of sport for Australian POWs of the Turks during the First World War', *The International Journal of the History of Sport*, vol. 31, no. 18, 2014.

Dale Blair, 'Beyond the metaphor: Football and war, 1914–1918, *Journal of the Australian War Memorial*, issue 28, April 1996.

Pamela Cohen, 'Behind barbed wire', *Sporting Traditions*, vol. 23, no. 1, November 2006.

The Fortian, November 1919, https://fortstreet-h.schools.nsw.gov.au/content/dam/doe/sws/schools/f/fortstreet-h/download-box/1919-NOV-BOYS.pdf.

Allan Grant, 'The Changi Brownlow – Peter Chitty', *Almanac Footy History*, footyalmanac.com.au.

'Sport and Australian military life': https://anzacportal.dva.gov.au/resources/sport-and-australian-military-life.

Thomas Kaye, interview with Tony Dell, podcast 21 September 2021, https://podcasts.apple.com/au/podcast/116-tony-dell/id1271200777?i=1000536036737.

David Leydon, 'Wilfred "Chicken" Smallhorn: The spirit of the ANZAC Fitzroy legend, Changi legend', 2023, www.fitzroyfc.com.au/latest-news/wilfred--chicken--smallhorn-the-spirit-of-the-anzac-fitzroy-legend-changi-legend.

Kersi Meher-Homji, 'Oldfield was the neatest stumper of them all', *The Roar*, 31 May 2010, theroar.com.au.

Brendan Moloney, 'The hardest course of all', *Golf in Victoria*, June/July 1996.

Craig Sampson, 'Great escape', *Forty Degrees South*, issue 78, 2015.

E.W. Swanton, 'War culture: Cricket in WWII', *Military History Matters*, 20 December 2013, www.military-history.org/feature/war-culture-cricket-in-wwii.htm.

Ian Syson, 'Fronting up: Australian soccer and the First World War', *The International Journal of the History of Sport*, 28 April 2014.

Thierry Terret, 'The military "Olympics" of 1919', *International Society of Olympic Historians*, vol. 14, no. 2, 2006.

Max Uechtritz, 'Remembering Wallaby "Mac" Ramsay – WW2 Hell Ship victim', *The Roar*, 29 June 2017, www.theroar.com.

au/2017/06/30/remembering-wallaby-mac-ramsay-ww2-hell-ship-victim.

Christopher Warner, 'War athletes: Keith Truscott', *Military History*, 19 April 2021.

Wartime, Issue 33, January 2006.

THESES AND PAPERS

Tony Cunneen, 'Be a Sport and Enlist: Leslie Seaborn and the Sportsmen's Unit in the First World War', https://supremecourt.nsw.gov.au/documents/Publications/The-War-Memorial-Project/Cunneen_20170327_Seaborn.pdf.

Xavier Fowler, 'Sport and the Australian War Effort during the First World War: Concord and Conflict', thesis, University of Melbourne, 2018.

Warwick Franks, 'Sport in prisoner-of-war camps, in the army and on the Home Front', https://crescentbeachcayman.com/defreitas/files/Cricket-in-Stalag-344---Sport-in-German-Prisoner-of-war-camps-during-World-War-II.pdf.

Liam Kane, 'Embattled coalition: Australians and Americans at war against Japan, 1941–1945', thesis, UNSW, 2020.

Barry Valentine, 'The "Victory" Tests 1945', Association of Cricket Statisticians and Historians, https://archive.acscricket.com/research/The_Victory_Tests_1945.pdf.

Colin R. Veitch, 'Sport and war in the British literature of the First World War, 1914–1918', thesis, University of Alberta, 1984.

NEWSPAPERS, PAMPHLETS AND BLOGS

The Advertiser, Adelaide, 21 July 1915, 14 November 2014.

The Advertiser, Geelong, 22 May 1917.

afl.com.au: 'How footy and Anzac Day overcame a tempestuous beginning', 25 April 2015, Ben Collins.

The Age, 13 August 1981.

The Argus, 10 May 1917, 16 July 1917, 29 July 1952.

Armidale Chronicle, 27 March 1915.

Army News, Darwin, 7 December 1941, 5 February 1942.

Army, 11, 25 August 2005.

The Arrow, 14 July 1917.

The Australasian, 10 April 1915.
The Australian, 16 January 1995, 11 April 2024.
Bcon, 19 April, 17 and 25 May 1948.
The Big Issue, 2 September 2021.
Brisbane Times, 23 October 2015.
The Bulletin, 27 January 1916.
The Cove, 23 September 2020.
Cricket.com.au: 'Aussies inspired by Gallipoli visit', Louis Cameron, 18 May 2019.
Daily Telegraph, 6 October 1919, 25 November 2013.
Dubbo Liberal and Macquarie Advocate, 28 August 1914.
The Guardian, 6 June 2013.
Ku-Ring-Gai Historical Society Inc. newsletter, Vol. 38 No. 11, December 2020.
Malaya Tribune, 3 March 1941.
Manning River Times, 24 June 2009.
The Mercury, Hobart, 18 December 1941.
Morning Bulletin, Rockhampton, 27 September 1945.
Morwell Advertiser, 12 February 1915.
Northern Miner, 28 May 1915.
North Western Courier, Narrabri, 18 June 1915.
The Observer, Adelaide, 27 March 1915.
'The Old Tin Shed', http://sydneystadium.blogspot.com/2010/11/digger-evans.html
RAAF News, 1 September 1968, 1 August 1970.
The Record, Emerald Hill, 18 December 1943
The Referee, 25 November 1914, 27 October 1915, 15 December 1915, 1 March 1916, 5 September 1917, 12 September 1917, 19 September 1917, 7 and 14 November 1917, 20 February 1918, 9 July 1919, 1 October 1919.
The Register, Adelaide, 6 August 1915.
Reveille, 1 January 1935.
South Coast Times, 16 June 1916.
The Sports Factor, 'Lest we forget – sport and war', Murray Phillips, ABC RN, 19 April 2002.
Sporting Globe, 18 November 1942, 29 September 1945, 13 October 1945, 27 August 1949, 25 April 1953.

Straits Times, 22 September 1941, 2 November 1941, 9 November 1941; and 23 November 1941.

Sun News-Pictorial, 18 May 1942.

The Sun, Sydney, 16 May 1915, 25 May 1915, 15 August 1915, 9 March 1941.

Sunday Telegraph, 23 June 2013.

Sunday Times, Sydney, 2 February 1913.

Sydney Mail, 13 September 1916.

Sydney Morning Herald, 27 July 1917, 5 January 1940, 7 June 1943, 22 April 2007, 21 April 2013, 3 June 2016, 30 October 2017, 10 November 2017, 25 April 2019.

The Winner, 17 February 1915.

West Wimmera Mail and Natimuk Advertiser, 16 April 1915.

Wodonga and Towong Sentinel, 18 October 1940.

The Yorker, The Melbourne Cricket Club magazine, Issue 51, 2013.

AUSTRALIAN WAR MEMORIAL

2/1st Infantry Battalion War Diary, March–April 1940: https://s3-ap-southeast-2.amazonaws.com/awm-media/collection/RCDIG1021830/bundled/RCDIG1021830.pdf.

'A regatta and water sports', 22 June 1917, AWM25 897/2.

Lex Arthurson: AWM MSS1377.

Harold Ball: AWM, PR05406.

Ben Barnett: AWM54 1010/4/10.

Nicky Barr: www.3sqnraafasn.net/subpages/AWMBarr.htm.

British Commonwealth Occupation Force (BCOF): S00016.

Ernest Brooks: AWM G00406.

Tony Burcher, see Laurie Field interviews: AWM MSS1489.

'Correspondence regarding Inter-Allied Games in Paris 1919', www.awm.gov.au/collection/C2740041.

Adrian Curlewis interview with Hank Nelson: https://s3-ap-southeast-2.amazonaws.com/awm-media/collection/S00035/document/1865596.PDF.

Frank Day: AWM PR03884.

Bill Flowers: AWM MSS1575.

George Glansford: AWM S00516.

Tom Hamilton, Private Record: AWM PR00219.

Mike Hubert: AWM PR01123.
D.R. Jackson: AWM MSS 1193.
Betty Jeffrey: AWM PR01780.
Stephen Joyce: AWM S02795.
Jim McKinley: AWM S00287, https://s3-ap-southeast-2.amazonaws.com/awm-media/collection/S00287/document/1865630.PDF.
Jack Massie: AWM 3DRL/3701(A).
Sid Middleton: https://s3-ap-southeast-2.amazonaws.com/awm-media/collection/AWM2020.8.1251/bundled/AWM2020.8.1251.pdf.
Donald (Norman) Morrison VX28610: AWM PR05395.
Jim Parsons: AWM S02779.
Tom Richards: AWM 2DRL/0786.
Arthur Schrock: AWM65 4573.
Stan Sismey: AWM, MSS1615.
Leslie Sutherland: AWM 2DRL0988.
Jim Welch and Jim Davies, *Ersatz Ashes*: AWM 3DRL/3566.
Tom Whyte: AWM PR04722.